T H A M E S
C H E L S E A
The Pavilion
Cadogan Place
Trinity Church
SLOANE SQUARE
LOWER SLOANE STREET
Royal Military Asylum
CHELSEA HOSPITAL
QUEENS ROAD
QUEENS ROAD EAST
Bridge Road
Chelsea Barracks
Botanical Gardens
Battersea Park Pier
G R O S V E N O R
CHELSEA BRIDGE
RAILWAY PIER
BATTERSEA STATION
LONDON & BRIGHTON WEST END BRANCH
Commercial Road
BELGRAVE
EATON SQ.
Ebury Street
Eccleston Street
Cadogan Street
Marlborough Road
Whiteheads Grove
Jubilee Place
Markham Street
Greene Row
Walpole Street
Franklin Row
S W

Gibson
26.10.73

CHELSEA REACH

Hammersmith Bridge on Boat Race Day painted in oils by Walter Greaves. Recognised as a masterpiece on its first exhibition in 1911, it has remained at the heart of the mystery surrounding the relationship between Whistler and Walter Greaves.

OXFORD MUSIC HALL NIGHT
CREMORNE
6
3d
TEMPLE BAR

CHELSEA REACH

The Brutal Friendship of
Whistler and Walter Greaves

by
TOM POCOCK

HODDER AND STOUGHTON

First printed 1970

ISBN 0 340 10992 0

Printed in Great Britain
for Hodder and Stoughton Limited,
St. Paul's House, Warwick Lane, London E.C.4,
by Richard Clay (The Chaucer Press), Ltd.,
Bungay, Suffolk

Foreword

by

SIR JOHN ROTHENSTEIN

In this book the author too generously writes that it was largely due to my enthusiasm that Greaves's reputation was kept alive and that *Hammersmith Bridge on Boat Race Day* was saved from becoming an anonymous masterpiece. But among the several people who have worked for this end – and they have included Sickert – the foremost, beyond question, in recent times is Mr. Pocock himself. That this should be so is due not only, or even primarily, to his affectionate insight into the work and personality of the artist, but rather to his understanding of his life and environment.

"To appreciate a work of art," wrote Clive Bell, "we need bring with us nothing from life, no knowledge of its ideas and affairs, no familiarity with its emotions. Art transports us from the world of man's activity to a world of aesthetic exaltation."

I think this is a heresy. Moreover I am convinced that there is little or nothing in the life and environment of artists which may not contribute to our understanding of their work. And this because their work may reflect their circumstances far more than is generally believed.

Walter Greaves invariably depicted his own environment, and with an empassioned precision. To an extraordinary degree he was the product of that environment: unless, as a boy, he had emblazoned his father's boats with heraldic devices, figureheads and the like, it is improbable that he would ever have thought of using paint to express his delight in his surroundings; unless those surroundings had been of an uniquely evocative character he would not have experienced that delight.

Mr. Pocock has given us an enthralling account of Chelsea – its history, its economy, its social structure, its appearance – and a moving portrait introducing, I believe, all recorded or remembered facts about Walter Greaves. But he has done more than this: he has shown how the place cast its spell upon the man and precisely how the man responded. Much more will, of course, be written about ever-changing Chelsea, but it is unlikely that this biography of Greaves will ever be superseded.

Some years ago in New York, John Sloan said to me, of a painting which had become a classic, "I hate *MacSorley's Bar*, as a father might hate one of his children who was praised always at the expense of the rest." Greaves was deeply happy when his *Hammersmith Bridge on Boat Race Day* was bought for the Tate, but, being his finest painting and the one longest on public view, it was invariably praised at the expense of the rest, which (except by Sickert) were virtually ignored.

It is, indeed, his masterpiece, but there are other works, paintings, drawings and etchings which give moving expression to his inspired love of the Thames, not least the panoramic yet detailed *Chelsea Regatta*, showing the Chelsea waterfront before its demolition to make way for the existing Embankment, and our sense of their quality is enhanced by Mr. Pocock's narrative. But even our knowledge of his masterpiece is extended. The date "circa 1862" has been generally accepted; likewise on occasion Greaves's statement that it was painted before he met Whistler, which was not earlier than 1863. Mr. Pocock, by careful scrutiny of the dresses, hats and hair-dos of the women on the bridge concludes that the picture was painted not in the earlier but the later 'sixties.

He notes that Whistler – The Master with whom Walter's tragic relations are related in detail – imposed his low tones upon Walter and his brother Henry, but that Walter's old love of pure, strong colour reasserted itself during Whistler's absences, and convincingly suggests that as he went to Valparaiso in the autumn of 1867 the picture was painted then.

Mr. Pocock has also discovered a photograph of a painting *The Boating Pond, Battersea Park* (which he has been unable to trace), which is (or was), to judge from the reproduction, a masterly work, showing, among other qualities, a command of composition not always evident in the work of Greaves.

When his interest in Greaves was first aroused, Mr. Pocock believed that there was not enough material to justify a book. Thanks to his zestful assiduity he has assembled enough to make a book that adds a fascinating chapter to British art history.

JOHN ROTHENSTEIN,
Chelsea.
April, 1970.

Preface

I first heard the story of Walter Greaves in the backstreets of Chelsea. In the 'thirties, when my family was living in Oakley Gardens, my father and I would exercise our dog with evening walks along Upper Cheyne Row, Lawrence Street and Justice Walk to Old Church Street and back. On one of these walks through the setting of the story, my father told me about the friendship between Greaves and Whistler and its strange sequel.

Some thirty years later, in a London saleroom, I saw and bought a small self-portrait of Walter Greaves. His eyes had caught and held mine and I was intrigued by the expression in them. Here was a young man on the sharp edge between confidence and lack of it. I remembered the story and began to brood on it. So much had been written of sexual love and so little about the sort of love that is called friendship that I hoped I might be able to discover more about this complex relationship between two very different men.

Although Walter Greaves was, in 1911, quoted as saying that he planned to write his autobiography, he never did so. Indeed the only two publications devoted solely to him are pamphlets: William Marchant's *A Reply to an Attack* and Dr. Christian Brinton's sentimental little tract published on the occasion of the first Greaves exhibition in New York. Otherwise, Walter Greaves was elusive, flitting through the biographies and autobiographies of Whistler and other artists and, at each encounter, becoming less easily understood.

It seemed to me – as it probably had to others – that there was not enough material surviving to support a book about Greaves. I therefore eventually wrote a series of articles about him and these were published in the London *Evening Standard* early in 1967 to coincide with an exhibition of his work arranged at Leighton House – Lord Leighton's exotic *palazzo* – by the Royal Borough of Kensington and Chelsea. As direct result of these articles I was put in touch with people who had known Walter Greaves and others who could sketch in many blank spaces of the portrait I planned. The result is this book.

Walter Greaves was a simple man caught up by powerful forces and whirled through a life of happiness and disaster that would have broken the spirit of anyone lacking his innate serenity. There remain mysteries and perhaps these will never be solved. But what has emerged, strong and clear, is a story of friendship that will find response in any person who has abandoned an old friend or been abandoned. It happened to be set in Chelsea during the years of its rise as the artists' quarter of London, so that, in setting the scene, something of the social background to that time emerges as backdrop to the people involved.

This book is very much a corporate effort by those who have been moved by the story of Walter Greaves and who love Chelsea. Some have led me to important and untapped sources, other have filled in small corners with detail. To all I am heartily grateful. Firstly, I must thank those who themselves knew Walter Greaves and talked about him to me: Mrs. Josephine Thompson (*née* Marchant), Mr. Roland Bevan, Mr. Ralph Burchett, Mr. A. Egerton Cooper, Mr. Harry Delaney, Mr. Frederick Ferebee, Mr. Alfred Hayward, Sir John Rothenstein and Sir Charles Wheeler. Of the many who helped with research, guidance and encouragement, I would particularly like to thank Mrs. Cicely Marchant, Mrs. Cynthia Thompson, Mrs. T. N. Sunderland of the Courtauld Institute of Fine Art and Miss Patricia Meara, the Reference Librarian at Chelsea Public Library; Mr. W. S. Hudson, Deputy Chief Librarian of the Royal Borough of Kensington and Chelsea; Mr. Cyril Edwards, Librarian for Chelsea; Mr. Richard Ormond of the National Portrait Gallery; Captain C. Townsend of the Royal Hospital, Chelsea; Mr. Robin Spencer; Mr. Peter Goodall; Mr. John Yeoman; the archivists and reference librarians of the Greater London Council at County Hall and in the public libraries of Battersea, Fulham and Wandsworth; the Chairman and Council of the Chelsea Arts Club; Professor A. McLaren Young, Mr. R. O. MacKenna and Mrs. Margaret MacDonald of the University of Glasgow; and my wife, Penny, herself a Chelsea girl.

TOM POCOCK

Contents

Illustrations

Acknowledgements

For permission to reproduce illustrations the author and publishers would like to thank:

The Trustees of the Tate Gallery (*Hammersmith Bridge on Boat Race Day*, *The Green Dress*, *Walter and "Tinnie" Greaves on the Embankment* by Walter Greaves and *Nocturne in Blue and Gold: Old Battersea Bridge* by J. McN. Whistler); The National Portrait Gallery (*Walter Greaves* by William Rothenstein and *Whistler* by Walter Greaves); The London Museum (*Whistler at Cremorne* and *The Female Blondin* by Walter Greaves); Manchester City Art Gallery (*Walter Greaves* by William Nicholson); The Chief Librarian of the Royal Borough of Kensington and Chelsea (*Upper Cheyne Row*, *Cheyne Walk*, *Cremorne Bandstand and Barges at Lindsey Jetty* by Walter Greaves); The Albright-Knox Gallery, Buffalo, U.S.A. (*Old Battersea Bridge* by J. McN. Whistler); The Chairman and Council of the Chelsea Arts Club; The Chairman and Council of the Chelsea Society; Messrs. Christie's; Sotheby and Co.; Mrs. Josephine Thompson; Sir John Rothenstein and Mr. Michael Rothenstein; Mr. G. W. Free of The King's Arms, Cheyne Walk, Chelsea.

Other illustrations, which are not from the author's collection, have been impossible to trace to their present owners and to them our thanks are due.

FOR PENNY

I

Arrangement in bricks and water

The wash of water against the river wall below his bedroom window was the earliest and most abiding childhood memory of Walter Greaves. The Thames, sweeping in a broad bend between Middlesex and Surrey, lay across the lane from the small house at the western end of Chelsea. It was more than the setting for the life of the Greaves family and more than their means of livelihood. It was to act upon and change the life of Walter Greaves, much as it changed his surroundings.

Like Chelsea, Walter Greaves had simple, almost pastoral origins. As was usual in nineteenth-century England, the roots of his family were embedded deep in the development and origins of their community, and the person was the product of the place. Upon this innocence was to be imposed sophistication and the happiness and pain that goes with revolution and transformation. But, at the beginning, the pattern of both the lives of the man and his community were as they had naturally evolved under the influences of geography, history and economics. It was a bright morning to be followed by storm, mist and moonlight.

Walter Greaves was born on 4th July, 1846, the third son and fifth child of Charles William Greaves, boat-builder and waterman, of Chelsea. His father, then a robust man of thirty-six, was totally absorbed by his river life. He, his fourteen-year-old eldest son, Charles, and the one workman he employed were seldom more than a hundred yards from the river. They built the pulling-boats and the rakish skiffs that were replacing the tubby wherries of the Thames watermen. They tended the ceremonial barges of the Corporation of the City of London, which were berthed at Chelsea. They undertook commissions to move passengers and goods by water. In summer there were visitors to be rowed across to Battersea, perhaps to The Old Swan tea gardens next to the riverside church. In winter there were sportsmen after duck in marshy Battersea Fields, or snipe-shooting up the creek which marked the western boundary of Chelsea.

Walter Greaves was to remember his father as "a bit of a sport", fond of shooting not only wildfowl but pigeons in the regular competitive shoots which were held at the raffish Red House tavern over at Battersea. And when, on occasion, dolphins came gambolling up the river from the sea, he shot at them, too.

Walter was christened at St. Luke's, the gaunt parish church in the Gothic style, half a mile from the river, where Charles Dickens had been married. Since 1824, when it had been completed at a cost of thirty thousand pounds, its Bath-stone tower, standing a hundred and forty-two feet above the new terrace cottages, had been an inescapable landmark. But the old parish church of Chelsea, now renamed All Saints', remained the waterman's landmark of weathered Caroline brick that was always the pivot of village life. Walter was born at 31 Cheyne Walk, rather more than a hundred yards downstream of the church and a few doors away from The Magpie and Stump tavern. Here, Henry had been born two years before and now the family needed a bigger house and moved upstream to Lindsey Row, and it was there, in 1852, that the last of the children, Alice, was born.

Charles Greaves was modestly ambitious for his family. He had developed his individual skill as a waterman into a business which proudly displayed a broad sign on the river wall, "Greaves. Boatbuilder". An artisan whose children and grand-children could be expected to move up into the great, expanding Victorian middle class, he had planned the pattern of his children's lives. His sons, Charles, Henry, ten years younger, and Walter would all be apprenticed to his boatyard and would in due course inherit and develop his business. His daughters, Eliza, Emily and Alice, would help his wife, Elizabeth, with the house and would learn such ladylike accomplishments as needlework and playing the piano.

Throughout his childhood, Walter Greaves was aware of the river. Sparkling blue in summer sunshine, leaden and sometimes flecked with ice in winter. At dawn and dusk an enticing blue haze that, for a few moments, gave the familiar scene an air of mystery. Across the river the spire of Battersea church and on the broad stream itself the sailing barges, their tan sails glowing by day and hanging black as bats' wings by night. But most exciting and, although he cannot have imagined this, most significant, both to his own life and to that of Chelsea, was the bridge.

About a hundred yards downstream of the Greaves's boatyard, Battersea Bridge spanned the river.

In the development of Chelsea, the bridge was both catalyst and watershed. In the first half of the nineteenth century, past events were seen to have occurred either before or after the building of the bridge. During the childhood of Walter Greaves, it was said of the very old that they could remember the building of the bridge. The bridge had transformed Chelsea from a village into a town. What had happened in Chelsea before the bridge seemed to belong to another age, and rapidly blurred from recollection into tradition and mythology.

Battersea Bridge was opened to traffic in 1771. It replaced the regular ferry between Chelsea and Battersea and was the only bridge between Westminster and the wooden bridge at Putney, which had been built in 1729. It was a massive structure of timber, bolted together, of nineteen spans. It was seven hundred and twenty-six feet in length and twenty-four feet wide, at night illuminated, by oil lamps and, after 1824, by gas.

To the Greaves boys, the bridge was a constant fascination; as Walter was to recall, "I was always well provided with thrills." When a big tide was on the ebb, the river sluiced between the narrow spans as dangerously as through the nineteen arches of medieval London Bridge, five miles downstream. It was a constant challenge to young watermen to shoot the arches in their skiffs and a constant danger to river traffic. Boats and barges often collided with the piers and sprang leaks and foundered or, when a powerful current ran, holed and capsized against the great baulks of the bridge. With mingled excitement and horror, Walter Greaves remembered the dangers of the bridge: how there was usually coal to be picked up on the Chelsea foreshore at low water from the wrecking of coal barges on passage upstream; and one terrible day when a barge from

Rochester sank and the boy watched while watermen dragged the corpses of an entire family from its cabin with boathooks.

It was this bridge that had changed Chelsea half a century before Walter Greaves was born. Before 1771, Chelsea village had sent the produce of its market gardens and nurseries to London by river or wagon. After that date, it was to be a major entrepôt, trading easily and lavishly with Surrey and beyond. Its docks expanded and road transport became an important industry with thousands of horses and ponies stabled in Chelsea to draw not only local produce to market but bricks for the streets of plain little houses which were being built for the new town of Chelsea across commonland, orchards and market gardens. Before 1771, the population of Chelsea village could always be numbered in hundreds, by 1800 it had increased to twelve thousand and, at the time of Walter Greaves's birth, to more than forty thousand.

By then, events before the watershed year seemed infinitely remote. It was not only their recession in time or the Chelseans' preoccupation with their own transformation: there was also the great historical barrier of world events, notably the French Revolution and the wars that followed. Chelsea, although a country town, was near enough to London to feel the immediate impact of events, and newspapers were on sale there only an hour later than in Fleet Street. Even after the fall of Napoleon, memories of the wars lingered more vividly in Chelsea than elsewhere. In the Royal Hospital, which Sir Christopher Wren had built for pensioned soldiers on the instructions of King Charles II at the end of the seventeenth century, lived hundreds of veterans of campaigns from Egypt to Waterloo. In dozens of small taverns that clustered about the Royal Hospital and the rambling riverside inns, the old soldiers told their stories, as did the sailors at Greenwich.

Along the waterfront of the little river port there was still talk of sea fights and a fading but chill memory of the press gang, personified in early Victorian Chelsea by one Jamie Cator, who used "to eke out his living by bringing down the floats of timber from the docks . . . and work on the sand-barges dredging in the river". Described as "a hard-featured, powerful old man" Cator was, according to one boy brought up on sailors' stories, "a remnant of the old press gang – and looked it every bit. He was morose, dark-featured, heavily marked with the small-pox, and had a deep scar from the corner of his mouth to the back of his jaw . . . He was dressed in oiled canvas trousers, a shiny black sailor's hat, with an old pensioner's undress blue short coat, and was not looked upon with respect."

More in accord with the popular image of the jolly British tar was the landlord of The Lord Nelson tavern in the King's Road at this time, who inspired a flattering rhyme:

Under brave Nelson of the Nile,
Our gallant landlord did his duty;
And peppered well Old England's foes,
Inspired by courage, home and beauty.

Now safely moored with friends around,
Of grog and grub he takes his fill;
Fighting his battles o'er again,
Or shuffling in the light quadrille.

The great wars and the building of late Georgian Chelsea – including the Greaves family's own modest house – was the beginning of all things known and understandable. Before that time everything not only seemed different but clearly had been different. For Chelsea had been no ordinary, bucolic village, like Battersea across the river, and the mythology which Walter Greaves learned as a boy was supported by evidence, mysterious but tangible, that these things had, in truth, happened.

The most exotic of this evidence was in the Old Church along the river bank upstream of the bridge. The thirteenth-century church encased in seventeenth-century brick, ripened by age to near-purple, the Old Church had the fascination of holding clues to a forgotten past.

Within, names since known as streets or houses, were cut in monuments, ornate and plain: names such as Cheyne, Lawrence, Stanley, Gorges, Northumberland and Dacre.

Without such reminders, it is probable that most citizens of Chelsea would have forgotten even more than they had. They had even forgotten where their most famous citizen, Sir Thomas More, had lived. They would point to the gabled greengrocer's shop by the river, which had a panelled back room and a Tudor staircase, and say that that was part of More's house.

It was, in fact, a fragment of the seat of the Earls of Shrewsbury, which had been demolished in 1813. Beaufort House, where More lived, had vanished from sight and memory. It had stood some two hundred yards from the Greaves's house but had been demolished in 1740 and now Beaufort Row, leading from the bridge to the King's Road, ran across its buried foundations. There were, had it been known, surviving traces: ancient garden walls, thick and bulging, rich plum-coloured but, when chipped, glowing Tudor rose.

Like the bridge that stood where his water-gate had been, More himself was of significance in the transformations of Chelsea. Before he settled there in 1520 it had been a simple farming and fishing village. But it was the first firm, relatively high ground on the north bank of the Thames west of London. Between the seats of the nobility along the Strand and Chelsea lay Westminster marsh, most of it so liable to flooding that the salient of land between Whitehall and Chelsea had become a place for slums and prisons. So, in the sixteenth century, when London had begun to expand westward the fashionable suburbs moved directly from Charing Cross to Chelsea.

Royal visits to Chelsea confirmed its popularity as the smart suburb for the court. King Henry VIII exchanged some expropriated monastery land for the manor of Chelsea and built a new manor-house, to be named Chelsea Place, near the river downstream from the church. Although by the time Walter Greaves was born nothing remained of Chelsea Place, which had been demolished in the mid-eighteenth century, but some dark brick garden walls, the house cast a lurid, romantic glare on local tradition.

Apart from King Henry, both Catherine Parr and Anne of Cleves, his queens, lived there. Princess Elizabeth was lodged there and Lady Jane Grey spent perhaps her last contented year in the house. The latter's fate, together with More's, helped conjure up stories of The Phantom Headsman of Cheyne Walk and add excitement to discoveries of "secret passages" beneath houses built on the sites of the vanished mansions. One such, discovered beneath the riverside inn, The Magpie and Stump, had clearly been connected with Shrewsbury House and was explored by Charles Greaves and three equally daring friends. The legend was that the passage, in which, as in others, a man could stand upright, led to Kensington Palace. Presumably fortified in the bar parlour above, the four men first forced open two heavy iron doors, then, holding candles before them, gingerly advanced into the dank, stale air of the tunnel. But soon this had become so foul and thin that the candles guttered and went out and the explorers retreated.

About a dozen mansions, built in the sixteenth and seventeenth centuries, had disappeared when Walter Greaves was born, sometimes leaving a few traces: vaulted cellars, garden walls, gateways or ancient trees.

A few old houses survived, most notably Lindsey House.

Built early in the seventeenth century as a residence for the court physician, the riverside mansion was bought by the Earl of Lindsey some fifty years later and for nearly a century was inhabited by the nobility. But London was expanding fast, pushing the fashionable suburbs farther west, notably to Twickenham and the reaches of the Thames upstream from Kew. Those mansions that survived were converted for use by institutions, or divided into apartments and so played an important part in the later development of Chelsea. For here would settle the camp followers of the rich and powerful. Here mistresses could be discreetly installed; here were buildings suitable for genteel educational establishments; here were premises for the luxury industries; here would be places of entertainment; and here was an environment for artists and writers: pleasant, economical and close to the doorsteps of their patrons.

The earliest and most glamorous of the Chelsea courtesans was Nell Gwynn, although her presence there has never been proved. In the nineteenth century it was taken for granted that not only had she persuaded the King to build the Royal Hospital but that she had also lived in Chelsea. Paradise Row, a terrace of red brick houses between the Royal Hospital and Cheyne Walk, and Sandford Manor on the Fulham bank of Chelsea Creek, up which Walter

Greaves would row when a boy, were pointed out as her homes. It was even said that the King's Road had been specially constructed for royal visits to her.

In fact, the King's Road, which remained a private royal thoroughfare until 1830, was designed primarily to link Whitehall with Hampton Court. Yet there is no reason to doubt that Nell Gwynn did stay in these houses and that her royal lover did visit her there.

The royal approval which King Henry VIII had given Chelsea was confirmed and garnished by King Charles II. He enjoyed both the jollities of riverside garden parties and the informality of swimming in a Thames free of London sewage, although on one such occasion his assassination was attempted by Captain Blood with a long shot from the reeds of Battersea Fields opposite. Chelsea became known as "Hyde Park on Thames", remaining the resort of the *bon ton* to a decreasing degree until the building of the bridge.

As the nobility moved from their mansions, schools for the children of gentlemen moved in. One such was established in the old home of the Lawrences to educate girls "in French, Writing, Arithmetick, Dancing, Musick and all Manner of fine Needlework" whereby, claimed the prospectus for 1752, "they will be qualified in Housewifry and Notableness". Other girls' schools were to follow, including one founded by Elizabeth Fry, the prison reformer, in 1825 and ominously named The School of Discipline.

Chelsea, with its river and open spaces, was ideal for naval and military academies and both were opened in the eighteenth century. In 1777, The Maritime School – later renamed The Naval Academy – was opened in a large house in Paradise Row.

The Military Academy was established first at Little Chelsea, between Chelsea and Kensington in 1770, and later at Stanley House, a surviving mansion at the western end of the King's Road. At Little Chelsea the grounds were laid out in the pattern of fortifications, and here, in 1784, one of the first experiments in military flying took place. With Blanchard, the aeronaut, at the controls the "grand aerostatic balloon . . . ascended from the military college at Little Chelsea. The gallant adventurers, after taking leave of their generous host, and a numerous circle of nobility and friends, arose with the most majestic grandeur, and, wafted by the prayers and plaudits of upwards of 400,000 spectators, in eight minutes were lost in æther."

Mansions and their outbuildings, which did not become schools, often housed light industries serving the wealthier suburbs. Most famous of these was the Chelsea china factory in what had been the grounds of Lawrence House. In Shrewsbury House, a school was replaced by a wallpaper factory. Chelsea Park, which had been part of More's estate, was, early in the eighteenth century, planted with mulberry trees for the breeding of silkworms. Although Chelsea silk was described as being "very rich and beautiful" the venture was a failure and the silk works were replaced by a tapestry factory and gradually new building encroached on to Chelsea Park until it finally vanished, leaving, as a reminder of its past, mulberry trees in little walled gardens.

By 1780, the shape of Chelsea had changed. The main road from London, past the Royal Hospital, no longer petered out at the western end of Cheyne Walk but crossed over Battersea Bridge, and the King's Road was increasing in importance. Now the heirs of Sir Hans Sloane, who had bought the manor of Chelsea in 1712 and persistently enlarged his estate, built Sloane Street, leading north from the eastern end of the King's Road to Hans Town, a neat residential development near the main road from London to the west.

Hans Town, planned by Henry Holland, the architect of the Brighton Pavilion, was to be a genteel suburb for the well-to-do middle classes. The lower end of Sloane Street attracted court dress-makers, hairdressers, silk mercers, milliners, drapers and fan-makers, whose small but exclusive show-rooms attracted customers from Mayfair as well as the expanding suburban villages.

Entertainment became a Chelsea industry early in the eighteenth century. At one end of the social scale it developed from the river-side taverns and Thames regattas; at the other, from the garden parties of the rich. Among the most lavish of these were given by the first Earl of Ranelagh, and for one visit by King George I to Ranelagh House, arriving in a procession of barges, Handel composed and conducted his Water Music.

In 1733 the property was sold to the lessee of Drury Lane Theatre, who set about exploiting the estate's reputation by converting it into a grandiose place of entertainment. In pleasure-gardens running down to the Thames, he built the Rotunda, a circular assembly hall, one hundred and eighty-five feet in diameter. The promenade itself was surrounded by fifty-two supper boxes, each with its private door opening on the gardens and the hall was lighted by a thousand wax candles in chandeliers.

Ranelagh pleasure gardens were opened in 1742 and survived for more than sixty years. Although its proprietors provided an orchestra, a resident organist (at one time the father of Fanny Burney, the diarist), various open air entertainments, food and drink, it was essentially a spectacular stage setting for occasions of varying amusement and success. It produced startlingly different reactions from its visitors.

In fine weather it was popular to go by water from Westminster Stairs, so that the first view of Ranelagh after dark was of lights flickering among the trees and the distant glow of the Rotunda "like a giant's lanthorn". The first sight of the Rotunda was always startling. "I found myself dumb with surprize and astonishment in the middle of a vast Amphitheatre; for structure Roman, for decorations of paint and gildings, gay as the Asiatic," wrote a French visitor. "Pleasure seemed to beckon her wanton followers . . . my eyes grew dazzled, my head grew giddy and all night I dreamt of Vanity Fair."

The entertainment provided varied from afternoon promenades round the Rotunda, while the orchestra played, to gossip and pausing for tea and bread and butter, and exotic masquerades.

Horace Walpole described one such masquerade, in 1749, as "the prettiest spectacle I ever saw . . . When you entered you found the whole garden filled with masks and spread with tents which remained all night *very commodely*. In one quarter was a maypole dressed with garlands, and people dancing round it to a tabor and pipe and rustic music, all masked, as were all the various bands of music that were dispersed in different parts of the garden; some like huntsmen with French horns, some like peasants, and a troop of harlequins and scaramouches in the little open temple on the mount.

On the canal was a sort of gondola, adorned with flags and streamers, and filled with music moving about. All round the outside of the amphitheatre were shops, filled with Dresden China, Japan, etc., and all the shopkeepers in masks. The amphitheatre was illuminated; and in the middle was a circular bower composed of all kinds of firs in tubs, from twenty to thirty feet high; under them orange-trees with a small lamp in each orange, and below them all sorts of the finest auriculas in pots; and festoons of natural flowers hanging above. There were booths for tea and wine, gaming-tables and dancing, and about a thousand persons. In short, it pleased me more than anything I ever saw."

The gaiety, the privacy of supper boxes and arbours, and the anonymity of masks and night, produced the inevitable scandals. The masquerade, described in *The Rambler*, is "an entertainment, which in an instant gives confidence to the timorous, and kindles ardour in the cold; an entertainment where the vigilance of jealousy has so often been eluded, and the virgin is set free from the necessity of languishing in silence; where all the out-works of chastity are at once demolished; where the heart is laid open without a blush; where bashfulness may survive virtue, and no wish is crushed under the frown of modesty."

A naked masquerade, "when the weather gets hot enough", was announced by *The Connoisseur*, whether seriously or satirically it is hard to tell. "One set of ladies intend to impersonate water-nymphs bathing in the canal; three sisters, celebrated for their charms, design to appear together as the three graces; and a certain lady of quality, who most resembles the goddess of beauty, is now practising, from a model of Venus de' Medici, the most striking attitudes of that character. As to the gentlemen, they may most of them represent very suitably the half-brutal forms of Satyrs, Pans, Fauns and Centaurs."

When a waiter from the Rotunda was sent to prison, the news prompted the remark, "What a horrid idea he'll give of us to those fellows in Newgate!" Finally, the Middlesex magistrates decided that the masquerades were "a nursery of Lewdness, Extravagances and Immorality which will, if not seasonably prevented, as it has already very much debauched, in a short time absolutely ruin his

Majesty's best subjects" and this particular entertainment was banned.

Others survived: balls, concerts, fireworks and balloon ascents. A favourite firework display was "A Representation of the FORGES OF VULCAN, FLOWING of the LAVA and the ERUPTION of MOUNT AETNA." Aviation included not only such novelties as the "grand Aerostatic Pyramid" thirty feet high and covered with caricatures and hieroglyphics, but the spectacular Night Balloon. This was a silk balloon beneath which fireworks were ignited when it reached a height of several hundred feet and which finally vanished "with a great explosion and a brilliant flame, leaving a prodigious cloud . . . visible at the distance of ten to twelve miles in all directions."

Yet there was an underlying melancholy to the revels. By day, the swish of long dresses round the Rotunda emphasised its emptiness; by night, the fact that the fashionable time to arrive was after the formal entertainment ended at midnight stressed its hollowness of purpose. Even Dr. Johnson, who approved of Ranelagh as a place of harmless enjoyment, was thrown into sombre retrospection: "Alas! Sir, these are only struggles for happiness. When I first entered Ranelagh, it gave an expansion and gay sensation to my mind, such as I never experienced anywhere else. But, as Xerxes wept when he viewed his immense army, and considered that not one of that great multitude would be alive a hundred years afterwards, so it went to my heart to consider that there was not one in all that brilliant circle that was not afraid to go home and think; but that the thoughts of each individual there would be distressing when alone."

The life of Ranelagh gradually petered out. Decoy dandies were sent to stroll in the Mall to remark in loud voices, "What charming weather for Ranelagh!" but patronage decreased and the shareholders complained as dividends fell below five per cent. So, after a last splendid ball in 1802, Ranelagh was sold and, in 1805, the Rotunda was demolished. Less than ten years later an old patron of the place, strolling through some unkempt wasteland near Chelsea, was shocked to hear that he stood on the site of Ranelagh. "All was desolation! A few inequalities appeared in the ground, indicative of some former building, and holes filled with muddy water showed the foundation walls – but the rest of the space, making about two acres, was covered with clusters of tall nettles, thistles and docks! I traced the circular foundation of the Rotunda, and at some distance discovered the broken arches of some cellars, once filled with the choicest wines, but now with dirty water! . . . No glittering lights! No brilliant happy company! No peals of laughter from thronged boxes! No chorus of a hundred instruments and voices! All was death-like stillness! Is such, I exclaimed, the end of human splendour?"

The social gap between the jollities of Ranelagh and the dozens of Chelsea inns and beer-houses was bridged by a unique establishment: the Bun House. This, together with its later imitators, stood throughout the eighteenth century and for twenty-five years after Ranelagh, on the border between Chelsea and Pimlico. An elaborate, arcaded confectioner's, its customers came from all classes, from the Hanoverian royal families to the huge crowds of Londoners who flocked to the nearby Five Fields at fair-time, or to Chelsea regatta.

The Chelsea bun was a novelty, endowed with near-immortality, for its recipe survived the demolition of the Bun House itself.

Even when Walter Greaves was a boy an old song was being sung:

As I was going to Chelsea one day,
I met with a pretty young girl on the way.
I kindly saluted, but this was her tone,
Why can't you be easy, and leave me alone?

Chorus:
Let me alone, and let me alone,
Why can't you be easy and let me alone?

I told her my name, it was harmless James,
I call'd her a thousand sweet delicate names,
I told her her heart was as cold as a stone.
No matter, says she, can't you let me alone?

I says, my dear love, I am not in my sun,
If you go to the Bun-house, I'll buy you a bun.
No, thank you, says she, I've got money of my own
To buy half a thousand, so leave me alone.

I says, my dear girl, with you I shall dine,
For at Finchback's I heard they sell very good wine,
And more than all that, there is wax-work to be shewn.
No matter, says she, can't you leave me alone?

I followed this damsel through field after field,
With a deal of persuasion, I brought her to yield.
Next day we were married, and she altered her tone,
And she teases me now if I let her alone.

The neighbouring Five Fields, upon which Belgravia and part of Pimlico was to be built, were the scene of summer fairs and the taverns of the district often had tea gardens, with rustic bowers and grottoes, skittle alleys and bowling greens. One, Strombolo House, was a miniature imitation of Ranelagh; another, The Dwarf's, owed its fame to the landlord, John Coan, The Norfolk Dwarf, whose reputation as an entertaining host to the carriage trade as much as to holiday crowds won him the description, "The Jovial Pigmy".

Later, other, more elaborate, pleasure gardens were opened on the fringes of Chelsea. In 1839, the New Vauxhall and Royal Bath Gardens announced a military spectacle: "The Taking of Fort Bhurtpore in Upper India in 1826 . . . The walls were 60 feet thick, and bastioned at intervals, the principal of which was mined with 2,000 lbs. of powder; when it exploded, the grenadier company of the British regiments being too near the mouth of the mine were nearly all destroyed. The British had 3,000 killed and wounded. The exhibition will call into exercise the whole energies of the establishment, assisted by hundreds of auxiliaries."

And, more in the tradition of Ranelagh, the Royal Manor House Gardens announced a year later: "An entirely new ballet in the vaudeville theatre. The extraordinary Herculean Feats of Signor Plimmeri, the Acrobat Fury! *Soirées Musicale*, by the celebrated Hibernian Prodigy, master Spencer Forde . . . concluding with a grand display of fireworks and a novel and terrific Pyrotechnic Tableau!"

Such entertainments and the tavern-life, the tea gardens, the coffee houses, the exhibitions of curiosities and the menageries that opened and closed in and about Chelsea were to develop into the

Cremorne pleasure gardens, which opened a year before the birth of Walter Greaves, and were to have a significant influence not so much upon popular music and light entertainment as upon painting.

Crime was reduced by the introduction of a uniformed police force in the early eighteen-thirties. The first constable to appear in Chelsea was many years later remembered as being "a tall, ungainly-looking countryman, dressed in a blue bob-tailed coat with white metal buttons, white duck trousers, heavy blucher boots, and a top hat and white gloves. For several days an admiring crowd persistently followed him up and down his beat, a little way behind like the tail of a comet."

While police patrols and the lighting of roads by gas almost put an end to highway robbery, Chelsea remained a violent, volatile place. While the middle classes enjoyed the home-made entertainments of the nineteenth-century parlour and made expeditions to pleasure gardens, or the theatre, the recreation of the working man was drink. They were physically strong, these men, working on the river and its wharves, in the market gardens, as carters and some even as stevedores in the docks east of the Tower of London, walking to and from their work each day. Fist fights outside public houses were common, as were brawls between drovers over their right of way and between rival watermen.

The rorty life of Chelsea in the eighteen-thirties was preserved in detail by the local gossip-columnist, Bo-peep, whose scandalous revelations were awaited with apprehension and glee. "We advise Chancellor, the omnibus man, not to invite young girls into his bus, and then endeavour to take improper liberties with them . . ." he wrote. "We advise Mr. Fairborn to behave better to his wife and not to keep so many fancy women . . . Bo-peep wishes to know why old Green, of Jubilee Place, and swell Cronchley, the grocer, visit Madame Frances of 11 Leader Street . . . We advise the slavey at Duncan's, Robert Street, not to seduce the red-haired pot-boy of the Wellesley Arms from his duty at the rate of four kisses a pint . . . We advise stumpy Moss not to get so drunk every night but to marry the girl he seduced . . . We advise young Marshall, of Alexander Place, to leave off dressing in such a stupid manner. Why not pay for the boats at Greaves?"

Walter Greaves was to remember the roughness of Chelsea life as part of the vigorous character of the place and as a fault more than balanced by boisterous good humour and generosity. He remembered the dangerously rough practical jokes played by Chelsea youths, such as the night when a gang of them crept up to the watchman's box in Cheyne Walk and tipped it into the river. Luckily for the watchman it floated like a boat until shouts for help brought a waterman to his rescue.

As a boy, Walter Greaves was not given to violent pranks, but even he was not beyond a little window-breaking. The field to the east of Cheyne Row, where Shrewsbury House had stood, was rented by his uncle to graze ponies and here Walter and his brothers used to play. Once Walter shied a stone through a back window of the house where Thomas Carlyle was writing his biography of Frederick the Great.

Walter Greaves and Thomas Carlyle, who were to become the two most familiar figures in the streets of Victorian Chelsea, became aware of their environment in totally different ways. For young Walter Greaves it was a slow-growing understanding and love of surroundings, intimately familiar since birth but acquiring, for him, a fascination that was to become an obsession that he could communicate. For Thomas Carlyle, Chelsea was revealed as suddenly and vividly as the rising of a curtain on an elaborate and teeming stage.

Carlyle was already thirty-nine when, in 1834, he arrived in Chelsea searching for a house to which he could bring his wife, Jane, to whom he had been married nine years. There was a terrace house, built in 1708, to let for thirty-five pounds a year in Cheyne Row, with all the qualities that had already begun to attract the middle-class intelligentsia to Chelsea. "Chelsea is unfashionable," wrote Carlyle to his wife, waiting in Scotland. "It was once the resort of the Court and great, however; hence numerous old houses in it, at once cheap and excellent."

The solidity of the house impressed Carlyle. "The house itself is eminent, antique; wainscotted to the very ceiling . . . broadish stair with massive balustrade . . . floors firm as a rock . . . Three storeys beside the sunk storey . . . on the whole a most massive roomy sufficient old house, with places, for example, to hang say three dozen hats or cloaks on; and as many crevices . . ."

But there were many other such terraces in London, so Carlyle's choice was finally decided by what he could see down the street, "flag-pathed, sunk-storied, iron-railed, all old-fashioned and tightly done up", past a line of pollarded lime trees.

"Our Row," he wrote, "runs out upon a beautiful Parade (perhaps they call it) running along the shore of the River; shops, etc., and a broad highway, with huge shady trees; boats lying moored and a smell of shipping and tar; Battersea Bridge (of wood) a few yards off; the broad River, with white-trousered, white-shirted Cockneys dashing by like arrows in their long canoes of boats; beyond, the green beautiful knolls of Surrey with their Villages; on the whole a most artificial, green-painted, yet lively, fresh, almost opera-looking business such as you can fancy."

Added to this was the peculiar quality Chelsea had inherited from its past inhabitants, one of special appeal to the historian and philosopher, whose imagination was swirling with thoughts of tumultuous events and giant personalities which he planned to describe at his desk in the eminent, antique house in Cheyne Row. "Chelsea is a singular heterogeneous kind of spot, very dirty and confused in some places, quite beautiful in others, abounding with antiquities and traces of great men . . ."

The Carlyles were unable to resist this appeal and took the house. So here they moved with their chests, trunks, furniture and their canary, Chico, who, as the cab jolted out to Chelsea, "struck up his lilt in the very London streets whenever he could see green leaves and feel free air". They also brought with them the frustrations and tensions of a sexually maladjusted marriage that was to give a sombre mood to their house and their circle. At once, Thomas Carlyle's influence began to radiate from the house in Cheyne Row. First with his history of the French Revolution, written there, then with the massive biography of Frederick the Great and works of history and philosophy that, to the Victorians, seemed to be impregnated with the eternal verities.

Forty-seven years Carlyle lived in Cheyne Row, surviving his wife by fifteen years, becoming to the people of Chelsea a figure as familiar and seemingly indestructible as Queen Victoria herself. As his drawing-room became a centre of pilgrimage for intellectuals, so "The Sage of Chelsea" became one of the district's curiosities, inspiring a mythology and iconography in his own lifetime. The working people of Chelsea, who lived around him, regarded him with a mixture of awe and uncertain amusement. The lean, grizzled old Scot with his wide-brimmed hat and walking-stick could be seen almost daily stumping through the narrow streets about the Old Church, or smoking a late evening pipe by the riverside. He was familiar but there was no familiarity. Mr. Carlyle was known as a silent, gruff old man.

Young Walter Greaves, guiltily remembering his smashing of The Sage's window, recalled an incident that illustrated the relationship between Chelsea and Carlyle. Down by the riverside taverns and wharves there was much casual jollity and exchange of gossip, but in this Carlyle never joined. His dour manner became so much a part of his legend that, among irreverent Chelsea youths, it became a sport to attempt to force him into conversation. Walter Greaves recalled that once he and other lads, who were hanging about the river wall, saw Carlyle approach, and one of them called out, affably but cheekily, "A fine evening, Mr. Carlyle?" Without pausing or glancing at his questioner, The Sage muttered, "Tell me something I dinna ken."

Thomas Carlyle had visited Chelsea and had stayed, but the literary and artistic men who had preceded him were mostly transient. At first they had come to Chelsea with the households of their noble patrons, then, as the nobility moved westward, stayed at Chelsea as being convenient both for London and the rural residences of the rich.

Hans Holbein had been introduced into Sir Thomas More's household by a mutual friend, Erasmus, and his portraits of that tragic family are given extra poignance by the knowledge that his success at Chelsea led to his engagement as the favoured painter at the court of King Henry.

Early in the eighteenth century Chelsea became for a time a political resort and was frequented by the Whig journalists Joseph Addison and Sir Richard Steele, the editors of *The Tatler* and *The*

Valter Greaves, the confident pupil. A detail from self-portrait (*above*) sketched on the balcony of Lindsey House in the late 'sixties.

The rejected friend. A pencil drawing of Greaves by William Rothenstein (*below*) made in 1915.

Jimmy Whistler, the friend and master. Possibly a self-portrait (*above*), or a joint effort with Walter Greaves, in the late 'sixties.

Whistler, the angry god. A portrait in oils from memory by Walter Greaves (*below*) from a series painted after Whistler's death.

The happy years. Whistler sketches the Thames and Cadogan Pier in a boat pulled by Henry Greaves (*above*) while coal is unloaded at the wharf beside Chelsea Old Church. In this, and other drawings by Walter Greaves, the date – "'60" – is suspect.

Whistler in his Lindsey Row studio (*below*) drawn, probably inaccurately in detail, from memory by Walter Greaves. The portrait of his mother is on the easel and his palette table on his left.

Spectator, and their friend the ebullient satirist Dean Jonathan Swift. The latter, who took lodgings in Danvers Street in 1711 for a few months, saw Chelsea with an unromantic, irritable eye. In his letters to "Stella" – Esther Johnson, whom he was later to marry in secret – Swift described Chelsea with almost photographic honesty. One purpose of taking lodgings outside London was to benefit from the walk to and from the city through the fields. "We are already mowing and making hay, and it smells so sweet as we walk through the flowery meads," he wrote, adding, "But the hay-making nymphs are perfect drabs, nothing so clean and pretty as further in the country. There is a mighty increase in dirty wenches in straw hats since I knew London." His regular walk from St. James's Street took him a little under an hour and was, he reckoned, a distance of two miles or "just five thousand, seven hundred and forty-eight steps".

During the first half of the eighteenth century there remained two great houses in Chelsea owned by rich families of good and eclectic tastes to offer patronage to the arts. There, Sir Robert Walpole, the statesman, entertained royalty, politicians, the nobility and intellectuals. There, his son Horace began to weave the mischievously glittering web of intrigue and gossip which, following the fashion, he later spun around himself at Twickenham. Their friend and neighbour in Chelsea, upon which he was to exercise a more lasting influence than they, was Sir Hans Sloane.

In his lifetime of ninety-three years, Sloane was to become a gentleman-scientist – of the species to which Prince Rupert had belonged – but his beginnings were those of a professional. He studied medicine in France and, late in the seventeenth century, had gone to Jamaica as physician to the Governor. There he married the rich widow of a planter and was able to indulge in his passion for collecting curiosities, notably geological specimens and plants, of which he brought some eight hundred varieties home with him to England.

Able and amiable and with a fashionable practice in Bloomsbury, Sloane became physician to both Queen Anne and the first King George. He was President of the Royal College of Physicians and, on the death of Sir Isaac Newton in 1727, became President of the Royal Society.

His and his descendants' long association with Chelsea began in 1712 when he bought the manor, Chelsea Place, and much surrounding land. His property included a riverside garden near the Royal Hospital, which had for about forty years been leased by the Apothecaries' Company for the experimental planting of herbs and rare plants. Sloane now gave this to the Company for an annual rent of five pounds in perpetuity and one of the most remarkable gardens in England began to exert its influence on the vegetation of the world. It was a place of import, export and experiment. Here were planted curious specimens brought home by such travelling naturalists as Captain James Cook and Sir Joseph Banks. From here were sent seeds from which three-quarters of the world's cotton crop is descended. Here varieties of medicinal herbs were grown for the treatment of such eighteenth-century disorders as "the King's Evil, Strein, Shortness of Breath, Kive-Heels and Surfeits, Cholick Pain and Thirsty Fever, Stitch, Hickock, Spleens, St. Anthony's Fire, Palsy, Husking-Cough, Vapours, Humours and Low-Spirits."

Generosity apart, Sir Hans Sloane enjoyed commercial aptitude, which some of his descendants were to inherit, occasionally to the detriment of Chelsea. This led him to buy Sir Thomas More's old mansion and grounds and demolish the house to enlarge his manorial estate. His collection of curiosities, which he hoped would remain as a permanent museum at Chelsea Place, he offered to the nation at what he claimed to be less than half their original cost to him. After his death in 1753, Horace Walpole, one of his executors, wrote mischievously that Sir Hans had considered the true value of his collection to be forty thousand pounds "and so would anybody who loves hippopotamuses, sharks with one ear and spiders as big as geese! You may think that those who think money the most valuable of all curiosities will not be purchasers."

But the Government did buy the collection – or most of it – and had it moved back to Bloomsbury as the nucleus of the British Museum. While Sloane's array of geological specimens, rare creatures preserved in spirits of wine, shells, insects, and a magnificent library, were of great value, he also assembled a bizarre collection of oddities and it was these that so amused Walpole. These included: "The singed hair of a woman killed by thunder . . . Part of the sail of the *Montagu* knotted together by a storm . . . A poysoned arrow which being tryd had no effect on a wounded pigeon . . . A Highlander's garters . . . A muskett bullet which being shot at a mark on a door went through and killed a young man on the other side . . . Britches of the runaway rebellious negros in the woods of Jamaica . . . A girdle to be worn by a child to prevent the effects of thunder, at which there hangs a silver purse, a medal of our Saviour, a nutmeg, a picture of the Virgin, a cross in alabaster, a hand in jet, a bell, an ewer, a piece of Spanish gold, a comb, a fork, etc."

The spirit of Sloane haunted Chelsea. Among the dark cedars and flowering trees of the Physic Garden his marble statue by Michael Rysbrack remained like a commanding phantom. His descendants were to name their developments such as Hans Town and Sloane Street after him.

Sloane was to have another influence, both entertaining and subtle, upon the development of Chelsea. While the best of his private museum went to Bloomsbury some of the gewgaws and knick-knacks remained in Cheyne Walk and became the nucleus of another collection. James Salter had travelled with Sir Hans as his valet in the seventeenth century, and in a house by the river near Chelsea Place he opened a coffee house. This was no ordinary coffee house and the whimsical Irish proprietor described it as a "knackatory", a caricature of his former master's collection along Cheyne Walk. Salter, a man of presence and humour, was nicknamed "Don Saltero" by one of his customers, a retired admiral, and he and his establishment became thoughout the eighteenth-century the meeting place not only of Chelsea worthies, but of literary men from London and an essential part of every foreign visitor's London itinerary.

Sir Hans went there to meet his fellow-Whigs, Addison and Steele, to talk politics in rooms cluttered with such exhibits as a piece of Solomon's temple, a starved cat found between the walls of Westminster Abbey, a fairy's or elf's arrow, Mary Queen of Scots' pin-cushion, the caul of an elephant and, so Steele joked, "Pontius Pilate's wife's chambermaid's sister's hat". After the Don's death, his daughter continued to preside over the knackatory until 1799, when it changed hands and the comic museum was sold. The auctioneer's marked catalogue shows that the whole collection sold for fifty-two pounds, eight shillings, including "Lot 42. The Pope's candle with which he curses the heretics and 3 bottles of preserved snakes, etc. 3s. 6d." and "Lot 99. The Tarantula, the bite of which occasions madness and death and is curable only by music. 5s. 6d." Don Saltero's survived as a tavern of the same name until 1867, when it was converted into a private house.

By the middle of the eighteenth century, Don Saltero's had become the meeting place of a "Chelsea set" of writers, wits and intellectuals, over whom presided an entertaining but caustic Scot, who was trying to combine journalism and the writing of novels and plays with the practice of medicine. Tobias Smollett was, for thirteen years, to become in Chelsea what Dr. Johnson became to Fleet Street, but he had no Boswell and the convivial evenings at Don Saltero's can only be imagined from a few snatches of reminiscence that have survived.

Smollett settled in Chelsea at the age of thirty with the wife he had met and married in the West Indies and his three-year-old daughter, Elizabeth. The household, which he maintained in style, included his mother-in-law and servants and so needed the space which abandoned mansions of the nobility now offered in Chelsea. The Smolletts took apartments in Monmouth House at the top of Lawrence Street, near the Old Church and facing the river. Here he wrote his novels *Roderick Random* and *Peregrine Pickle*, which were praised, and *Sir Launcelot Greaves*, which was not. Here, to help pay his debts, he put together his unworthy *A Complete History of England* and tried his hand at a wide range of other writing and journalism.

The alternate success and failure of his writing led him to sudden and surprisingly bitter attacks on his more notable friends, including David Garrick, the actor-manager, who had presented his plays. Smollett's circle, who visited him at Chelsea, included such as Oliver Goldsmith, the essayist, John Wilkes, the political writer, Laurence Sterne, the novelist, and Dr. Samuel Johnson, for whom Smollett invented the title "The Great Cham of Literature".

Smollett's kindness was remembered longer than his irascibility and, in particular, his generosity – despite his own chronic money troubles – to "unfortunate brothers of the quill", whom he would dine on Sundays with full-blown fare of roast beef and Yorkshire pudding, port, punch and beer. The Smolletts' stay in Chelsea ended when his daughter, an intelligent child who wrote poetry, died of tuberculosis in 1763, despite the care of her adoring doctor-father and the renowned health-giving properties of Chelsea air. Broken-hearted, Smollett and his household began their wanderings on the Continent, he failing both in health and humour. Even so, he could write to a Chelsea friend in that year, "I cannot help respecting Chelsea as a second native place, notwithstanding the irreparable misfortunes which happened to me while I resided in it."

Monmouth House, haunted by this restless ghost, stood another seventy years. Then, in 1834, Thomas Carlyle looked from the upper windows of the house in Cheyne Row, which he was to buy, and wrote that, from the back, he could see "into mere leafy regions with here and there a red high-peaked old roof looking through; and see nothing of London except by day the summits of St. Paul's Cathedral and Westminster Abbey, and by night the great Babylon affronting the skies . . ." From the front windows, he wrote, "We . . . could shoot a gun into Smollett's old house (at this very time getting pulled down)" and, describing briefly his fellow-Scot's life there, added, "Don Saltero's coffee-house still looks as brisk . . ."

Although the most notable Chelsea figure of his time, Smollett was a temporary settler. Already, native talents were beginning to emerge and one of them, James Gillray, certainly knew and enjoyed the hearty eccentricities of Don Saltero's, which must somewhere be reflected in his ribald cartoons. Gillray, who was aged only six when Smollett left Chelsea, was the son of an old soldier, who had fought at Fontenoy and, after losing an arm, had become an out-pensioner of Chelsea Hospital. For forty years he was sexton to the graveyard behind Lindsey House, which in the mid-eighteenth century was acquired by the Moravian Brotherhood, a religious sect from Central Europe. In the sexton's lodge, James spent his childhood until first apprenticed to a letter-engraver and then, showing signs of emerging brilliance, began to study at the Royal Academy.

Although James Gillray was, as a caricaturist and political cartoonist, the first Chelsea-born artist of fame, artistic skills had already begun to spread into the village at another level. The year in which this began is not known exactly but the place was within a hundred yards of Smollett's old home in Lawrence Street.

Of all the ingredients that make up Chelsea mythology none is more tantalising than the history of the Porcelain Manufactory. The time and manner of its beginnings are unknown. After perhaps fifty years it vanished so completely that its appearance and exact site were forgotten at a time when print engravers were meticulously recording prospects of London and its environs. In another half-century the only proof that this magical workshop had existed at all were its wares bearing the anchor trade-mark, china made from a secret composition. "A Display of Elegance and Taste reigns almost uninterrupted," one of the factory's advertisements had announced. "A continued variety of antique, select and peculiar Forms and Shapes, aetherial Colours and elaborate Decorations, that alternately rise with increasing beauty and which distinguish Genius . . ."

Here, and in the salerooms of St. James's, the Georgian arbiters of taste bought the porcelain figures, the dinner services, the busts, the handles for canes, the scent bottles and cutlery, the dishes and tureens fashioned with elegance and frivolity that were the incongruous produce of a robust riverside village smelling of tar and horse dung. The first Chelsea ware that can be identified was fired in 1745, or thereabouts, and the proprietor of the factory was a Charles Gouyn, but this was not its beginning. There was to be speculation that porcelain had been made at Chelsea for nearly fifty years before this time, the skills being introduced by experienced craftsmen from Dresden or Venice.

The greatest years of Chelsea china began when the factory was managed by Nicholas Sprimont – probably from about 1750 for about twenty years – who was himself succeeded by William Duesbury, under whose direction the factory was moved to Derby in 1784. The buildings were immediately demolished, disappearing so completely that speculation over its site has continued ever since. The probability is, however, that the manufactory was strung out along the western side of Lawrence Street on either side of Justice Walk. Remains of kilns were identified in the cellars of a little old public house, The Prince of Wales, on the corner of Justice Walk;

broken fragments of porcelain have been dug up in the gardens of Georgian houses at the north-west corner of Lawrence Street; in 1842, a pit filled with other such waste – a glorious mine of glowing colour and graceful shapes – was found in the mud when foundations for new buildings were being dug and several cartloads were hauled away to a rubbish tip.

A few hints and memories link this elegance with the rough practicality of Georgian London. An old foreman of the factory remembered, years later, that Dr. Samuel Johnson had visited the factory, perhaps while on a visit to Smollett, and tried his hand at conjuring up porcelain of his own. Amused, the management allowed him access to all parts of the factory but the mixing room where the secret ingredients were prepared. Full of confidence and the picnic meals his housekeeper brought to him from Fleet Street, The Great Cham was as clumsy with his hands as he was deft with words and, in any case, his efforts inevitably collapsed in the firing kilns. Admitting failure at last, he observed characteristically that "the china, though beautiful, was too dear".

Another link is through an account book in which work of extreme delicacy is listed with bluff Georgian disregard for spelling: "A Groop of figars; 1 pr. of Britanyas; a bote; 4 Chellsey playts; 1 pr. of tewlips; a large pugg dogg, a tea cettle, a hartychoack . . ."

The importance of the Porcelain Manufactory was that here were trained and worked hundreds of villagers. In Lawrence Street, several generations were taught to model and paint, some becoming renowned for their skill in painting flowers and insects, abstract decoration and the brilliant coloured clothes such as were then being displayed a mile down the bank of the river at Ranelagh. Memories of this industry were as fragile as porcelain but probably traces of its artistic influence survived in Chelsea.

The boy Walter Greaves and his brother Henry, apprenticed in their father's boatyard and growing their muscles as watermen, could see much on the river that had survived the changes. At Whitsun, there was the regatta, which was described with Rowlandsonian relish by one of his contemporaries: "The waterside on regatta day was like a fair, as there was always two or three mountebanks, a circus and dancing booth on the various pieces of vacant ground in the neighbourhood of the river. Some of the performers, dressed as clowns, played a kind of river tournament, sitting straddle-legged on beer barrels afloat, tilting at each other with long poles; the fun was to see them tumble each other into the water. Then there was the old woman drawn in a washing tub by four geese. There were rowing races for watermen and prizes were given for running in sacks, and climbing the greasy pole for a leg of mutton fixed at the top, and a prize for running along a greased pole placed horizontally from the stem of a coal barge . . . After each display, the performers would march with a band to their different places of entertainment."

Among this almost medieval jollity would appear the noble shapes of the ceremonial barges of the Lord Mayor of London, the Aldermen and the Livery Companies. These were berthed at Chelsea, where at the succession of small boatyards, they could be refitted and painted. The painting of these barges was the task Walter and Henry Greaves most enjoyed. This was not like slapping paint and varnish on to their father's clinker-built skiffs or tarring the sides of Thomas barges, for these magnificent craft were emblazoned with heraldic devices, figureheads and gilding. On their sides and carved cabins the Greaves boys could paint romantic, medieval emblems from the Age of Chivalry, then seeming to Victorian England the most noble and golden of all the golden ages of an idealised past. They could paint coats of arms in the bold heraldic colours of argent and gules, vert and rouge. They could draw inspiration, not from any cultivated school of art, but from the bright and meticulous armorial bearings and lettering on carriages and stage coaches that came spanking down the Brompton Road or stabled at Chelsea; from the curious designs of castles and roses that the barge people painted on the narrow-boats that were towed down the canals to the Thames; and from inn signs, for there were some about Chelsea which, it was said, had been painted by George Morland in payment for drink.

The boys began sketching the barges' figureheads and then designing both these and elaborate coats of arms, including one particularly splendid fantasy for their own family with the proud words, "The Greaves Arms" beneath it, a sketch of which

Walter was to keep all his life. Walter and Henry Greaves became fascinated by the anatomy of ships and boats and the interlocking intricacies of their rigging. And, for them, interest in the mechanics of water-craft was linked with that of the riverside warehouses and docks, and these with the old buildings among which they stood. The early-Victorian architect Augustus Pugin lived nearby and it is possible that he interested the boys in the anatomy of buildings, perhaps, describing in contrast the slow evolution of the comfortable Old Church with the Gothic mimicry of St. Luke's.

The realisation that there was more to Chelsea than familiar prettiness and the homely patina of age came to Walter Greaves through two men, both painters. Joseph Turner and John Martin both settled beside the river at Chelsea, the former a few paces upstream from the Greaves's house, the latter a few paces downstream. Both exercised a profound effect on the district and the simple waterman's family who were their neighbours.

The date of Turner's arrival in Chelsea remains as obscure as was so much of his private life. In piquant contrast to the blazing truth of the light he transferred to canvas, his own ways were devious and secretive. When Turner bought the six-roomed house at the extreme western end of the Chelsea waterfront he was aged about sixty and had long been recognised as a painter of genius. As an artist he bridged the gulf between the formal painters of the eighteenth century and the Impressionists who were to follow at the end of the nineteenth. In the first years of Queen Victoria's reign, he already seemed to belong to a fast-receding past, for here was a man who had sketched the battle-damage to the *Victory* after Trafalgar.

A year or two before 1840, Turner, whose known residence was off Cavendish Square, invited his painter friend John Martin to walk with him across Hyde Park and Brompton, then through the market gardens to his "small place in Chelsea". Martin's son, Leopold, who accompanied them, found the house "miserable in every respect". But Turner proudly led them upstairs, where he "pointed with seeming pride to the splendid view from the single window, saying, 'Here you see my study; sky and water. Are they not glorious? Here I have my lesson, night and day!' "

Later, Turner was to become more secretive and flinch from old friends who recognised him in Chelsea or on one of the steamboats which had begun a regular service to the City.

Turner had had much in common with John Martin, who was thirteen years his junior. Like their immediate predecessors and contemporaries, both were fascinated by the play of light. Turner had inherited this interest from Dutch painters of the seventeenth century through John Constable, who had transposed the wet, windy, salty skies of Holland to Suffolk. Constable had died at about the time Turner bought his Chelsea vantage point for viewing sky and water, having described the latter's work as "airy visions, painted with tinted steam".

Other painters had been fascinated by light in different ways: Joseph Wright of Derby by artificial light – candles, log fires and fireworks; William Etty by the glow of light upon human skin. John Martin, like Etty a Yorkshireman, tried to marry his passion for dramatic lighting effects with the monumental Biblical or Classical subjects that were then the fashion and he did this to wildly theatrical effect.

Years before Martin followed Turner to Chelsea in 1848, the two had taken different paths. Turner had become uncompromising and his sea-pieces baffled a generation that had become used to recognising whether the ship was a first-rate man-o'-war or a brigantine, and whether her predicament had been brought about by French broadsides, or a gale driving her on to the rocks. Instead, the painting entitled *The Landing of the Pamphilus* was not so much a Classical set-piece with armoured heroes and naked heroines, or a heart-rending scene of shipwreck, but a great swirl of light diffused through cloud, wind, rain and sea. Such painting was, according to one critic, just the "fruits of a diseased eye and reckless hand".

John Martin had remained with the fashion. His thundering skies lowered over the fall of Babylon or Nineveh, Belshazzar's feast, a crisis in *Macbeth* or The Last Judgement. Although Turner painted at Chelsea for about a dozen years and Martin for half a dozen, neither left recognisable paintings of the river which had drawn them to its banks. Yet it is probable that some wild Turner sunset was conceived there and that the thunderstorm raging over Martin's Sea of Galilee may, in fact, have been pelting Putney.

That both these men were remarkable and that they found something remarkable in Chelsea must have been obvious to the Greaves family, living between Turner's cottage and Martin's apartments in Lindsey House. Turner was a mystery to Chelsea, so much so that he was long thought to be a retired admiral named Booth, which was, in fact, the name of his housekeeper that he had assumed locally for anonymity. Probably it was from Chelsea that Turner travelled by water to Wapping on those private missions when he painted the intimate little watercolours which were first assumed to represent sunsets. After his death, they were discovered by the inhibited Ruskin to be sexual and feminine and so were burned. When painting the realities of sunset, the best vantage-points were on the south bank of the Thames, and Turner would hire Charles Greaves to row him across to Battersea Fields, where Battersea Park was to be planted, or to the churchyard of St. Mary's, Battersea, which jutted into the river, commanding a mile of wide water beneath the setting sun.

Yet the waterman did not know until later who was the weather-beaten old man with the bright seaman's eyes and the beaky nose. Walter later said, "Although he knew Turner well, he never knew the man he was, that is, not until afterwards. My father said that Turner was fond of sketching in Battersea and used to send his landlady, Mrs. Booth, across the river before him with his luncheon. When he did that he would always accompany her as far as Lindsey House to ask my father what the weather was going to be like, and if he received an unfavourable reply he would say to her, 'Don't go far. Greaves says it's going to be wet.' My father rowed Turner several times on the water, who always, he said, was dressed the same way, in a dirty faded brown overcoat and top hat."

Walter Greaves was only five years old when Turner died and was never certain whether he remembered him, or whether this was only another Chelsea mirage of the past, but he did remember his formidable old housekeeper. John Martin, however, he knew well from dramatic childhood memories. Martin's interest was not in watery sunsets but in spectacular, stormy night skies. These would be the nights when the wind rattled the windows of the Greaves's little house, the river slapped against the wall and thumped the moored skiffs together and, out in the stream, the Thames barges strained and creaked at their cables. "Whenever there was a storm," Walter remembered, "and my father had to stay up all night to look after the boats, Martin used to say to him, 'If there are good clouds and a good moon, ring my bell.' And when there were, we would ring the bell, and in a little while Martin would come out on to the balcony of his house and start working." If it was not too late Walter, then aged seven or eight, would be sent round to ring the bell, or, if that failed to wake the old painter, throw stones at his window, and he could recall the curious sight of the specialist in illustrating The Day of Judgement, bustling out on to the balcony in night-shirt and night-cap with his sketching materials, lit by a fierce moon glaring through scudding clouds and full of happy anticipation.

In those years there was another link, perhaps an unconscious link, which helped bind together these influences on Chelsea and the Greaves family.

Earlier in the century, when Charles Greaves was a boy, there had lived in one of the separate houses that by then comprised Lindsey House, an ingenious family of French extraction, the Brunels. Sir Marc Isambard Brunel had brought his family to Chelsea in 1808 for a variety of reasons, including its proximity to Battersea, where he owned sawmills, and to the river – for one of his interests was the development of the steam engine for marine propulsion. The family was beset by financial troubles, in 1814 the sawmills were burned down and, ten years later, the family left. The Brunels moved just as Sir Marc's most dramatic ambition was to reach fruition: the driving of the first tunnel beneath the Thames.

Sir Marc's imaginative and forceful son, Isambard Kingdom Brunel, was only eighteen when the family left Chelsea, but for a year he had been helping his father with plans for the tunnel. His own later achievements – notably as Chief Engineer of the Great Western Railway and designer of the colossal ocean liner, the *Great Eastern* – made him a giant of the Victorian Age. His monuments standing today in iron, brick and earth show him to have been an artistic as well as an engineering genius.

The Brunels maintained their link with Chelsea and exercised their own influence upon it, although the extent of this remains one of many speculations. John Martin, the painter, was a friend of the younger Brunel, and it was their old Chelsea house that he occupied from 1848 and it was from the two-storey balconies of iron piping, which Sir Marc had built up the front of his house, that he painted his wild night skies. But Martin was also an amateur inventor and one of his preoccupations was the increase in the driving-power of steam engines. So it was that, in 1841, Isambard Brunel invited him to take part in an experiment designed to prove the great Stephenson wrong in his belief that railway trains could never much exceed a speed of fifteen miles per hour. The pair, together with two companions, time-keeping clerks and an experienced engine-driver, boarded the Great Western Railway's most powerful locomotive for the trial run between Southall and Slough. One of the party recorded, "With Mr. Brunel's eye on the steam-pressure and hand on the safety-valve, we were off, and in half a mile we were running at top speed. To the great satisfaction of Mr. Brunel, and the astonishment of all, it was discovered that the distance of nine miles to the station at Slough had been run in six minutes, or at the rate of ninety miles an hour, a very different result from that which Mr. Stephenson's early calculations would have led one to expect."

The scene conjures up Turner's awe-struck painting *Rain, Steam and Speed – the Great Western Railway, 1844*, in which a high-funnelled engine charges across one of Mr. Brunel's viaducts, its carriages rocking and rattling behind, in a swirl of steam and rain. The combinations of circumstances ask: did Turner also know the Brunels? He had his secret cottage near them at Chelsea; he knew John Martin; he painted the Great Western Railway. It is reasonable to suppose that he did.

Thus, to Charles Greaves and his sons, there would seem to be a natural intimacy between art and industry. Turner and Martin they knew to be no dilettanti and the Brunels seemed almost as much artists as engineers. Even the Thames Tunnel was a popular subject for print-engravers and Isambard Brunel's bridges and viaducts, cuttings and embankments, railway stations and ships were vast and beautiful monuments to inventive genius and mechanical power.

That to draw and paint was a natural occupation – as natural as shooting snipe or rowing in the regatta – must have always been accepted by the apprenticed Walter and Henry Greaves. Together, as boys, they began to draw river scenes and the streets of Chelsea. Walter, it seems, had a flair for composition, while Henry, as his brother later said, was "a great one for detail". In their street scenes – jointly signed "H. & W. Greaves" – Henry would lovingly draw in each brick, each crack in plaster, each cobblestone and scatter of horse dung and every shop window would be meticulously filled with its wares.

But it is at this moment, so fresh with youthful enthusiasm and promise, that mystery begins to creep across the remembered life of Walter Greaves like a Thames fog in slow swirls and eddies; sometimes half-revealing and sometimes distorting some seemingly recognisable shape, occasionally clearing to unveil a clear view only to close and blanket it again all the more thickly.

It is ironical that this first of the mysteries should concern a scene brilliant with life and colour. All that is now certain is that in the possession of the Tate Gallery in London is a large painting in oils called *Hammersmith Bridge on Boat Race Day*. It is one of the great British paintings of the nineteenth century and one of the great primitive paintings of the world. Caught alive in bright poster colours is a scene of joy, energy and vivacity. It is a painting of people, crowded together in talk and excitement, swarming over the old suspension bridge at Hammersmith, while a racing pair shoots underneath. Its combination of colour and composition whisks away a century and there, suddenly, is the dash and gaiety of a Victorian holiday.

It is clearly a highly original work of art. It was painted by Walter Greaves and is usually said to be his greatest painting. It owes nothing to the influence of any other known painter and this has always been explained by the fact that the artist said that he had painted it at the age of sixteen.

Certainly, as a boy, Walter Greaves must often have pulled one of his father's skiffs upstream to watch the regattas held above Chelsea. This particular scene, he later said, was the view from a window of a riverside inn at one end of the bridge, from which he had sketched it. The big canvas itself, he said, had been painted at home in Chelsea.

This painting and the fact that it was said to have been painted as early as 1862 has always been at the vortex of the controversies that have swept around the bewildered figure of Walter Greaves. On the face of it, this seems to explain much of the triumph and tragedy that was to follow. It appears to be the work of a young painter with a natural eye for composition and colour; the colours and the bold design could well have originated from his earlier painting of heraldic devices on ceremonial barges in his father's boatyard.

Yet a closer look at those teeming figures introduces a shadow of doubt. To study the clothes and hairstyles of the women – both of which were changing rapidly at that mid-century – and comparing them with other paintings and fashion plates of the period, shows that they seem to belong to a later time. This evidence points to the picture having been painted nearly ten years later than its artist claimed. This disparity could probably be put down to the weakening of Walter Greaves's memory, which became marked after middle age. But, whatever the reason, the probability that *Hammersmith Bridge on Boat Race Day* was painted near to 1870 adds a new and more deeply mysterious element to the events which were about to take place beside this reach of the river, and to the human relationships which were to be formed in that particular decade.

2

Harmony in friendship

The house at the corner of Sloane Street and Hans Street lay only a mile and a quarter from the Greaves boatyard. Yet in that short north-easterly journey through Chelsea a complete transformation took place. A few yards up from the river the watery, tarry smells and the noise of creaking capstans and winches were lost and replaced by the sounds and smells of stables, horses and carts. Then the neat terraces of modest houses built at the turn of the century over market gardens and open land between surburban villas, some still standing in well-ordered walled gardens. Next, the gentility of Hans Town – so convenient for Hyde Park and Mayfair. Finally Sloane Street, separating the well-to-do citizens of north-east Chelsea from the prosperous inhabitants of the gleaming stucco residences which the speculator Thomas Cubitt had erected during the second quarter of the century over what had once been the Five Fields, so finally merging the little riverside town with the capital.

Sloane Street was gracious and, compared with the great radial highways carrying the wagons, coaches and carriages to and from London, quiet. The opening of the first Chelsea Bridge, near the site of Ranelagh in 1858, had meant that some Surrey market-gardeners now took this road to London. Yet its traffic was mostly from the mews stables of Hans Town and Belgravia and its sounds that of street vendors and the hurdy-gurdy. On the corner of Sloane Street and Hans Street stood the plain, handsome house of Francis Seymour Haden and his American wife, Deborah. He was a fashionable surgeon with a growing practice – but with a social standing far higher than that of the ordinary Victorian doctor – and considerable talent as an amateur artist. She was an American, the daughter of a Major Whistler, an engineer whose greatest achieve-

The delights of Cremorne pleasure gardens. A hansom cab draws up at the illuminated gates at dusk (*left*). A sketch in charcoal, chalk and pastel on brown paper by Walter Greaves.

In sunshine, Whistler leans against the Venus fountain while Walter Greaves and one of his sisters share a bottle of beer (*below*). In the background of this drawing by Walter Greaves is the Chinese bandstand.

The Green Dress. Eliza Greaves painted in oils by her brother (*left*) wearing the Tudor-style dress which changed its colour from the blue that Whistler claimed as his own so that its exhibition was regarded as an act of betrayal.

The life class. A drawing of the nude figure in charcoal and chalk on brown paper (*right*) made by Walter Greaves at Whistler's side in Barthe's Chelsea studio. The model was likely to have been Mary Lewis.

ment had been the planning and construction of the railway between Moscow and St. Petersburg. The Whistler family – three children, including Deborah, by his first wife and four sons by his second wife – were, like many restless Americans, compulsive travellers. Deborah had met her handsome English husband while the family was visiting London from Russia and now, in 1859, ten years after her father's death, James, her half-brother, was to stay with her at 62 Sloane Street.

The journey to London and the long cab ride from the boat-train at London Bridge Station was familiar to James Whistler, who had stayed with the Hadens several times since their marriage twelve years earlier. But this visit was to be different. At the age of twenty-four James Abbott McNeill Whistler had come to stay not for a holiday but to change lives, and to change Chelsea and change the course of art.

The young man, who had arrived in Chelsea with few belongings and little money, cut a figure of incongruity but one which, partly through his own doing, would have attracted little attention in this quarter of London a century later. His slight, muscular body and *bouffant* black curls were bedecked in clothes which surprised his conventional brother-in-law; perhaps he still wore his individualistic clothes, notably a wide-brimmed straw hat with a broad ribbon dangling from its crown and what appeared to be dancing pumps. But Seymour Haden was not only polite and tolerant; as an artist he knew that such individualistic eccentricities were the traditional, anarchical dress of the Parisian art student, and it was from the studios and *la vie de Bohême*, which surrounded them, that Jamie Whistler had arrived. No doubt, Haden must have thought, the young man would grow out of such absurdities. For these were the years when British artists would dress and live in the style of successful men of property or business, and certainly there was nothing in the appearance of Haden to connect him with the copper plates and acid bath of the etcher in his own studio.

As with young Walter Greaves at the far side of Chelsea, experience and environment had acted upon a natural talent. It had been planned that James Whistler should follow his father into the Army and he had entered West Point military academy. There he had acquired a certain military panache, a fierce patriotism and physical strength, but not a commission. Amenable neither to discipline nor horsemanship, and failing to attain the required aptitude in history and chemistry, he left West Point after less than three years. Later, he could sometimes joke about his failure, but the memory of it rankled and he would always refer to himself as "a West Point man" without a hint of self-mockery.

As an alternative he tried to enter the naval academy of Annapolis. In this, too, he failed, but he did, in 1854, find a junior appointment in the United States Coast and Geodetic Survey. There, for a few months, he worked as a draughtsman, learning the exact and demanding technique of etching charts. With the American Civil War and its terrible casualty lists drawing nearer, it is curious to speculate on the course of events had James Whistler taken part in the passing-out parade at West Point instead of becoming, in Washington, a student of etching.

The discipline of an office was as irksome as that of the parade ground and an understanding mother encouraged his flair for draughtsmanship by allowing him to study art in Paris with a small allowance from home. At once he found the discipline not only of the teaching studio but of fashionable artistic doctrine equally tiresome and, while he left an indelible mark on the artists' quarter of Paris on the Left Bank of the Seine, he was seldom seen at an easel in the studio of the painter Gleyre, in whose class he had enrolled.

Parisian taste in pictures was then *louche*, with classical and romantic subjects providing painters with excuses to produce the luscious, sentimental and often erotic works that were in demand among the prosperous middle class which had emerged since the Revolution and First Empire. The life class was the centre-piece of the art student's education but its disciplines tended to be overlaid by fashion, as in the studio of Bouguereau, where students were taught to copy his voluptuous, waxy nudes. To James Whistler such painting seemed both ridiculous and degrading. While he accepted some of the technical knowledge imparted by Gleyre – such as painting in oils upon a black background – he joined the small *avant-garde* of students who followed the ideas of Courbet, whose realism, discarding the careful composition and the fevered imagination of his contemporaries, opened the door to the later Impressionists and to Whistler.

Realism versus romanticism was one of the most favoured subjects for debate in the cafés of the Latin Quarter, where art students would argue for hours at the tables for the price of a cup of coffee. This was the Paris James Whistler had hoped for. He had probably read Henri Murger's *Scènes de la Vie de Bohême* and its world of artists and models living passionate intellectual and sexual lives in picturesque poverty was the Paris he was determined to find. While the English art students, whom he quickly got to know, had brought their manly Victorian ideals with them across the Channel, Whistler transformed his dapper West Point image into that of the gay bohemian. The young men from London – including Edward Poynter, Aleco Ionides and George du Maurier – cooked plain English food in their lodgings and kept fit with Indian clubs and boxing gloves. Whistler once sauntered in and, seeing two of them sparring among their easels, remarked that if they wanted a fight it would be less exhausting to hire porters to do it for them.

To these conventional friends, the Latin Quarter was a picturesque and enjoyable environment but little else. The cafés were cheap and convenient for good talk over coffee, and the models from the life class were, outside the studio, for jolly banter and even flirtation. But Jimmy Whistler combined earnest, but unconventional and sometimes solitary study of art with *la vie de Bohême* as it was lived by the French students. He lived in the cheapest lodgings – one a quiet little hotel near the soaring, sonorous church of St. Sulpice, another a towering, tottering rookery above a roaring street-market off the Rue de Seine. In the weeks before his allowance arrived from America, furniture and clothes were sold or pawned, bills were unpaid and free meals sometimes charmed out of friends and *patrons*. And, unlike most of his British contemporaries, he led an active sex life.

Whistler lived with two young girl models in Paris. One of these, noted for her lovely body and fiery temper, had been nicknamed *La Tigresse*, but it was his own pet name for her, *Fumette*, that he gave to her in the etching which caught and preserved her feline femininity. To his apprenticeship in etching charts he was now adding artistic touches to the drawing on copper plates with a needle, helping to bite the plates in the acid bath and pull the proofs at the press. It was in his Parisian etchings, and those made during a long ramble with a friend to Alsace and back, that were seen the beginnings of a skill which was to be compared with that of Rembrandt.

Many years later, Whistler's contemporaries from London were to look back on these years through different eyes. Ionides, who was to introduce him into London Society, with affection. Poynter, when a knight, President of the Royal Academy and rich from the painting of faintly erotic Classical scenes in the style of Bouguereau, with disdain. Du Maurier was to describe the scenes and characters of the time in his novel *Trilby*.

Trilby, the little model dominated by the hypnotic personality of Svengali, was said to have been inspired by Whistler's *Fumette* and the idle American art student Joe Silby by her lover. Although it is said, probably with justification, that this portrait was shadowed by later memories of an older, sourer Whistler, it seemed so accurate and certainly stung its subject on so sensitive a nerve that, when *Trilby* was first serialised in *Harper's Magazine*, he insisted on threat of litigation that du Maurier delete a devastating description. When the story was published as a book, this had been done. Du Maurier had written of the young American: "Always in debt, like Svengali; like Svengali, vain, witty and a most exquisite and original artist; and also eccentric in his attire (though clean), so that people would stare at him as he went along – which he adored! But, unlike Svengali, he was genial, caressing, sympathetic, charming; the most irresistible friend in the world as long as his friendship lasted – but that was not for ever. The moment his friendship left off, his enmity began at once."

Such sharp observation of Whistler's character seldom, if ever, came at once. The first impression was almost invariably that of a feckless charmer. The second was of an artist of brilliantly original talent. Later, the amusing vanity shaded into arrogance and the mischief sharpened into malice and only those who understood the causes of this behaviour, or could stand up to it, survived as friends. So it was as a delightful, if irresponsible, clever, if eccentric, art student that Jimmy Whistler was received by his brother-in-law in Chelsea. In Seymour Haden, gentlemanly tolerance and the knowledge of his wife's love for her half-brother was reinforced by the recognition of real merit as an artist and a shared absorption in etching. It says much for Haden that, at first, he not only welcomed young Jimmy, who was at least neat and clean, but also extended the hospitality of the elegant house in Sloane Street to his French artist friends, who had never seen a modern bathroom and probably would not have used one if they had.

It was Haden who first introduced Whistler to the Thames. Rivers had already flowed through his life and imagination: the stimulating sparkle of the Hudson at West Point; the grandeur of the Neva at St. Petersburg; the romantic melancholy of the Seine at the bottom of the narrow streets of the *Quartier Latin*; and now the Thames, ten minutes walk from the house in Sloane Street. At this time the river was still free from the constriction of granite embankments, handsome but severe, which were to be constructed during the 'sixties and 'seventies along its northern shore from Blackfriars to Battersea Bridge. At Chelsea, it still lapped the watergates of the Royal Hospital and the Physic Garden and against the stairs and the old brick river walls. On the far bank were the reedy flats of Battersea Fields, where snipe could still be shot, and the village of Battersea with its riverside church and the first factories.

Haden's Victorian romanticism took him upstream to Fulham, Putney and Richmond, where Georgian country houses could be seen through the splendid chestnuts, surrounded by sloping lawns and rose gardens. Whistler's taste for undisciplined bohemianism and disciplined artistic realism took him downstream to the wharves and docks of Wapping and Rotherhithe. The journey to this reach by cab was long, and by steamboat or skiff was complicated by loading and unloading, weather and tides. So for a time Whistler took lodgings by the river, enjoyed the jolly, undemanding company of watermen in the taverns and etched an exquisite series of plates. These showed the rough, working Thames, which were later to confound the more conventional of his critics when his sophisticated impressionism provoked them to jeer that he could not draw.

Walter Greaves, many years later, said that he first met Whistler at this time. This is possible. Whistler may well have travelled to the docks by water from Chelsea and the Greaves boys were always about on the waterfront. And it was to be said that a bearded figure painted in oils by Whistler on the balcony of The Angel tavern at Rotherhithe was one of Greaves's watermen.

The first fascination with the Port of London now gave way to an awareness of the broad serenity of the river that flowed between Chelsea and Battersea. Perhaps Whistler first saw it from the deck of one of the paddle-wheel steamboats which plied between the piers of London and its riverside suburbs. Perhaps he walked along the King's Road, where villas still stood in thickets of lilac and laburnum among the shops, saddlers and inns, towards the old village of Chelsea and, like Carlyle, experienced a first view of the river with theatrical intensity.

One evening, certainly, he must have stood at the western railings of wooden Battersea Bridge and watched the broad sweep of water beginning its southward turn between Battersea, Wandsworth and Putney on the south bank and Chelsea, Fulham and Hammersmith on the north. From here, from his own rooftop and from the waterside church at Battersea, Turner had watched and painted the light. Now Whistler experienced and absorbed its subtle changes of mood between the fading of the strong, vivid Canaletto colours of late afternoon – sunlight on blue water and red-brick houses – through sunset to twilight, dusk and dark. The magical transformation of the scene – not only of river, fine houses and ancient trees – but of the factories which had begun to cluster along the Battersea shore, inspired him. Many years later, when an acknowledged, although controversial, genius he could not help himself from dropping his sardonic wit and becoming, for a moment, serious and almost sentimental and describing the experience in unforgettable language. "When the evening mist clothes the riverside with poetry as with a veil," he said, "and the poor buildings lose themselves in the dim sky and the tall chimneys become campanili and the warehouses are palaces in the night and the whole city hangs before us in the heavens . . ."

That Whistler should decide to settle here was almost inevitable. He was becoming restless in Sloane Street. Against his love for his sister and the shared interest in etching with her husband was set the propriety and formality of the household ruled with unassailable assurance by Haden. For his part, Haden was becoming irritated by his brother-in-law's studied flouting of convention and by the less contrived, but still tiresome bohemianism of his young artist friends from Paris, whose ignorance of English etiquette had lost any quality of entertainment. So Whistler increasingly wandered from the comforts of Sloane Street – the chintz-covered furniture, the gleaming dining-room table, the crisp linen and the gas-heated hot water geyser in the bathroom that so alarmed his French friends – to take rooms of his own. He lodged in Wapping, in Old Bond Street and then in Bloomsbury, near Clipstone Street, where a group of young painters had founded the Artists' Society twenty-five years before and with hearty bohemianism had taken turns in bringing models of picturesque poverty in from the streets. Then he had moved to lodgings in Chelsea. At first these were in one of the charming little seventeenth-century houses set behind gardens in Paradise Row, on the road that led from Westminster, past the Royal Hospital to Cheyne Walk.

It was inevitable that the lively, inquisitive American should then meet and find entertaining an English equivalent of the talented eccentric of the *Quartier Latin*: Charles Algernon Swinburne. At this time Swinburne was living a few hundred yards from Whistler's lodgings, in the fine house – 16 Cheyne Walk – in which Dante Gabriel Rossetti had set up his bizarre household. Like Whistler, small, slight and striking in appearance – but with red hair and green eyes in place of the black curls and glittering eyes of the American – and with unfettered poetic imagination; but unlike Whistler in his lack of self-discipline, for Swinburne was usually drunk and his perverse, masochistic sexual tendencies were no secret.

Whistler formed strong mutual friendships with both Swinburne and Rossetti, not only because he admired the poetry of one and the painting of the other, but because of their gentlemanly manners that reminded him of Southern etiquette, or of the idealised code of the English upper classes which he unconvincingly affected to despise. The friendship with Swinburne, of whom Whistler's mother was to become protectively fond, lasted a quarter of a century and although the intimacy was lost after a few years, this was long for a Whistlerian friendship and its inevitable violent end was brought on, not by the artist's volatile temperament, but by harsh criticism of him by the poet. His respect for Rossetti lasted until the latter's death in 1882 when Whistler said simply, "Rossetti was a king."

In Chelsea at this time both Rossetti and Carlyle were kings, and much as Whistler might admire them he was not cast for the role of crown prince and he hankered after a kingdom of his own. This he established at the far side of Chelsea from Rossetti's household, upsteam of Battersea Bridge. In 1863 he rented a small house – then 7 Lindsey Row but later called 101 Cheyne Walk – next to the faded but still magnificent mansion Lindsey House, which had been divided into five separate houses. This was the unfashionable end of Chelsea, where Turner had tried to live incognito; tough, and the nearest London equivalent to the riverside streets of the *Quartier Latin*. What had drawn him there was not primarily the possibility of establishing his own bohemia but the blue river light. This was the misty, mysterious blue that he had just seen for the first time in oriental art – the prints of Hokusai, the eighteenth-century Japanese artist, and blue-and-white china – that had just been recognised and embraced by the *avant-garde* in Paris and which he was to help introduce to London.

So it was that Walter Greaves, now seventeen and living two doors away from Whistler's new house, first heard strange rumours of the arrival in Lindsey Row of "a Japanese artist". He and Henry would stare curiously at the windows of Number 7 and were eventually surprised to see, seated on a sill, sketching the river, not a pig-tailed Japanese but a neat, lithe young man with black curls. Soon after came what almost certainly must have been the first meeting. "One day we were painting on the river," Walter Greaves remembered years later, "when Whistler, whom we knew by sight as a neighbour, came up to us and watched us at work. He said suddenly 'Come over to my place', and we went there and he showed us his work and his Japanese things. I lost my head over Whistler when I first met him and saw his painting."

The two Chelsea boys were, like so many before and after, captivated by Whistler's wit and charm. This was never more potent than when he was putting forward his theories on art and taste to a receptive and admiring audience. Soon after, the invitation was returned and, for the first time Whistler entered the cosy, self-contained world of the little house on the corner of Lindsey Row and Milman's Row. It was a world which he could dominate without effort if he felt so inclined, but it also offered relaxation after the emotional and social tension of Sloane Street and the intellectual challenge of the Rossetti household. Here the clever extrovert could exercise his egocentricity and be rewarded with unquestioning adoration.

Later, Whistler was to call the Greaveses "a sort of Peggotty family" and so they were. Charles Greaves, the simple, sturdy boat-builder, was in his fifties and, although not himself a man of culture, would talk of Turner and encourage his sons in their recreation of drawing. His wife, Elizabeth, was warm and kindly, ready to laugh helplessly at Jimmy Whistler's quips and mimicry. These included the miming of clockwork toys and firework displays, and she was easily deceived by harmless practical jokes, as when the American pretended to be two men quarrelling in the next room and frightened her out of her wits.

Then there was the eldest son, Charles, in his early thirties, who took after his father and worked in the boatyard, being much pre-occupied in the evening with courting. The three girls, Eliza, Emily and Alice, were gay and quite pretty; Eliza and Emily were in their early twenties, but Alice, who when Whistler first entered the family circle was only eleven, was to be his favourite. After supper in the Greaves' parlour, Walter or Henry would strum on the piano and Jimmy would prance round the room with one of the girls in a dance that was part-waltz, part can-can, or sing comic plantation songs. Whistler was fascinated and awed by the fresh beauty of young girls and, with them, the randy resolution with which he usually pursued desirable young women was replaced by delicacy and even reverence. They responded with trust and affection and soon "Tinnie", as Alice was nicknamed, was posing for Whistler, as his niece Alice Haden had, and, as she grew up, little exchanges of confidences developed into flirtation.

But it was Walter and Henry with whom Whistler struck up the strongest friendship. He thought them "very intelligent and nice boys" but, above all, they were to introduce him to excitements which he had never expected to find in a London suburb. The two boys – Henry was two years older than Walter – knew Chelsea, Battersea and the river intimately. With them he explored the jumble of old inns, stables, wharves and warehouses and rickety houses held up by ancient pride, which clustered round the dark tower of the Old Church. Here the country smells of hayfields, horses, farmyards and dung mixed with town smells of smoking chimneys and brewery and with river smells of wet timber, mud, hemp and tar, all mingled and blown together by fresh breezes from the wooded Surrey hills. Here the country noises of farm carts, cocks crowing, donkeys braying and church bells blended with town noises of hooves and wheels on cobbles, the cries of street vendors and the hammering of blacksmith and artisan and with river sounds of lapping water, thumping hulls and creaking rope.

The most enticing distraction – one with which not even Paris could compete – lay some three hundred yards up the river bank from Lindsey Row. The Greaves boys would escort Jimmy Whistler from their house, past the coal wharf where the sailing barges discharged their cargoes into wagons, then along the narrow lane which ran between the gently-sloping stone embankment and the three inns – the Queen's Arms and the King's Arms, standing side by side and the Aquatic Stores – past their father's professional rivals, Alexander's boatyard, to where Turner's cottage marked the end of the riverfront houses. Ahead lay billowing oaks and elms in an elegant profusion that could only have been planted to ornament "a spread of fine home scenery" around a gentleman's country seat. Elegant wrought-iron gates and a striking archway in the Gothic taste led into this park. By day, the prospect provided a scene of pastoral ease in contrast to the busy wharves and lanes of Chelsea. By night, the archway was brightly illuminated with gas lamps and, beyond, lights glittered wickedly through the leaves and sometimes the darkness would be torn and dashed by exploding, flaring, showering fireworks. This was Cremorne.

The pleasure gardens of Cremorne suddenly bloomed, flourished exotically for some forty years, then, almost as suddenly withered, died and rotted on the Thames-side mud, leaving no trace. The influence of this place upon Whistler was to be profound but, in these early years, it was just a fitting exercise ground for his high spirits and capacity for enjoyment.

Cremorne House, built more than a century before, was one of the last country houses in Chelsea. In its day it had attracted visitors as varied as John Wesley and Queen Charlotte. The last Lady Cremorne, after whose family the name of the house had been changed from Chelsea Farm – was a great-grand-daughter of William Penn, founder of the State of Pennsylvania. She had left it to her cousin, Granville Penn, who had no need of it and eventually sold it to a Charles Random de Berenger, the Baron de Beaufain as he styled himself.

As rakish as he was talented, "The Baron" had served a sentence in the King's Bench prison for his part in the Stock Exchange swindle of 1814, which had ruined and driven into exile Lord Cochrane, the most original naval genius since Nelson. De Berenger was what the Regency admired, "a man of bottom", a sportsman and *bon viveur* and, as a crack shot, a potential duellist to be avoided. As such, he was able to expiate much of the scandal that had surrounded him, at least among the bucks whose company he most enjoyed.

The Cremorne estate, with its wide but secluded lawns and river frontage, seemed the ideal setting for a commercial venture, which de Berenger's imagination must have longingly planned in the confines of the King's Bench: a sporting club. This was to be named "The Stadium" and, in 1831, *The New Sporting Magazine* described its prospectus. "The Club is to be divided into three branches. *No. 1.* The department for cultivating perfection in shooting generally. *No. 2.* For aquatic pursuits, sailing, rowing, swimming, fishing, waterfowl shooting and bathing. *No. 3.* The department of general purposes, and for investigating improvements. Its care, says the prospectus, will be to promote, by a variety of means, all matters connected with the manly, skilful, or useful exercises, not already set forth, such as fencing, archery, riding, driving, skating, coursing, hunting and racing."

The Stadium opened the following year, gentleman members paying a subscription of two or three guineas. A coat of arms, depicting pole vaulting and golf as well as the listed activities, and a new brochure were designed by George Cruickshank. "The Baron's" initial success was such that he opened a "Ladies' Links" and club-room, "which Gentlemen cannot enter unless by consent of the Ladies occupying such."

But, unlike its successor, the Hurlingham Club, Cremorne was not a financial success, probably because the ladies and gentlemen it hoped to attract could generally indulge in all such seemly sporting activities in the privacy of their own gardens. Other attractions had to be introduced. Manly exercises were to include tilting and mock jousting tournaments. There was to be music and dancing in the evenings when at a "Grand Miscellaneous Concert, the lovers of Terpsichore might sport the light fantastic toe." But the most notable promotion was aeronautics. Older Chelseans could remember the sensational balloon ascent by Blanchard in 1784 and now aviation was to become a regular dramatic event at Cremorne.

Simple balloon ascents no longer aroused such excitement, so that each flight had to include some bizarre or dangerous antic, becoming over the years increasingly so, as the public appetite for such spectacles jaded. In 1837 Charles Green, "the intrepid aeronaut", ascended from the gardens in the balloon *The Nassau* accompanied by a lady with a tame leopard crouched at her side. Green became the chief attraction of Cremorne and was to make, in all, five hundred and twenty-six flights from the lawn without accident, although he once nearly crashed at Harrow.

De Berenger died in 1845 and the proprietors who followed him over the next thirty years strove to exceed his aerial spectacles. A Madame Poitevin ascended as Europa and the Bull with a wretched heifer, which had to be slaughtered on their descent. The clown Tom Matthews sang "Hot Codlins" before take-off and then, at three thousand feet, "Pigs Pettitoes" – or so the gaping crowds below were assured. Trapeze acrobats hung from balloons and fireworks were lit, dangerously, in the swinging gondolas.

Balloons, often carrying half a dozen passengers or more, would be blown off course to come down in Essex fields or marshes, and sometimes crashed against trees or chimney pots while taking-off or landing. A large French captive balloon, nearly a hundred feet in diameter, would lift thirty passengers to a height of two thousand feet at a charge of ten shillings each. This balloon, raised and lowered by a 200-horse-power steam-engine, which could be heard as far away as Sloane Square, once broke its moorings but managed to land its terrified passengers without injury.

Such flights became near to Roman gladiatorial spectacles and newspaper reports of them referred to "shrieks of alarm" and "shouts of enthusiasm" and one aerial acrobat, hanging by his heels from a balloon over Cremorne, aroused "mingled alarm and pleasure". Inevitably there were fatal accidents. The parachutist Latour crashed to his death in 1854 and, twenty years later, De Groot, "The Flying Man", tried to descend from the balloon *The Czar*, from a height of five thousand feet above Chelsea, by the use of bat's wings thirty-seven feet long and an eighteen-foot tail. But *The Czar* drifted towards the pinnacles of St. Luke's church tower at three hundred feet and "The Flying Man" attempted an emergency landing, crashing to his death on the pavement kerb of Sydney Street.

Yet some serious attempts to develop powered flight were made at Chelsea, the most notable being the flight of Delamarne's dirigible in the summer of 1865. This early airship was two hundred feet long with a diameter of fifty feet and was powered by hand-worked propellors and steered by a massive rudder at the back of the gondola. This was reported somewhat patronisingly by *The Chelsea News*: "Bye the bye, I will mention the little excitement which arose in the King's Road on the night of the first ascent of the incomprehensible sailing balloon from Cremorne Gardens. Despite the announcement of the first advent, its appearance in the air filled everyone with surprise, particularly, I observed, in the King's Road, where all came out to see what appeared to be like in the distance the upper part of one of Taylor's furniture waggons, minus the wheels and its connections, floating grandly in the air as if taken up by a whirlwind and made to revolve on its own axis . . . The car has four vanes attached to it, two acting vertically and two laterally, which rotate rapidly on the motion of a machine inside. They are designed to have a power similar to that of a screw propellor, but we cannot think they are at all powerful enough to produce much effect. Mr. Delamarne has made an experiment, but, as yet, there is not evidence of its success. He may be on the right track, but there are some grave faults in the mode of applying his ideas: these he may be able to remedy in time, and in any case his attempt to navigate the air is deserving of encouragement."

Disaster almost ended another Cremorne display when, in 1861, "The Female Blondin" crossed the Thames by tightrope between Chelsea and Battersea. Leaden weights to which the guy-ropes were attached had been stolen and, when she was two-thirds of the way across, the tightrope began to sway violently and she would have fallen had she not had the presence of mind to drop her balancing pole and swing down by her hands. She did fall while performing at Highbury Barn the following year and was crippled, but it seems likely that she returned to the scene of her Chelsea triumph to marry. Her name was Lucy Young and, in 1864, Charles Greaves Junior married a Lucy Young. "The Female Blondin" was a favourite subject for dramatic drawings by Walter and Henry Greaves. The Greaves family had a season ticket to Cremorne and it is pleasant to think that the boatman, having worshipped the trim little figure in flared skirt and pantaloons swaying on the rope above the river, was able to give her a home at the scene of her greatest triumph.

Dangerous spectacles were only part of the constantly shifting patterns of entertainment offered by Cremorne and to which the Greaves boys introduced Jimmy Whistler.

By day, the twelve acres of Cremorne were pleasantly laid out gardens surrounded by oaks, elms and ash, trimmed bay trees in tubs, more than twenty thousand flowering plants, replaced after they had bloomed, and discreet bosky arbours. Entertainment began in the early evening with whatever aeronautical or acrobatic spectacle that had been arranged. For those not immediately enticed into the bars and "delightful lavender bowers", there were side-shows, shooting galleries, a fortune-teller and a variety of curiosities and freaks such as "Natator, The Man-Frog" who stood on his head, smoked a pipe, ate sponge-cake and performed frog-like evolutions, apparently in a tank filled with six feet of water. There was a circus, a marionette theatre, an American bowling-alley and, above all, a bandstand. This, shaped like a pagoda and brilliantly illuminated after dark, was surrounded by a circular dancing-platform which, it was said, sometimes swirled with two thousand couples. As the band, fifty-strong, played thumping waltzes, London shop-girls and their escorts danced before the nightly firework display. The lighting of the Catherine wheels and the firing of rockets announced the arrival of the smarter patrons, strolling down the avenue illuminated by gas lamps held aloft by plaster goddesses. For them there would be supper at Cremorne House – now an hotel – or in the tiers of intimate supper-boxes, until the fashionable late hour to begin dancing.

Occasionally the fireworks display was extended into a grand pyrotechnic spectacle combined with a naval or military tattoo, representing perhaps the siege of Acre, of Gibraltar, or a scene of carnage in a current campaign. For naval displays all fourteen paddle-steamers of the Citizen steamboat company, which plied between the City and the suburbs upstream, would be pressed into service, their unwarlike silhouettes hidden by billows of smoke from blank cartridges, maroons and Bengal Fire.

These pageants, like the flying displays, were sometimes touched by real danger, as when, in 1855, five hundred soldiers re-enacted the storming of the Mamelon Fort at Sebastopol and the stage erected before the fortress scenery collapsed beneath their charge. On this August night Jane Carlyle was sitting up alone at Cheyne Row and next day wrote of the accident to her husband. "And last night the results of Cremorne in the King's Road were – what shall I say? strange, upon my honour! First I heard a measured tread, and then, out of the darkness, advanced on me eight soldiers carrying, high over their heads, a bier! on which lay a figure covered with a black cloth, all but the white face! And before I had recovered from the shock of that, some twenty yards further on, behold, precisely the same thing over again! I asked a working man what had happened. 'It was a great night at Cremorne, storming of Sebastopol; thirty or forty soldiers were storming, when the scaffolding broke, and they all fell in on their own bayonets!' The two who had passed were killed, they said, and all the others hurt! But a sergeant, whom I accosted after, told me that there were none killed and only three hurt badly."

Cremorne was open, during the season, for fifteen hours a day and the entrance fee was a shilling. Drunkenness, brawling and improprieties in the bushes became usual and the management made desperate attempts to raise the standard of behaviour with generally unsuccessful attempts to lure the *bon ton* with fancy dress parties and well-to-do foreign visitors to the Great Exhibition of 1862 with advertising: "*Le Jardin et Hotel de Cremorne ten minutes de distance de l'Exposition! Table d'hote tous les Dimanches Deux shillings et sixpence.*"

Jimmy Whistler, who was always handy with his fists, enjoyed late night visits to Cremorne, either escorting one of the Greaves girls, or his Irish mistress Jo Heffernan, or jostling through the crowd of young blades and soldiers in tight red jackets, flanked by the protective Walter and Harry Greaves. But it was not just the public flouting of English convention, the possible opportunity to use those quick fists or the vague and exciting atmosphere of devilment in shrubberies suddenly illuminated by the glare of fireworks. Cremorne with its coloured lights, pyrotechnics, exotic pagoda and minarets and the elegant, trailing dresses of the women was a restless kaleidoscope of colour when seen with detachment. Of these evenings at Cremorne, Walter Greaves later said, "What enjoyable evenings those were when we used to sit with Whistler at the windows of the hotel and look down on the wonderful scene below; the whole place ablaze with thousands of lamps, and the crowds of dancers, with their multi-coloured dresses, all moving round the brilliantly lighted bandstand to the strains of the 'Derby Gallop' and the noted waltzes of the day."

Although Whistler only sketched the night scene at Cremorne in black and white, he remembered the colours well enough next day to paint them in his studio at the back of the house in Lindsey Row. He remembered the girls as lightly-trailing shades of delicate colour, the gas lamps and fireworks as a glow and sparkle, the whole mingling into a combination of shape and colour that need have little or nothing to do with a Victorian pleasure garden.

But most magical was the sight of Cremorne from the river. The Greaves boys were skilled watermen, knowing instinctively how far up or down stream each tide would carry them, and the technique of shooting the arches of Battersea Bridge when a strong ebb tide

Chelsea, the Greaves brothers' favourite subject. An annotated sketch of Upper Cheyne Row (*above*) made as the foundation for a detailed street scene such as that in Cheyne Walk (*below*), where children dance to the hurdy-gurdy and the King's Head and Eight Bells tavern and the Old Church are prominent in the background.

"The Female Blondin" crossing the Thames from Cremorne to Battersea by tightrope was a favourite dramatic subject for Walter Greaves. In 1861, Lucy Young, while performing this feat, caused a sensation by her escape from disaster.

Thomas Carlyle on a solitary walk through Chelsea. A stock figure in the Greaves brothers' topographical drawings, he is shown in Duke Street, which ran from the northern end of Battersea Bridge to the Old Church and was swept away by the building of the Embankment.

was running. They had started taking Jimmy Whistler on boating expeditions and teaching him the short, sharp stroke of the Thames boatman, "The Waterman's Jerk".

On the river he would laugh and chatter, but would be reduced to an awed silence when the boat had been pulled across the stream from the shingle beach by the Greaves boatyard and towards Battersea church. "Whistler was a rare fellow for colours and the illuminations at Cremorne always had a great fascination for him," Walter Greaves remembered. "We used to row down the river and linger opposite the gardens when he loved to pick the pinks, blues and other colours out amongst the lights."

The river had brought Walter Greaves and Jimmy Whistler together in shared experience of its beauty and a compulsion to express this in paint. Talk of the night-time river was one of the few subjects of conversation that would bring total sincerity to Whistler's tone and even sentiment to his eye. It was to offer new arrangements of colour, tone and shape, strong enough to break the chains of conventional artistic theory. For Walter Greaves it was a more simple, direct force and he spoke of it as such. "I never seemed to have any ideas about painting – the river just *made* me do it. You see, you have to have them if you paint in a studio; but if you are outside all day, as I was, by the river, all you've got to do is to watch the red-sailed barges passing. And then there was the bridge. I suppose Battersea Bridge got a bit on the brains of all of us."

The old wooden bridge, sometimes dangerous, always beautiful, reminding the American painter of a Japanese bridge seen by Hokusai, and to the Chelsea waterman the familiar and loved bridge that linked his home with Battersea, was to exercise a profound effect upon both their lives. Getting on the brains of both, it haunted their imaginations. But, long after its waterlogged timbers and piles had been uprooted and replaced by iron and stone, at the time when it should have been remembered with tranquillity, the bridge was to have a shattering effect upon the life of Walter Greaves. But that was to come after half a century. Now all was laughter and excitement both for the cosmopolitan sophisticate and the simple riverside family upon which he had settled like the exotic, bemusing, stinging butterfly that was to become his chosen symbol.

3
Nocturne

"He taught us to paint and we taught him the Waterman's Jerk," Walter Greaves said about Jimmy Whistler. "We all treated him like a brother."

In these middle years of the eighteen-sixties there was fair, if incongruous exchange. The Greaves and Whistler households were in startling contrast. The Greaves, often seven of them crowded together in the neat house, lived according to the genteel ordinances of the rising lower middle class, observing its etiquette and providing their own modest entertainments. Whistler, on the other hand, lived at least two different lives. When his mother stayed with him, his mistress and model, Jo Heffernan, was kept in the background. He escorted the old lady to Chelsea Old Church on Sunday and never sniggered at her intense and primitive piety. Such thoughtfulness enabled her to forgive or overlook those caprices of her son's that did not escape her, as when she surprised the parlour-maid posing for him naked in his studio at the back of the first floor.

"Whistler was continually in and out of our house and our families were very united," said Walter Greaves. Sometimes Jimmy would send round dessert to the Greaves family after dinner and he and his mother would share it with them. He was usually gay, sometimes serious: "He was fond of making sketches of my sister, 'Tinnie', in chalk on brown paper; he used to say she had such a wonderfully shaped head." Then the mood would change: "One day he came to our house and said he was going to act in a piece at the Albert Hall called 'Twenty Minutes Under an Umbrella'. My sister 'Tinnie' rehearsed it with him; there was a lot of flirtation in it – Whistler was always up to that sort of thing – and the play was a great success." It was a time of happiness, to seem even more idyllic in retrospect. "He was very fond of my mother," Walter remembered, "and, in fact, would do anything for any of us . . . Whistler's mother was very fond of the members of our family; she was a charming old lady and extremely sympathetic, if a little strict . . . She was a very religious lady and used to say that she liked being up in her bedroom because there she felt nearer her Maker."

But, already, innocence was slipping away. Whistler was suggesting that the brothers' painstaking drawings of Chelsea streets and waterfront were dull, and intriguing them with talk of Hokusai and Hiroshige, showing them his limp-back books of Japanese coloured woodcuts and his blue-and-white china. It was all bewildering but fascinating.

The sophistication that was being forced upon the Greaves boys found an echo in their changing surroundings. The rumbustious simplicity of Chelsea – innocence, perhaps an inappropriate word – was being lost. This was most apparent on the river. As a change from homely jollities and adventurous expeditions to Cremorne, Walter and Harry would take Jimmy on the river, sometimes in one of their father's fast skiffs, or, for voyages downstream to Wapping or upstream to Putney in a heavier boat pulled by two pairs of oars. Whistler was enchanted by the novelty: "All his spare time he loved to be on the river. He soon learned to row and we have often spent whole nights on the water, especially moonlight nights; he would generally dress in ducks, with a sailor hat and a little blue coat – quite a dandy. He was quite pleased with himself and used to say to 'Tinnie', 'Don't you think I make a nice little sailor-boy?' "

But the river was changing. Upstream the view from Battersea Bridge was no longer of a wide, clear sweep of water seeming to stretch as far as the tree-tops of Richmond Park. In 1863, Battersea Railway Bridge was opened half a mile upstream to link the London and South-Western Railway's Clapham Junction with the Great Western Railway's Willesden Junction north of the river. To Whistler this offered new arrangements of form and light: plumes of wind-blown steam by day and lighted carriage windows reflected on the river at night. But to Walter Greaves it represented the loss of something familiar and beautiful.

Half a mile downstream Battersea Fields had been transformed from a damp wilderness into a grand Victorian garden. The inns on the marshes – The Red House, The Albert Tavern and The British Flag, the Tivoli Gardens and The Balloon tea gardens – had attracted more than the watermen, market-gardeners, carters and ostlers of Chelsea and Battersea, and on a hot summer Sunday in the early eighteen-fifties as many as fifty thousand people would crowd the pleasure grounds, fifteen thousand of them crossing the river from Chelsea.

The upholders of Victorian morality, seeing the London pleasure-gardens as dangerous survivals of Georgian immorality, were trying to replace them with gracious parks in which flower-beds, woodland vistas and manly recreation would enlighten and improve mind and body. One such, a Lieutenant-Colonel J. J. Sexby, V.D., had denounced Battersea Fields. He wrote, "And surely if ever there was a place out of hell that surpassed Sodom and Gomorrah in ungodliness and abomination, this was it. Here the worst men and the vilest of the human race seemed to try to outvie each other in wicked deeds. I have gone to this sad spot on the afternoon and evening of the Lord's Day, when there have been from sixty to one hundred and twenty horses and donkeys racing, foot-racing, walking matches, flying boats, flying horses, roundabouts, theatres, comic actors, shameless dancers, conjurers, fortune-tellers, gamblers of every description, drinking booths, stalls, hawkers and vendors of all kinds of articles. It would take a more graphic pen than mine to describe the mingled shouts and noises and unmentionable doings of this pandemonium on earth."

In 1853, the Battersea Park Act had put an end to all this. Over the following years barges and lighters unloaded thousands of tons of earth from the excavations for the new Victoria Dock at Canning Town to raise the level of Battersea Fields and form a wide embankment along the river. In 1858, the year before Vauxhall Gardens finally closed, Queen Victoria opened Battersea Park. Prince Albert's plan to move the Crystal Palace, that had been the centre-piece of the Great Exhibition of 1851, from Hyde Park to Battersea had not been adopted, but other sophistications were to follow. Of these the most exotic were The Subtropical Garden, planted in 1864 beside the fifteen-acre lake and sheltered by high, wooded embankments, where the evening chorus of starlings was heard among rustling palms and Battersea market-gardeners could stare in awe at bizarre blooms transplanted from remote corners of the Queen Empress's domain.

Saddest of all for Walter Greaves was the knowledge that the Chelsea waterfront, which he knew so intimately, was under deferred sentence of destruction. As early as 1839 the Commissioners of Woods and Forests had proposed the embanking of the river at Chelsea and, in 1846, approved a plan for an embankment and wide road between Vauxhall and Battersea bridges and a suspension bridge at Chelsea. Work had begun but the unexpectedly high cost halted work at the Royal Hospital and Chelsea won a short reprieve. But now the need for a new main sewer to run under the embankment road, westward from Chelsea, became urgent and work was finally resumed in 1868.

The sense of foreboding that hung over much of Chelsea was not felt in 7 Lindsey Row. Whistler needed an audience in which to see his attraction reflected. Like many young Americans who visited England during the coming century, he was socially ill at ease. English by ancestry, but American by birth and cosmopolitan by upbringing, he thrust down the roots he lacked and tore them up for transplanting when he pleased. He liked to boast about his training at West Point, affected military smartness and a delicate swagger, yet was conscious that as a soldier he had failed. The only stabilising factors in his life were his immediate family – notably his mother – and his interest in art. The rest was ephemera and, while he enjoyed entertaining, he also required that his audience be appreciative and undemanding.

His house and studio were often busy with visitors. Old friends from Paris, new friends in Chelsea, flirtatious models and sometimes his intellectual peers from Rossetti's exotic establishment. Into this exciting scene now moved Walter and Henry Greaves, wide-eyed with anticipation fulfilled.

The influences that had acted upon Whistler up to this time were complex. The natural aptitude had been given extra delicacy by learning to etch in Washington; in Paris, he had followed the "Realist" teaching of Courbet, who sought to replace the fashionable, painstaking neo-Classicism by capturing atmosphere at the cost of strict accuracy and reflecting life as it was rather than it was imagined once to have been; in London, he had been fascinated by the very different set of rebels, the Pre-Raphaelites, who tried to escape from the ugliness and injustices of enveloping industrialisation by flight into an imaginary golden age of medieval chivalry and purity, recorded in immaculate craftsmanship. A French contemporary whose work interested him was Edouard Manet, also an admirer of the painting of Goya, Velasquez and Franz Hals.

The Greaves brothers had, he would have admitted, influenced him by introducing him to the Thames at Chelsea and Cremorne by night. Otherwise they were useful technicians to have about the studio. Unable to afford the cost of buying stretched canvases and frames, it was convenient to have at his disposal two skilled shipwrights. Soon they were neglecting their work in the boatyard to help make frames and prepare canvases in Whistler's studio, delightedly working without pay in return for Whistler's assurance that they were not only his pupils, but his favourite pupils.

Most of Whistler's greatest pictures were painted in Chelsea and the Greaves brothers watched their creation and the progress of the artist's developing style. Already he had caused an artistic sensation with his *The Music Room* and *At the Piano*, both painted at the Hadens' house and using a domestic scene not to tell a story, as was the fashion, but to display an arrangement of form and colour. This was followed by *The White Girl*, a full length portrait of his mistress, Jo, in a long white dress, her famous russet hair falling to her shoulders. Now at Lindsey Row he painted *The Little White Girl*, in which Jo is again seen in white, leaning pensively on a mantelpiece and reflected in the mirror above, a Japanese fan in her hand.

The Royal Academy had rejected *The White Girl* in 1862 and it was then refused by the *Salon des Beaux Arts* in Paris, only to achieve even greater fame by its inclusion in the imaginative idea of the Emperor Napoleon III, the *Salon des Refusés* in 1863. There it shared principal attention with Manet's *Déjeuner sur l'Herbe*, which shockingly showed a nude model seated among a group of fully-dressed artists at a picnic. The Academy did accept *The Little White Girl* two years later, but the reaction of public and critics to both paintings infuriated Whistler. The former was named by a London gallery owner, who exhibited it, *The Woman in White*, as if illustrating Wilkie Collins's novel, without the artist's permission. In Paris, a critic felt certain that the picture told a story: "*le lendemain de l'epousée cette minute troublante ou la jeune femme s'interrogé et s'étonné de ne plus reconnaitre en elle sa virginité de la veille.*" Whistler's explanation of his intention – "My picture simply represents a girl dressed in white, standing in front of a white curtain" – was ignored.

Even the sophisticates of Cheyne Walk could not bring themselves to look at a painting for its own beauty rather than for some obvious or hidden message. Yet Whistler was flattered when *The Little White Girl* inspired Swinburne to write a charming poem ("Come snow, come wind or thunder,/High up in air, /I watch my face and wonder/ At my bright hair . . .") and he had it printed on gold paper and pasted to the frame. Although many years later he still considered that the poem had been "a rare and graceful tribute from the poet to the painter – a noble recognition of work by the production of a nobler one". When Rossetti emulated Swinburne, Whistler tartly advised him "to take out the picture and frame the sonnet".

Although Whistler would have none of the romantic story-telling of the Pre-Raphaelites' art, he admired their rebelliousness and their professional skill. He had introduced Rossetti to the pleasures of Japanese art and, in their shared enthusiasm, was in turn influenced by him. Experimenting with Japanese taste, he asked the daughter of a mutual friend to pose for him in Japanese dress against a background of his oriental collection. The clothing, the carpet, the screen, vase and fan in the background are unmistakably oriental, but the head of *La Princesse du Pays de la Porcelaine* is unmistakably that of one of those romantically brooding young ladies created by Rossetti to satisfy his wish-fulfilling view of womanhood.

Most of the young women Whistler dressed up as geishas were, for all their exotic surroundings, quite obviously English models. Walter Greaves saw in the bright, pure colour of these paintings in oils something of the unabashed flamboyance with which he had decorated the City barges and, daringly, he tried his hand at a figure in

Japanese dress. Into his own sketches he began to introduce a frond of creeper or a flower in a tall vase among the homely scenery.

Whistler, having no intention of pretending that his figures were Japanese and being interested only in arrangement and harmony of form and colour, reached the extreme of his baffling experiments with oriental style in *The Balcony*, a title which he considered too descriptive, adding, *Variations in Flesh-Colour and Green*. In this, four English girls in Japanese dress sat among blossom, tea bowls and an oriental string instrument on a balcony, from which could be seen across a river what were clearly the factory rooftops and tall chimneys of Battersea.

Bizarre were the experiences and impressions that crowded in upon the Greaves brothers at this time. Whistler liked having them about his studio both as assistants and to help prepare the elaborate meals he could sometimes offer his visitors, and also as sounding-boards for his views on art and artists. In return they expressed continual admiration. Whistler had an irresistible capacity for winning friendship which lasted throughout his life, even when he had become as well known for quarrelling and discarding old friends.

The brothers took to dressing like Whistler in dark, wide-brimmed, low-crowned hats set at an angle or with the brim turned up. Henry grew a tuft of an "imperial" below his lower lip as Whistler had and, although Walter kept to his drooping black moustache, he affected coloured ties and gloves as did Jimmy. There was almost certainly no conscious homosexual element in their adoration. There was a strongly feminine streak in Whistler and he had an instinctive understanding of women and his most durable friendships were with women. But he was feline as a tom cat, always had a recognised mistress and, in the eighteen-sixties, took a second mistress, fathering a son whom he simply described as "an infidelity to Jo".

The Greaves brothers, like many heterosexual young men in later years, felt a wildly romantic affection for the unpredictable Whistler. This excitement became more piquant when sexuality was added to its setting, disturbing the two young men from a prim family circle in which their mother and sisters set a pattern of respectability.

This sexuality was at once apparent in Whistler's studio. There was the voluptuous presence of Jo, made to seem more daring by Mrs. Whistler's disapproval of moral laxity. There were often models about the place because Whistler liked to watch them move and note their attitudes in relaxation. Models often came to parties in the studio or accompanied Jimmy and the two boys to Cremorne, where there were prostitutes on parade and fights over women were commonplace.

Of all the river expeditions the three made, the most stimulating were the early morning visits to Putney. When the tide was flowing, they would sometimes be out on the river by five, pulling upstream past the water-meadows, the new factories and the white gleam of Hurlingham House among the trees, to land at Putney for breakfast with Charles Augustus Howell. These occasions would be attended by women, for Howell's house always seemed to be full of them and his sexual habits were even more irregular than Whistler's. An *entrepreneur* of great skill, Howell was also extremely fly, as was soon discovered by those with whom he had dealings: Ruskin, Rossetti and Whistler. Yet he combined dishonesty with a flair for making money for others as well as for himself and dazzling salesmanship, knowing exactly who was collecting blue-and-white china, or etchings, and marking up his prices accordingly. A liar on the grand scale he recounted complicated and ingenious fantasies about his past life, which none believed but all enjoyed. Whistler relished his company simply because he was outrageously amoral and unconventional. For the Greaves brothers, the visits to his lair, pungent with immorality, were, particularly in the fresh air and light of early morning, lurid experiences.

A more conventional eroticism was introduced into their lives by a young artist of their own age, Albert Moore. Whistler had already quarrelled with some of the artist friends from his Paris days and their place was taken by the Yorkshireman whose pictures seemed to most Victorians to comply with the conventions of their taste. There was a demand for mildly erotic art so long as it was thinly disguised. William Etty's glowing nudes had been too obviously carnal to be widely acceptable except when arranged in Classical attitudes—*The Sirens and Ulysses*, *Pluto Carrying Off Prosperine*, *Leda and the Swan*, *Andromeda and Circe*. Leighton, Alma-Tadema and

Poynter were among the artists who became famous and rich by the device of neo-Classicism, dressing or undressing their girl models in the diaphanous draperies of Athens and Rome. Moore, another neo-Classicist of great proficiency, had more to offer, as is shown by the interest shown in his work by Whistler to whom such painting usually seemed disingenuous and absurd.

Albert Moore's naked girls were also in and out of Roman baths, or seductively sprawled in clinging robes upon marble seats, yet he saw them primarily as a vehicle for his sense of composition and colour. Although he could, like the others, call a picture *The Shunamite Relating to Her Maidens the Glories of King Solomon*, he preferred such simple titles as *Blossoms*, *Dreamers*, *Pomegranates* or *A Summer's Night*.

Whistler admired both Moore's break with convention and his decorative style, and the admiration was mutual. Encouraged by Whistler, Moore began to speak of his subjects as "arrangements" and pay even more attention to composition and colour than to historical accuracy. Whistler, in turn, showed a new interest in figure-drawing. Hitherto, under the influence of the Realists, his models had been friends and relations, or people in the street who had caught his attention. Now he, too, caught a little of the excitement of the Romantics and neo-Classicists in the decorative possibilities of the human body.

Although some of his most successful paintings and etchings had been figure subjects, Whistler sometimes found difficulty with anatomy. The figures he now began to draw in pencil and pastel colours were charmingly light and airy, or, as he liked to say, "dainty". But he was conscious of the need to work more on drawing from the life and joined a group of artists who gathered regularly in the evenings at the studio of Victor Barthe for this purpose.

Barthe, a Frenchman, had fought as a Zouave in Algeria and on the outbreak of the civil war in America had decided to offer his services to the Confederate Army as a mercenary. On his way through London he had spent his passage money and was giving French lessons to make good his loss, when he met an English girl and married her. They settled at 4 Limerston Street and he began to earn a living as an artist, antique dealer and costumier. Barthe made exact copies of period costume both for the theatre and for artists wanting to dress their models for some elaborate, set-piece historical "subject picture". He also built a studio in his back garden and it was here that the evening life classes were held.

They were convivial evenings of smoking, joking and sketching and sometimes Whistler would stroll across the King's Road with the Greaves brothers carrying brown sketching paper, charcoal and chalk to join them. Another young artist, James Christie, who years later was to help found the Chelsea Arts Club, described their visits.

"Whistler was not a regular attender, but came occasionally, and always accompanied by two young men – brothers – Greaves by name. They simply adored Whistler, and were not unlike him in appearance, owing to an unconscious imitation of his dress and manner. It was amusing to watch the movements of the trio when they came into the studio (always late). The curtain that hung in front of the door would suddenly be pulled back by one of the Greaves, and a trim, prim little man, with a bright, merry eye, would step in with 'Good evening', cheerfully said to the whole studio. After a second's survey, while taking off his gloves, he would hand his hat to the other brother, who hung it up carefully as if it were a sacred thing, then he would wipe his brow and moustache with a spotless handkerchief, then in the most careful way he arranged his materials and sat down. Then, having imitated in a general way the preliminaries, the two Greaves sat down on either side of him. There was a sort of tacit understanding that his and their studies should not be subjected to our rude gaze. I, however, saw, with the tail of my eye, as it were, that Whistler made small drawings on brown paper with coloured chalks, that the figure (always a female figure) would be about four inches long, that the drawing was bold and fine, and not slavishly like the model. The comical part was that his satellites didn't draw from the model at all, that I saw, but sat looking at Whistler's drawing and copying that as far as they could. He never entered into the conversation, which was unceasing, but occasionally rolled a cigarette and had a few whiffs, the Greaves brothers always requiring their whiffs at the same moment. The trio packed up, and left before the others always."

While there was smirking at this in the studio and the brothers' imitation of mannerism and dress was touchingly ridiculous, they were, after all, Whistler's pupils. Looking at his drawing of the model rather than the naked girl herself may also have been due in part to embarrassment. The sight of female nudity set among so much hearty masculinity must have shocked them as pleasurably as Manet's *Déjeuner sur l'Herbe* had sent a thrill of delighted outrage through Paris.

Whistler enjoyed the company of his models. Professionals were less likely to wilt, or even faint, than the subjects of commissioned portraits during the long hours he demanded of them. The Italians, who made a career of modelling, were the most proficient, but the cockney girls were more fun, full of the latest gossip from the Kensington studios of the neo-Classicists. One of these, Mary Lewis, also posed for Barthe's life class and was responsible for bringing on one of Whistler's increasingly frequent displays of pique.

George Moore, the future novelist, was a member of the class and noted with irritation the manner with which Whistler sometimes dominated the studio with his sharp jokes and how the other artists would crowd round him during rest periods. But on one occasion young Oliver Brown, the son of Ford Madox Brown, whose exquisitely-detailed narrative paintings were the antithesis of Whistler's art, began to read aloud from a novel he had written while Mary and the artists were enjoying a break. The girl was enthralled and, as she again took up her pose, asked him to continue while the class worked. At the end of the sitting, Mary and the others stayed on while Brown continued reading. Whistler deprived not only of his monopoly of attention but also of his dramatic exit, left, looking, as Moore put it, "as cross as an armful of cats".

Walter Greaves had difficulty in mastering figure-drawing. The little figures with which he had peopled his pencil and wash drawings of Chelsea streets had been marionettes, perfectly placed in the composition, but sometimes being without shadows, giving a haunted effect to the scene. In Barthe's studio, under Whistler's guidance, he was at last able to introduce a flowing line into his figures instead of building them up with torsos, heads, arms and legs.

The first decade of the friendship between Walter Greaves and

Whistler was a time of discovery for both. But, for each, it was usually discovery at different levels and time-scales. In most respects, Greaves followed in Whistler's wake. Artistically, he humbly acknowledged Whistler the master and did his best to imitate him; personally, he was able to wear similar, if cheaper and more threadbare clothes but, as a meek and inhibited man, he was unable to play Whistler to the life.

Having mastered and used Realism and etching, Whistler was now on the brink of a new discovery. What he was to discover had always been there for the recognising but it took a strange adventure to bring it to his attention. Although settled in Chelsea, Whistler was still restless. There were visits to Paris and, in 1866, an extraordinary expedition to South America, and it was there that he was to make his new discovery, a rediscovery of the Thames beneath his Chelsea windows.

The civil war in America had been making Whistler uneasy. For years he had assumed the martial pride and sense of honour of a West Point man and the style of a Southern gentleman. But when war broke out between the North and South, he had not returned home to fight. His mother had come back to England from a visit to America after a dangerous journey through the theatre of war, to take charge of his household, replacing Jo at Lindsey Row and lecturing him on propriety as if he were an adolescent. His elder brother, William, had served as a surgeon in the Confederate Army and, in 1865, had reached England with secret despatches for Whitehall after travelling in civilian clothes through the Union, in constant risk of being arrested and executed as a spy. It was irritating enough to be eclipsed by young Oliver Brown in the life class studio, but to have his assumed personality over-shadowed by the real achievements of his own family was insupportable.

The need to demonstrate his courage and support his self-created legend combined with the necessity of a temporary break with his bohemian life. The arrival of his mother meant that Jo would retire into the background and that he must be free to make his mark at a higher social level. The opportunity for both came when, at the end of the American civil war, London became a refuge for despondent and footloose Confederate officers. Some of these told Whistler that they were sailing for South America to help the Chileans and Peruvians free themselves from Spanish domination. They invited Whistler to join them.

Unlike Carlyle, downstream in Cheyne Row, Whistler did not indulge in the cult of hero-worship when the object was anybody but himself. Nor would he have been moved by the plight of the Chileans, or stirred by a war of liberation. But the invitation to Valparaiso did offer the opportunity both to prove his martial prowess and to make the break he required. So, early in 1866, leaving his mother under the care of the Greaves family, Whistler sailed for Chile.

As a martial exploit, the Chilean expedition was farcical. Whistler did, in fact, watch a desultory bombardment of Valparaiso by Spanish warships but, on his return at the end of the year, he would tell this story either showing himself as the modest hero, or as a clownish coward, according to his mood. But what Whistler saw of battle was unimportant. What made the expedition of such critical importance was what he saw of Valparaiso harbour when the warships lay peacefully at anchor in the blue dusk. This scene he painted in oils. In constrast to his fanciful war stories, it was a scene of utter tranquillity.

Whistler had discovered the night. Painters had long used darkness for dramatic effects – the moon glaring through storm clouds on to ruined castles, or battles lit by ghastly fires – but now Whistler could see the infinite subtleties of tone in failing or growing light and this understanding he brought to the Thames at Chelsea. That alone had made the journey to Valparaiso worthwhile.

But the expedition had not proved itself valuable as a demonstration of a West Point man's valour. He became increasingly pugnacious and quick with his fists. He brawled on the voyage home and had to be confined to his cabin. On a visit to Paris, soon after his return, he was twice taken before a magistrate on charges of assault. The object of his second attack had been his own brother-in-law, Seymour Haden. The two men had been drifting farther apart for several years. Whistler was irritated by the amateur etcher's criticisms of his work and that of his friends. Haden, moreover, had become the symbol of restrictive Victorian propriety and this had come to a head over the latter's haughtiness towards a mutual friend, resulting in a furious quarrel in Sloane Street. But now there was Haden in Paris, in Whistler's Paris. A quarrel was quick to ignite and Whistler knocked Haden through a shop window. He was fined by the magistrate and Haden, on his return to London, had his brother-in-law expelled from the Burlington Fine Arts Club. The two men never spoke to one another again and Deborah, conscientiously loyal to her husband, had to beg for scraps of news of her brother from other members of the family and friends. For Haden, who was to be knighted in 1894, the only link with Whistler was when their etchings were by chance exhibited together.

Whistler did not let the family feud worry him unduly for he was returning to start a new phase of his life. Jo was now to be quietly discarded – although she never expressed bitterness and remained faithful to the memory of their love affair for the rest of her life – and her place in the Whistler household was firmly taken by his mother. They moved from the modest Chelsea house to grander apartments at 2 Lindsey Row, part of Lindsey House.

The friendship between the Whistler and Greaves households had been further strengthened by the care the latter had shown for old Mrs. Whistler and for years afterwards Walter would be asked to stay at 2 Lindsey Row whenever her son was away. Whistler and his mother would often call on the Greaves family and Jimmy continued his mild flirtation with Tinnie Greaves, saying, "You are the pride of one end of the Row and I am the pride of the other."

Walter and Harry helped Jimmy move house and decorate the new apartments. This painting was done in a rush to be ready for Whistler's first party but, even so, wet paint rubbed off on his guests' clothes, mostly in the drawing-room where the walls were yellow tinged with pink, the woodwork white. The dining-room was painted blue – light walls and dark woodwork – and purple Japanese fans were tacked to walls and ceiling. The studio – again at the back of the first floor – had grey walls and black woodwork. Doors were sometimes painted yellow and white and the sparsely-furnished rooms, which were never to look lived-in, were in striking contrast to the cluttered studios and over-stuffed drawing-rooms then in fashion.

Delighted as the Greaves brothers were to welcome Jimmy back to Chelsea, there was now an element of strain in the relationship. Pleased to be called "my pet pupils", they were nevertheless bewildered by his new enthusiasms and frustrated at his insistence that they abandon their own liking for drawing Chelsea streets and filling them with activity like the stage of a toy theatre.

So dependent were the brothers upon Whistler's authority and day-to-day instruction that during his long absences from Chelsea it was easy to slip back into their original style, working together on elaborate street scenes, signed, "H. and W. Greaves". Looking back on these early years, Walter was to say, "My brother and I had painted grey and filled our pictures with numerous detail. But Whistler taught us the use of blue and made us leave out details. At first, I could only try to copy him . . ."

However much Whistler had distorted their natural talents, he had taught them to handle colour and, when he was not there to impose his own taste for low-keyed tones upon them, their old love of pure, strong colour, remembered from barge-painting days, returned. Perhaps during Whistler's expedition to South America or, at the end of 1867, when his mother visited the family in America and he spent seven months in Bloomsbury, Walter was sitting in an upstairs window of a riverside inn at Hammersmith watching racing skiffs skim under the bridge and was inspired to paint his most strikingly original picture. Nobody was ever to claim that his *Hammersmith Bridge on Boat Race Day* owed anything to Whistler's influence or that it was not a masterpiece. But the date it was painted was to become another shadowy corner in the life of Greaves.

The artist himself was to say that he had painted this canvas before he had met Whistler. Yet the picture can be dated by the dress of the figures swarming on Hammersmith Bridge. Women's fashions were changing fast at that time. Here the women are wearing their hair in the *chignon* style, which was introduced in about 1864, but changed six years later with the addition of a forehead fringe. They are wearing the crinoline skirt but without the bustle that came into fashion in 1870. This and other sartorial evidence points to *Hammersmith Bridge* having been painted in the late eighteen-sixties.

The setting for a friendship. Lindsey Row (*above*), drawn by the Greaves brothers and showing their father's boats waiting for hire. The Greaves's house is on the extreme left; Whistler's first house is that on the immediate left of Lindsey House; his second is at the far end of the mansion.

Battersea Bridge (*below*) in a Whistlerian Nocturne painted in oils by Walter Greaves soon after 1873 when the two centre spans were thrown into one.

The Chelsea waterfront in the eighteen-sixties. A photograph of houses and shops which were to survive more than a century, the King's Arms remaining a public house and the Queen's Arms being converted for a time into artists' studios

An extraordinary vagueness about dates was to have catastrophic effects upon the later life of Walter Greaves. Many of his drawings bore dates which seemed to bear little relation to the events depicted. He sketched Harry at the oars of a dinghy in which Jimmy Whistler sits sketching and the date is 1860, when, almost certainly, they had not met. There are several explanations and perhaps the truth derives, in part, from all of them. One is that the brothers feared Whistler's sarcasm if he should see work which he had not inspired, and deliberately inscribed early dates so that they could claim to have finished with their own style on becoming his pupils. Another is that dates were sometimes added years later, when their memory was failing and could be wrong by five or ten years. Another is that among the Whistlerian mannerisms they affected was a deliberate vagueness about dates and places and an almost superstitious fear of being pinned down in time. Whistler would make contradictory statements about the date and place of his birth and many events of his life, inventing incidents to please a fancy, or simply to confuse. A later pupil, Walter Sickert, described this habit, saying, "It was Whistler's incessant preoccupation to present himself as having sprung completely armed from nowhere." It may have been Walter Greaves's preoccupation, too, but it was his tragedy that he was completely unarmed.

Of the two brothers, Walter fell most readily under Whistler's spell, appreciating much of the thought behind the theories. Harry, less enthusiastic, hung back, clinging to his passsion for detail, bemused by Jimmy, who, when told that the Battersea factory chimneys in a drawing were not straight, replied, "But they are Whistler's." Even Walter, who could understand the Whistlerian atmospheric effects, was aghast at what he could do to their beloved boats.

Walter Greaves never overcame the feeling that Whistler was in some way misusing the sacred river, failing to understand the boat-builder's skill which they had mastered as boys. Years later, he told a visitor, "Mr. Whistler put in his boats wherever he wanted them, but we left our boats just as they were." And he exactly described the difference in outlook, saying, "To Mr. Whistler a boat was always a tone, to us it was always a boat."

During his first years in Lindsey Row, Whistler had painted the river – the familiar view of sailing barges, paddle-steamers, the spire of Battersea church, the growing factory chimneys and Battersea Bridge – but he had painted it by day. But now, since his experience at Valparaiso, he became fascinated with it in the failing light of evening and after dark. In daylight, the river scene demanded detail and the Greaves brothers were usually at hand to remind him of it. But at twilight, this was lost in soft monochromes and he could use expanses of water as planes for dramatic effect, as the Canaletto he so much admired had used the still blue water of Venice to emphasise the splendour of the buildings.

His voyages of exploration on the river with the Greaves brothers at the oars now generally began at sunset. As the light faded the shapes of boats and buildings would first be thrown into strong relief then slowly swallowed up in a mysterious haze or milky light, now green, now grey, now blue. Finally it would be dark and in the first moonlight the silhouettes of riverside buildings would stand black against the lighter sky, the gold points of their lighted windows glinting and wriggling on the swirling river. Whistler's affectation to despise beauty in nature was unconvincing. He might have replied to the remark, "The stars are fine tonight" with "Not bad, but there are too many of them", but even he was to say that, in the fading light, "Nature . . . for once has sung in tune, sings her exquisite song to the artist . . ."

Although Whistler never publicly acknowledged his debt to Walter Greaves, to him he owed his understanding of the river and the great painting that this produced. Sir George Clausen, the painter, who knew both men, said of Greaves, many years later, "I think Whistler owed the inspiration for his river pictures to him." But, at the time, Walter certainly regarded himself as no more than the friend and pupil privileged to row the boat bearing "The Master", as Whistler considered himself.

When he began experiments in painting the night river at the beginning of the eighteen-seventies, Whistler called his pictures "Moonlights". Later, a rich and intelligent patron, Frederick Leyland, a Liverpool ship-owner, suggested he call them "Nocturnes". Whistler was delighted with this and generously acknowledged, "I say, I can't thank you too much for the name 'Nocturne' as a title for my moonlights. You have no idea what an irritation it proves to the critics and consequent pleasure to me – besides it is really charming and does so poetically say all I want to say and *no more* than I wish."

Speaking of his Nocturnes, Whistler was more insistent than ever that these pictures told no story whatsoever, although he well knew that if he described some canvas as illustrating a night scene from a novel by Wilkie Collins, or Charles Dickens, it would be immediately accepted, admired and sold handsomely. When he painted a figure trudging through the snow in a deserted street towards the glowing window of a tavern and called it simply, *Nocturne in Grey and Gold: Chelsea Snow*, he explained, "My picture of a *Harmony in Grey and Gold* is an illustration of my meaning – a snow scene with a single black figure and a lighted tavern. I care nothing for the past, present or future of the black figure, placed there because black was wanted at that spot. All that I know is that my combination of grey and gold is the basis of the picture. Now this is precisely what my friends cannot grasp. They say, 'Why not call it *Trotty Veck*, and sell it for a round harmony of golden guineas?' I reply simply that I will do nothing of the kind. Not even the genius of Dickens should be invoked to lend an advantageous aid to art of another kind from his."

Speaking of the same Nocturne, Whistler joked that he had only to entitle it, "Father, dear Father, come home with me now" for it to become "The Picture of the Year".

For all his dislike of narrative painting, Whistler was always flattered when his work inspired another. As *The Little White Girl* had inspired Swinburne, so W. E. Henley wrote and dedicated a poem to Whistler after seeing one of his river Nocturnes:

Under a stagnant sky
Gloom out of gloom uncoiling into gloom,
The River, jaded and forlorn,
Welters and wanders, wearily – wretchedly – on;
Yet in and out among the ribs
Of the old skeleton bridge, as in the piles
Of some dead lake-built city, full of skulls,

Worm-worn, rat-riddled, mouldy with memories,
Lingers to babble to a broken tune
(Once, O, the unvoiced music of my heart):
So melancholy a soliloquy . . .

This so pleased Whistler that he allowed Henley to use one of his Nocturnes to illustrate the poem. But such sombre brooding was far from Walter Greaves's view of the Nocturnes. He later complained that Whistler had made him follow his example against his will, saying, "Mr. Whistler made us paint those Nocturnes; he would have us paint them." Yet he was so infatuated by the river in all its moods that he came to understand and to experiment himself.

It was, of course, impossible to work in colour on the river at night and so Whistler took to sketching outlines on scraps of paper and committing the colour to memory, a technique he had developed on his nocturnal visits to Cremorne.

Whistler's feats of concentration and memory on these occasions always impressed his companions. Walter Greaves recalled, "We often used to stay up all night on the river, rowing him about. When he came to a view which interested him he would suddenly stop talking and sketch it with white chalk on brown paper, just showing the position of the lights and the river banks and bridges, Just as suddenly he'd start laughing and talking again. The next day I'd go round to his studio and he'd have it all on canvas. He got me into the way of working like that."

Another remembered how, strolling beside the river at night, Whistler would suddenly see the view he sought, stop and stare. He would then turn his back on the river and chant to his companion, "The sky is lighter than the water, the houses darkest. There are eight houses, the second is the lowest, the fifth the highest; the tone of all is the same. The first has two lighted windows, one above the other; the second has four." If his companion corrected him on the smallest detail, he would stop, turn and stare again at the view he was memorising and repeat the performance – sometimes a dozen times before it was perfectly imprinted on his memory. Then with a brisk "Good night" he would be off to bed, the scene to be painted next morning gathering shape and tone in his mind's eye.

Thomas Way, the lithographer, remembered another such occasion: "We had left the studio when it was quite dusk and were walking along the road by the gardens of Chelsea Hospital when he suddenly stopped, and pointing to a group of buildings in the distance, an old public house at the corner of a road, with windows and shops showing golden lights through the gathering mist of twilight, said, 'Look!' As he did not seem to have anything to sketch or make notes on, I offered him my note-book; 'No, no, be quiet,' was the answer; and after a long pause he turned and walked back a few yards; then with his back to the scene at which I was looking, he said, 'Now, see if I have learned it,' and repeated a full description of the scene, even as one might repeat a poem one had learned by heart. Then he went on, and soon there came another picture which appealed to me even more than the former. I tried to call his attention to it, but he would not look at it, saying, 'No, no, one thing at a time.' In a few days I was at the studio again, and there on the easel was the realisation of the picture."

Soon Walter Greaves was helping Whistler prepare to paint Nocturnes on the morning after an expedition on the river. Immense care was taken to make ready the materials for painting before the artist began to concentrate on the picture. Sometimes the Nocturnes were painted on very absorbent canvas, or on panels, or simply, sized brown holland. For blue Nocturnes, Whistler like a red background and the brothers would bring him mahogany panels from their father's boatyard. When the background was not deliberately used to force up the colour laid on it, it would be chosen to match the prevailing tone of the picture. "The sky is grey and the water is grey," said Whistler once, "and, therefore, the canvas must be grey." Before painting Whistler would reshape his brushes, melting the glue over a candle and pushing the hairs into the required position. His colours, said Greaves, were heavily mixed with linseed oil and turpentine into what Whistler called "sauce", so fluid that it could be washed on to the canvas like watercolour. These colours, once prepared, were arranged on a large palette, fitted on to a table designed to hold his brushes and tubes in sunken boxes.

Once the artist and his assistants had made ready, the painting would begin with sweeps of the brush, so dripping with "sauce" that sometimes the canvas had to be thrown to the floor to prevent the paint running off. Sometimes perfection would be immediate, sometimes repeated attempts would have to be made, occasionally ending in failure. Often a Nocturne would be completed in only an hour and a half and neighbours remembered often seeing them standing against the garden wall to dry in the sun. Others would be laid out on the roof or, at this time of experimentation, might be allowed to dry slowly in the studio.

With his Nocturnes, Whistler finally established his reputation as an artist of originality, or, in the other view, eccentricity. He painted Nocturnes for the rest of his life and gave the adjective "Whistlerian" to the English language as an immediately recognisable description of moody evening light. The sweep of the river before Lindsey House, the scene of his greatest triumphs in this style, became known as Whistler's Reach. For the artist, who sought only beauty for beauty's sake, the flattery was as irritating as the misconceptions. His wit was, however, more than able to keep both in their place. Once a voluble lady told him that she had just seen the Thames with "an exquisite haze in the atmosphere which reminded me so much of some of your little things. It was a really perfect series of Whistlers." The artist replied, "Yes, madam, Nature is creeping up."

In return for practical help in the studio, Whistler instructed Walter Greaves in the painting of Nocturnes, sometimes making him paint the same scene with the same blends of "sauce". When Whistler was painting his *Variations in Pink and Grey: Chelsea* – the view of the waterfront and river from a first floor window in Lindsey Row, in which the pink evening light blended with the pink of almond blossom – Walter was told to try his hand with the same colours on brown paper. But as Greaves painted stiff little figures walking beside the river, it is probable that Whistler leant across and with a few swift dabs of pink, grey and orange paint gave him the figure of a girl with a parasol in the most delicate Japanese manner – but that is only conjecture from the contrasting styles of figure-painting. The work of master and pupil could veer together so as to become, at times, almost indistinguishable.

Each working on a canvas of identical size, the two men painted the same view of Battersea Reach, the foreground an expanse of empty water separated from the sky by the dark line of wharves, factories, Battersea church and the railway bridge; spire, chimneys and lights reflected on the water. The two paintings, exactly similar in so many ways, were to the practised eye, different. It was not only that Whistler had painted sprigs of oriental foliage in his foreground; the feeling of the two pictures was different. Whistler was painting beauty, which happened to be in an arrangement of water, bricks and sky, and painting it with romantic delicacy. Walter Greaves was painting a view he knew and loved and he laid on his paint with a confidence and strength born of intimacy with his subject.

In time, he was able to initiate his own Nocturnes, both borrowing ideas from Whistler and contributing his own. In *The Balcony*, his Whistlerian view of a misty Battersea church and solitary lights across the water was dramatically framed by the railings and creeper of a balcony. In his *Moonlight Over Battersea*, the illuminated face of a clock on a factory glared fiercely across the river beneath a benign moon. The furled sails of Thames barges hung in black crape swags against a green sky in *Battersea Reach – Moonlight*. Painting the river at dusk, he would sometimes introduce the graceful white ghost of a sailing boat, white hull and sail emphasising the sombre background in the gathering gloom. At least once he painted beside this boat the equally elegant figure of a man in white. This was Jimmy Whistler, no longer needing to be at his pupil's side.

At some time in the early eighteen-seventies, Whistler painted his *Nocturne in Blue and Gold: Old Battersea Bridge*. Almost unrecognisable as the familiar bridge at low tide, the tall, arched spans and the boat and waterman beneath seemed to belong to some Japanese fantasy, the only sign that this was the Thames being the dark, humped roofs, towers and chimneys on the riverside and a scatter of gold from an exploding rocket, made part of the night sky by Cremorne.

At about this time, Walter Greaves probably painted his Nocturne, *Passing Under Old Battersea Bridge*. In this, two lighters and a bargee are silhouetted sharply in the black frame of a narrow arch of the bridge. In the dim distance can be seen another bridge. It was a highly original work, owing little beyond its misty background to Whistlerian influences.

But because, some forty years later, Walter Greaves either could not or, with his Whistlerian dislike of dates, would not remember exactly when he had painted this picture the consequences for him were to be disastrous.

4

Discord in gold

The regatta of 1871 was the wake of old Chelsea village. Less elaborate than it once had been, it was still the event of the year and the prizes for the rowing race between the Royal Hospital and Cremorne – a purse of sovereigns was first prize – were subscribed by the citizens of Chelsea. But now, at last, the old waterfront was to go and the granite embankment was to advance westward from the Royal Hospital to Battersea Bridge.

This year the narrow streets and the taverns were more crowded than usual and Walter and Henry Greaves looked hungrily at the scene, determined to print it vividly on their memories. In this they succeeded and, many years later, Walter remembered that "what with guns firing, flags flying, bands playing and the immense crowd of people, Chelsea was pretty lively . . . This regatta, like the other river races made a remarkably artistic display of colour, especially as it took place on a fine summer's day, with blue skies and white clouds. The Adam and Eve, the headquarters of the sports, was crammed with people and one wondered how it stood the strain of such a weight, being a very old building.

"The Old Church entered into the gaiety, flying the white ensign from the top of its tower, and from the windows of the other old buildings, people would be urging on their favourite rowers, whilst crowds would run along the shore and cheer them along. The umpire accompanied the race in a four-oared boat rowed by four watermen. The Duck Hunt, which ended the day's sport, was a man in a small dinghy being chased by two larger boats and eventually caught, causing considerable amusement amongst the onlookers, who afterwards adjourned to the various inns for refreshment and song-singing. Of course, the old Battersea Bridge had its share of the crowd, as likewise the steamboat pier, which put the finishing touches to the scene."

Walter Greaves watched the final race from the Chelsea end of the old bridge, looking down on to the crowded beach – the race was rowed at slack low-water – and to the three crowded, flag-fluttering balconies of The Adam and Eve. He later painted this scene in oils and produced the largest and most lively of the etchings he was making under tuition from Whistler. Again it is a highly original and distinctive work, owing nothing to The Master. The design is bold, making dramatic use of the dark, upright timber piles of the steamboat pier in the foreground. The little figures in his crowd have come to life as they did on Hammersmith Bridge and the picture catches and preserves a vigorous, happy moment.

The last prizes presented, the last song sung, the demolition gangs moved in. Pony carts and cabs were stopped from jingling under the wide arch of Arch House, beside the Old Church into narrow Duke Street on their way to Battersea Bridge. In their place tramped the navvies – big, whiskered men with corduroy trousers hitched up below the knee with string. Sledge-hammers and pick-axes reduced to rubble the old rosy and russet walls and roofs of The Adam and Eve, Alldin's Coal Wharf, the row of shops and the rickety sheds, privies and greenhouses in the yards and tiny gardens watered by the river. No longer could Henry Greaves carefully draw the shop windows of the tobacconist, with its clay pipes and jars of shag; Morgan the egg-merchant; Welles's furniture and junk shop; the bills advertising Cremorne; the sign "Steamboats to the City Every 15 Minutes" and the dung-littered cobbles.

The new Chelsea Embankment was a monumental piece of engineering, conceived and designed by Sir James Bazalgette, the most remarkable town-planner in nineteenth-century London. It was a new structure, built out into the river leaving the houses of Cheyne Walk still sheltered by the trees that had once lined the bank. Along the old foreshore were laid huge sewers to carry the effluent running down the drains from Chelsea and Kensington away to the east, only draining into the Thames when a rain flood forced open the heavy wooden overflow gates. These sewers were encased in concrete beneath the wide road and pavement, and the grey granite river wall was topped by globe gas-lamps on standards decorated with dolphins.

However much the Greaves family mourned the disappearance of the old waterfront, to many, including Carlyle, it was a symbol of progress and industry, worthy of the capital of a still-expanding Empire. This road, running from Westminster Abbey to Chelsea Old Church marked the final inclusion of the suburb into the city. Looking forward to its construction, twenty or more years earlier, Thomas Faulkner, the Chelsea bibliographer and historian, had foreseen a "handsome terrace" offering a "*coup d'œil* that would not then be surpassed in any city of Europe, not even by the celebrated terrace at Cologne."

Three years after the last Chelsea regatta, crowds again thronged the streets leading to the river for the formal opening of the Embankment by the Duke and Duchess of Edinburgh. The new riverfront gave Chelsea a new and totally different quality. The road itself was so far in advance of its time that it was not to take its full capacity of traffic for another ninety years. Then, it was a wide, airy riverside promenade, used more by pedestrians than carts and cabs. Walter Greaves, for all his nostalgia for the picturesque past, appreciated its beauty. A few years after its completion he painted himself and Tinnie seated on a bench by one of the plane saplings, which had been planted along the pavement by the parapet. It was a small painting in oils – unconsciously influenced by Manet through Whistler – and, to demonstrate the new social distinction which the Embankment imparted, Walter showed himself attired in silk hat and frock coat and Tinnie carrying a pink parasol. The unaccustomed view of distant cabs gave him a new artistic quirk. Once he had been amused by the sudden appearance of a chimney-sweep's brush as it pushed out of a Duke Street chimney-pot and the brothers often included this in their drawings. Now he was struck by the dainty movements of a distant horse and many of his paintings, sketches and etchings were to include a dark little horse, elegantly prancing.

The Victorian cult of the picturesque had already embraced Hampstead and its Heath but Chelsea had not generally been considered as being more than quaint. Now the Embankment and its neo-Classical grandeur showed off the beauty of Cheyne Walk, and the gardens which were planted in front of the eighteenth-century houses on either side of Albert Bridge made even the ramshackle old buildings at the bottom of Lawrence Street beside the Old Church seem properly picturesque. Hitherto, most artists had settled in Chelsea because of the few who had chosen to live there for its beauty, and not because of any attraction in the place itself. The main influx of artists did not begin until Chelsea had been joined to London by the Embankment and the beauty of the river was no longer something to be discovered at the bottom of a lane but was exposed for all to see. The twinkle of distant oil-lamps at night was replaced by a mile of gas-lamps slashing the water with light.

As the settlement of Chelsea by artists and writers became a migration, the place was dominated by three principal courts, two artistic and one literary. To the east was Rossetti's bizarre establishment, cluttered with ideas and bric-a-brac, its garden a human and animal menagerie. Rossetti had at various times stocked his large, leafy garden with peacocks, owls, parakeets, a jackdaw, a raven, rabbits, hedgehogs, dormice, squirrels, kangaroos and wallabies, a deer, raccoon, Irish deerhound, chameleons, lizards, salamanders and "The Bull of Bashan", bought at a Cremorne sideshow, which once chased him into the house. So many neighbours complained of the shrieks of the peacocks that Earl Cadogan, his landlord, had to include a clause in future leases forbidding these birds on his property.

These were hardly more curious than his collection of friends and, indeed, himself. There were among them the flawed genius Swinburne, indulging in drink, drugs and flagellation, capering naked through the house and writing his verse in the first-floor drawing-room overlooking the river; Howell, ingeniously spinning profitable introductions and sales when not absorbed in seduction; Holman Hunt, visiting from his house by the Old Church, where he painted Christ in *The Light of the World* in high Pre-Raphaelite manner and slept with a child-mistress from the cottages behind the Cross Keys tavern in Lawrence Street. Other frequent visitors to this bower of romantic idealism were Ford Madox Brown, who, like Holman Hunt, had taught Rossetti to paint in earlier years, Edward Burne-Jones, another Pre-Raphaelite, and, of course, Whistler.

As protocol demanded, Rossetti paid at least one return visit to Whistler's court in Lindsey Row but Swinburne was a frequent visitor and Mrs. Whistler took a motherly interest in the delicate, wayward young man with the weak chin, girlish mouth and mop of red hair, nursing him during one of his frequent illnesses. Swinburne sometimes had to be reproved like a small boy and once, after he had neglected his regular visits, she addressed him as "Mr. Swinburne". Sitting at her feet, he looked up, anguished. "Mrs. Whistler, what has happened? It used to be Algernon!" "You have not been to see us for a long time," replied the old lady. "If you come as you did, it will be Algernon again."

Not far from Rossetti's house another painter of the school, Daniel Maclise, had lived for nearly ten years before his death in 1870. But he played little part in the intellectual activities of Cheyne Walk. Embittered by the cool reception of his murals for the Houses of Parliament he had become a solitary, complaining about the noise of granite blocks for the Embankment being unloaded from barges at the old dock near his house and dragged away in carts by teams of horses. But Walter Greaves knew him, if only by sight, and sketched him standing alone and aloof outside his gate.

The literary court of Chelsea was in Cheyne Row, mid-way between Rossetti's and Whistler's. Thomas Carlyle had lived in Cheyne Row many years longer than the other two and his sombre house was already an established shrine, but he might have had a rival had not Leigh Hunt and his family left his house in Upper Cheyne Row for Kensington in 1840. A former friend of Shelley and Byron, Hunt was already fifty and bringing up a large family when he had settled in Chelsea at the same time as Carlyle and for the same reasons. Trying to maintain an impractical wife and seven children by journalism, combined with writing books, plays, verse and essays, Hunt's was an early prototype of the untidy, disorganised bohemian Chelsea household: "hugger-mugger" was Carlyle's description of it and "poetical tinkerdom". Hunt, like so many of his successors, was a cheerful, generous man despite surroundings which his neighbour found so distressing. "In his family room," noted Carlyle, "where are a large sickly wife and a whole school of well-conditioned wild children, you will find half-a-dozen rickety chairs gathered from half-a-dozen different hucksters and all seeming engaged, and just pausing, in a violent hornpipe. On these and around them and over the dusty table and ragged carpet lie all kinds of litter – books, papers, egg-shells, scissors and last night when I was there, the torn heart of a quartern loaf. His own room above stairs . . . has only two chairs, a bookcase and a writing table; yet the noble Hunt receives you in his Tinkerdom in the spirit of a King, apologises for nothing, places you in the best seat, takes a window-sill himself if there is no other, and then, folding closer his loose flowing 'muslin cloud' of a printed nightgown, in which he always writes, commences the liveliest dialogue on philosophy and the prospects of man . . ."

But then Carlyle was always complaining and particularly of noise, which filled the Hunts' home; a demolition gang had been knocking down Smollett's old house when he arrived, street cries and the noise of horses and carts drove him to attempts to sound-proof his attic study and, at the end of his life, there was the racket of building across the street as Peabody Buildings were erected to house the inhabitants of demolished rookeries and cottages. Hunt, while sharing Carlyle's immediate liking for the district, found no such disturbance. His own first description of his house was in the same tone as his neighbour's: "The house was of the old-fashioned sort which I have always loved best, familiar to the eyes of my parents, and associated with childhood. It had seats in the windows, a small third room on the first floor, of which I made a sanctum . . ." Outside, "there were a few lime trees in front, which in their due season diffused a fragrance" and he felt that living in Chelsea was like being "at the end of the world". But there were also the street cries and in these Hunt found "a quaintness and melodiousness", specifying "an old seller of fish, in particular, whose cry of 'Shrimps as large as prawns!', was such a regular, long-drawn and truly pleasing melody, that in spite of his hoarse and, I am afraid, drunken voice, I used to wish for it of an evening, and hail it when it came."

Although Walter Greaves was born six years after Hunt left Chelsea, this was recognisably the place he would know and love.

After his wife's death in 1866, Carlyle became increasingly morose, remembered as "a gloomily serious, silent and sad old man gazing into the final chasm of things". Even the charitable Walter Greaves remembered him as "a gruff man and hardly answered when you spoke to him", walking by the river in his familiar wide-brimmed hat or smoking his pipe by the water's edge late at night.

Although both Carlyle and Whistler enjoyed stimulating conversation and lived so near to one another, there was no contact between them until they had been neighbours for a decade. Then, one day in 1872, a mutual friend in Chelsea, a Madame Venturi, a generous hostess to both men, suggested to Carlyle that Whistler should paint his portrait. The Sage agreed to visit Lindsey Row and see some of Whistler's work and thus ensued one of the remarkable brief confrontations of the century, something akin to the unexpected meeting of Nelson and Wellington in Whitehall.

As he began experimenting with Nocturnes, Whistler balanced the exercise of his imagination by beginning his greatest sequence of portraits. The first was of his mother. It showed her seated, in profile, her hands folded upon her lap, a look of calm resignation on her face. Whistler put much loving work into the portrait, admitting privately some time later, "one does like to make one's mummy just as nice as possible". But characteristically he called the picture, *Arrangement in Grey and Black No. 1: The Artist's Mother*, saying, "Take the picture of my mother . . . as an Arrangement in Grey and Black. Now that is what it is. To me it is interesting as a picture of my mother; but what can or ought the public to care about the identity of the portrait?"

There was a deceptive simplicity in the composition and colouring of the painting and even in the materials used, for Walter Greaves, who was present when Whistler was working on it, remembered that the exquisitely painted handkerchief in the hands had been "nothing but a bit of white and oil". Its seeming ingenuousness led to the irritation of the critics. The Selection Committee of the Royal Academy wanted to reject it but changed their minds grudgingly after a protest, so that it was exhibited in 1872.

This picture was in Whistler's studio when Carlyle called with Madame Venturi. "He seemed to feel in it a certain fitness of things," said the artist. "He liked the simplicity of it." Carlyle was not only a man of taste, he saw that not only would Whistler be likely to portray him without irrelevancies – most portraitists would have set The Sage in his study with piles of calf-bound books, a skull and an hour-glass – but, if he could give a simple old lady the air of an elderly Isis, what could he not do for the leading philosopher of his age? Soon afterwards Carlyle arrived for his first sitting.

It was a meeting of opposites, each entrenched behind ideas and prejudices, both equally demanding. Carlyle, old, gruff, unhappy after a life of sexual frustration, seeing himself as the interpreter of the greatness in leaders of men. Whistler, young, sparkling, fully conscious of his physical attraction, seeing himself solely as his own prophet, albeit unrecognised by the surrounding Philistines. The artist was accustomed to making extraordinary demands on his sitters – with the exception of his mother – by asking them to hold poses until they were near collapse. This sitter regarded the artist as a technician he could use and give orders to, and began doing this on the first day. Seeing Whistler ready with brushes and palette – and not realising the time needed to arrange the composition and mix the colours – he sat down and ordered, "And now, mon, fire away!" There was no reaction, so he added, "If ye're fighting battles or painting pictures, the only thing to do is to fire away!"

Carlyle quickly became restive at the number of sittings Whistler demanded (having imagined that two or three would be enough) and annoyed when, shifting his position on the hard, upright chair, the artist snapped, "For God's sake, don't move!" He decided that time could be saved if Whistler used larger brushes and, to humour him, the artist held a number of these, quite unsuited to his method of completing a painting which was like that of a duellist, standing well back from his canvas then darting forward to dab a touch of paint with a long, delicate brush. The Sage tried to pass the time by lecturing the artist on subjects he considered worthy of attention, but, so absorbed was Whistler in his work that he rarely answered. But once, when his own profession was mentioned, he did stop to listen. Carlyle had once sat to George Watts, a painter devoted to idealised "High Art", and, in attempting to make small talk, he related, "There was Mr. Watts, a mon of note. And I went to his studio, and there was much meestification, and screens were drawn round the easel, and the curtains were drawn, and I was not allowed

Battersea Reach in summer. Thames barges unloading alongside Lindsey Jetty, painted in oils by Walter Greaves at the window of his family's house.

Battersea Reach in winter. Both Whistler and Greaves painted Nocturnes when snow and ice on waterfront and foreshore gave new lights to a familiar scene.

Sunlight at Cremorne. The Chinese bandstand etched by Walter Greaves.

Sunlight at Battersea Park. *The Boating Pond*, painted in oils by Walter Greaves.

to see anything. And then, at last, the screens were put aside and there I was. And I looked. And Mr. Watts, a great mon, he said to me, 'How do you like it?' And then I turned to Mr. Watts, and I said, 'Mon, I would have ye know that I am in the hobit of wurin' clean lunen!' "

Whistler remembered this and imitated the accent – so strongly that a friend recorded it phonetically – primarily because it demonstrated The Sage's lack of artistic appreciation and also perhaps because he was amused that the shabby old man should appear to share his own fastidiousness in dress. Yet Carlyle complained that Whistler showed more interest in the hang of his coat than in his face and finally insisted that a model wear the coat as he was certainly giving no more sittings. Whistler had no alternative but to comply, recognising The Sage to be as stubborn and uncompromising as himself. As Carlyle left the studio, he passed a little girl, Cicely Alexander, arriving to pose for a portrait which Whistler was painting at the same time. Told this by the maid, Carlyle shook his head sadly, muttering, "Puir lassie! Puir lassie!" Whistler later professed to find the sitter for the portrait, which he had called *Arrangement in Grey and Black No. 2*, "a delightful person", but was himself described by Carlyle as "the most absurd creature on the face of the earth".

Walter Greaves was in the studio for much of this time and remembered the tensions and the impatience. Still much in awe of Carlyle, he made sketches of him and he said he was given three sittings of his own. But he later remarked sadly, "I never got to know him even when I painted his portrait." The many portraits of Carlyle by Greaves showed him wearing the famous hat, which in Whistler's picture rests on his knee. In quality they varied – as his work always did – but they were executed with great care both in oils and pencil. Certainly the Greaves portraits are not imitations of Whistler, for while the latter had simply arranged a sad old man in a perfectly balanced painting, the best of Greaves's show the sitter's intelligence and strength of character.

Pleased as he was with the Carlyle portrait, Whistler found relief in painting a pretty young girl for his *Harmony in Grey and Green*. The Greaves sisters had made, to Whistler's specification, "a carpet of black and white tapes" for Cicely Alexander to stand on and

Walter proudly spoke of it as "very uncommon". But the child, painted standing in a white and green dress, holding a feathered hat at her side, wears a sulky expression as if pleading to be allowed to go home. This was accurate portraiture for, as a grown woman, she vividly remembered the agony of posing for Whistler through seventy sittings.

"I rather considered that I was a victim all through the sittings," she said, "or rather standing, for he never let me change my position, and I sometimes used to stand for hours at a time. I know I used to get very tired and cross, and often finished the day in tears . . . He was most kind in other ways . . . He never made any objection to my poking about among his paints, and I even put charcoal eyes to some of his sketches of portraits, and he also constantly promised to paint my doll, but this promise was never kept."

Whistler liked to entertain his sitters. When his mother was in Chelsea, it tended to be a formal affair with a maid in attendance. But when she was away he held parties – what Walter Greaves called "times" – with Walter and Henry acting as stage-managers and Jimmy's mistress acting as hostess. Cicely Alexander, being the young daughter of a rich patron, was, of course, entertained by Mrs. Whistler at "delightful American luncheons", which, because of her son's reluctance to leave his studio, would often start at four o'clock. She remembered "hot biscuits and tinned peaches and other unwholesome things". The biscuits were probably the buckwheat cakes which Whistler liked to bake himself and canned food was not considered seemly or healthy at the well-ordered dining-room table.

The parties were sometimes boisterous affairs, particularly when Jo was his mistress and her bucolic Irish father might call, or her sister, who dressed up as a French nurse-maid to take Whistler's illegitimate child for riverside walks, or any number of shadowy figures from the fringe of artistic society. Dancing was often called for and the Greaveses played the piano. This was not taxing, because Walter said that Whistler "only liked one tune and he couldn't dance – not really".

When in a jocular mood, Whistler spared no thought for his neighbours' peace and would hire a passing hurdy-gurdy to play in his front garden. But when the pet pigeons of a drunken and irascible retired sea captain next door became a nuisance, Walter was told to make a complaint. Knowing the captain's reputation for violence, he refused and Whistler announced that he would go. Walter timorously watched him enter the next house and, a moment later, fly out pursued by the captain, waving a sword.

As word of Whistler's unconventional brilliance as a portrait-painter spread – largely by the Leylands, and the Alexanders on Campden Hill – the number of smartly-dressed visitors increased and sometimes their carriages lined the kerb outside Lindsey Row.

The entertainments at Lindsey Row became more pretentiously formal as Whistler's circle of acquaintance expanded. He entertained not only his sitters and potential patrons but the artists who had begun to settle in Chelsea in increasing numbers, an influx significant enough to prompt Victor Barthe to establish his evening life class. The new arrivals tended to drift towards the courts of Rossetti or Whistler, the romantic rebels to the former, the *avant-garde* to the latter.

The most significant of the romantics was William de Morgan, a friend of Burne-Jones and a disciple of William Morris and his belief in the renaissance of hand-crafts. In 1872 de Morgan took a house at the top of Cheyne Row – replaced at the end of the century by the Roman Catholic Church of the Holy Redeemer – in order to be near the site of the Chelsea china factory which he intended to emulate. De Morgan's pottery, manufactured here for ten years, followed the Pre-Raphaelite taste in mood and colour. Then, after working with Morris at Merton Abbey for seven years, he returned to Chelsea where he lived and worked on the north side of the King's Road – first in The Vale and finally in Old Church Street – until his death in 1917.

An artist, who admired Whistler and was admired by him, arrived in Chelsea a year after de Morgan. Charles Keene's illustrations for *Punch* and his etchings were well known to Whistler when he arrived and the two men were members of the same etching club. But Keene, whose beard and baggy tweeds made him instantly recognisable as an artist, was too much of an individualist to be drawn into orbit around The Master. A bachelor, he lived alone in

Paradise Row – and later in the King's Road – in a comfortable jumble, smoking memorably strong tobacco and simmering stews for the supper which invariably ended with bread and jam. Exquisite as was his taste, Keene had no time for Whistler's fastidious stage-setting in the studio; his own was cluttered with his illustrator's properties: armour, musical instruments, old clothes and a wooden horse with a saddle. Despite differing attitudes to their way of life, Keene, like Whistler, passed from the draughtsmanship of his etching days towards Impressionism.

Whistler's motive in establishing a court at Lindsey House was not solely because of his enjoyment of lively company or his need of an audience. The portrait of his mother was the last painting of his to be exhibited in the Royal Academy and, henceforth, he was waging war against the arbiters of conventional taste and for this he needed both support and publicity. Remembering the success of the *Salon des Refusés* in Paris a decade earlier, Whistler arranged his own exhibition at a Pall Mall gallery. Walter Greaves was there to help decorate the invitations with the butterfly signature, which Whistler probably evolved from his monogram, addressing the envelopes and setting out with bundles of them to post through Chelsea letterboxes. The exhibition, which opened in the summer of 1874, did not help his cause; for those critics who condescended to review it were unsympathetic, damned him with faint praise or brushed him aside as having failed to fulfil his early promise. Henceforth his antipathy towards the critics was to be open war, as against the Academicians.

Whistler was a deeply serious artist, hoping to convert others as easily as he had the Greaves brothers, and he lured potential converts to his studio by issuing standing invitations and leaving the door open. Inside, Walter Greaves was usually there to usher guests into The Master's presence, or, if he were out, show them his studio and his latest work. Walter was not, of course, paid for working as Grand Vizier of the studio any more than he was paid for walking, or taking the boat over to Battersea to buy Whistler's raw materials – colours, copal mastic, linseed oil, turpentine, size, black lead, canvas and wood – from shops that were cheaper than those north of the river, in particular from Freeman's in Lombard Street upstream of the church. "We never were paid so much as a penny for what we did," said Walter, "but we never minded that." Nor did he enjoy any social benefit, for Whistler's guests, whom he helped to entertain, did not invite him to their studio parties.

The Whistler household was, in itself, exciting enough for the Greaves brothers. It was always full of surprises and contrast. One week Mrs. Whistler would be in command and the men had to be careful, remembering not to be seen painting on Sundays – once she had returned from church to find them painting murals of ships in the hall and had preached them a sermon – and to hide their life class drawings when she was about. The next week, Jimmy's mistress might be in command; after his return from Valparaiso, Jo had been replaced by another model, Maud Franklin, a more sophisticated, delicate creature. Maud was more temperamental than her predecessor and she and Jimmy had violent quarrels, but she remained his mistress for about fifteen years and bore him two daughters. Like Jo, she was not invited to the houses of his more respectable friends nor the rich patrons who had been attracted by his striking portrait-painting. But she accompanied him to galleries, the theatre and studio parties, often leaving the house in the care of Walter Greaves.

Whistler enjoyed good food and wine when he could afford it and, when he could not, disguised the fact with elaborate presentation. His rich friend, Luke Ionides, who had helped introduce him into the world of London art patrons, remembered calling at Lindsey Row one afternoon and finding Whistler busily tidying the reception rooms. Asked if he had any money on him, Ionides said, "I told him I had twelve shillings. He said that was enough. We went out together, and he bought three chairs at two-and-sixpence each, and three bottles of claret at eighteen-pence each, and three sticks of sealing wax of different colours at twopence each. On our return he sealed the top of each bottle with a different coloured wax. He then told me that he expected a possible buyer to dinner, and two other friends. When we had taken our seats at table, he very solemnly told the maid to go down and bring up a bottle of wine, one of those with the red seal. The maid could hardly suppress a grin, but I alone saw it. Then, after the meat, he told her to fetch a bottle with the blue seal; and with dessert the one with the yellow seal was brought and all were drunk in perfect innocence and delight. He sold his picture and said he was sure the sealing-wax had done it."

Walter Greaves often had to help with such rushed performances, on one occasion sending a workman from his father's boatyard to borrow saucepans, a kettle and frying pans from Madame Venturi, and Jimmy himself persuaded Mrs. Leyland, the wife of his principal patron, not only to put up the muslin curtains in the dining-room but to lend him her butler. Sometimes Jimmy himself cooked – but usually only the buckwheat cakes – and pored over the cookery book which he called "The Family Bible". More suited to his talents was the decoration of the room, taking his time in placing nasturtiums, or a single lily, or waterlilies in a large blue-and-white Japanese china bowl, on which a short-sighted lady guest once tried to sit. Finally came his own *toilette:* the tying of the tie and the arranging of the black curls so that they displayed the single white lock on his forehead to effect.

Dinner parties were supplemented by Whistler's introduction of the Sunday breakfast for which his guests were invited for twelve but their host was unlikely to appear before two. These were generally, in effect, lunch parties but the food could be formal and varied or startlingly simple, and the wine excellent or the cheapest. Usually there was some American speciality: one guest spoke of "the inevitable buckwheat cakes, and green corn and brilliant talk", and among the drinks was the rum-based Mint Julep, which Whistler introduced to London.

When feeling expansive Whistler would offer his guests a meal such as *Potage Poitron; Soles Frites; Bœuf à la Mode; Chapon au Cresson; Salade Laitue; Marmalade de Pommes; Omelette au Fromage.* Sometimes the butter would be tinted green to match a picture or the curtains. But one Italian landscape painter, invited to breakfast and hoping for such a feast, reported afterwards, "I go. My cab fare two shilling, half-crown. I arrive. Very nice. Goldfish in bowl. Very pretty. But breakfast! One egg, one toast, no more. Ah, no! My cab fare back, two shilling, half-crown. For me, no more!"

But, whatever the dishes, Whistler could be relied upon to enhance or compensate. His speciality was pouring the wine when his guests were seated and his diminutive stature – he stood five feet, four inches – was no disadvantage. A friend described his "delightful way of waiting upon guests. He would go round with a bottle of Burgundy in its cradle, talking all the while, emphasising every point with a dramatic pause just before or just after filling a glass . . . There were minutes between one guest and the next . . . it was fully two hours before the story and breakfast came to an end together."

Continual entertaining, combined with the extravagant buying of oriental *objets d'art* and his tailor's bills, resulted in a permanent financial crisis. "Whistler used to think that money business a great joke," said Walter Greaves, "but I could never see it in that light. He used to say that he liked owing money because it made people call and enquire after his health." Indeed, Whistler delighted in telling tales of his escapes from creditors, usually with at least a touch of cruelty. Friends were usually paid in the end, persistent tradesmen might be persuaded to accept a picture instead of cash, but otherwise the extraction of money from Whistler required resilience and a ruthlessness to match his own. The debtor's attitude is well illustrated by a friend's account of his reaction to a loud and purposeful knock on his front door, when for once it was not ajar. "Psst! That's one-and-ten," he had whispered. After another knock, "Psst! Two and six." Asked to explain, Whistler said, "One pound, ten shillings; two pounds, six shillings. Vulgar tradesmen with their bills. They want payment. Oh, well!" Another, gentler, almost pleading knock. "Dear me, that must be all of twenty! Poor fellow! I really must do something for him. So sorry I'm not in."

On another occasion a Jewish creditor had called and Walter had retreated before him to the first floor and it was obvious that he would not leave until he had been paid. Whistler, who had been listening from the studio to Walter's mumbled excuses, suddenly bounded into the room, barking, "Are you the chap who killed our Lord? Come on, Walter: open the window and out with him!"

The terrified visitor fled.

Victor Barthe, who had sold some tapestry to Whistler, attempted to collect his money and the subsequent escapade as told by him was recorded phonetically at the time. "But vill he pay, zis Vistlaire, vill he pay?" Barthe had been asking, until he finally went to Lindsey Row to make a personal demand. A cab was outside the door, the maid said that Whistler was not in but, hearing his voice upstairs, Barthe pushed past. "Upstairs, I find him, before a little picture, painting, and behind him ze bruzzers Greaves holding candle. And Vistlaire he say, 'You ze very man I vant; hold a candle!' And I hold a candle. And Vistlaire he paint and he paint and zen he take ze picture and he go downstair and he get in ze cab and he drive off and ve hold ze candle and I see him no more. *Mon dieu, il est terrible, ce Vistlaire!*"

On another occasion, Whistler decided to take two of the Greaves girls to a promenade concert at Covent Garden. With them went Horace Gee, a charming drifter, whom Whistler had once invited to stay the night because of bad weather but who stayed for three years, drinking his host's whisky and becoming another courtier such as Walter and Henry, spending much time, as Whistler said, "with the Greaves, the boat people, a sort of Peggotty family, playing with Tinnie Greaves." As soon as they had sat down in their cab at Chelsea, Whistler told Tinnie that he had no money. "So what's the use of going out?" asked the embarrassed girl and suggested returning home. Whistler would have none of that and ordered the cab to drive on. After a while he stopped the cab outside a little tobacconist's shop and charmed the old woman behind the counter to lend him several pounds. Jumping back into the cab, Jimmy announced, "Now, Miss Tinnie, we can enjoy ourselves!" They did and returned late to the Greaves's house to dance while Gee, who was a deft pianist although he could not read a note of music, played. Whether the old woman was ever repaid is not recorded.

Having so little money themselves, the Greaves brothers were never exploited in this way. They were happy to work unpaid to the dismay of their father, who foresaw exactly what lay ahead when there was no longer a family home and business to provide food and lodging. At times Whistler thoughtfully encouraged Walter's development as an artist, taking him to see an exhibition of Velasquez and explaining his admiration for the deliberately muted colours and the strong, careful composition.

Walter was relaxing company – and even Whistler needed a rest from the continual display of personality and provocative ideas – but on him witticisms would be wasted. It was to an over-enthusiastic female admirer, not to Greaves, who exclaimed that there had only ever been two artists of true merit, Whistler and Velasquez, that Whistler remarked, "Why drag in Velasquez?" When asked later whether he had meant this seriously, he had snapped, "No, of course not. You don't suppose I'd couple myself with Velasquez, do you? I simply wanted to take her down." Walter Greaves would never have presumed to make so definite an assertion to The Master, however flattering.

Now considering himself to be an artist and no longer a boat-builder or waterman, Walter Greaves and his brother had ambitions to exhibit their work. The Master's reaction to this varied according to his mood. Once, Walter had painted a portrait of Tinnie without his knowledge. The canvas had been prepared by both brothers in the first-floor sitting-room of their house and Walter had painted his sister in black and white Tudor costume; achieving the effect of the ruffles and lace with a thin wash of grey paint after the rest of the painting was dry. The picture took Whistler by surprise and his first reaction was generous, "A charming harmony, the best you have done. Ha, ha! You are getting on." But when Walter said that he hoped it would be exhibited at the Royal Aquarium hall, Westminster, The Master replied, "No, no. It must not go there, it's only a fish shop." Whistler tried, but failed, to arrange its exhibition at the Grosvenor Gallery and it was, after all, hung at the Royal Aquarium in 1876.

The Master was possessive towards his two pupils and Walter said that "he would never allow us to exhibit anything without his permission". There were moments when rebellion seemed possible. Asked whether he preferred his own style to that imposed upon him, Walter replied, "I do, but Mr. Whistler wouldn't have us paint like that." And, again in retrospect, "Mr. Whistler made us paint those Nocturnes; he would have us paint them."

Not surprisingly Walter Greaves assumed that so long as he copied the adored and feared Master, he could do no wrong. But his increasing talents now seemed to arouse an edge of jealousy in Whistler. In 1874, Whistler had started a portrait of Florence Leyland, a young daughter of his shipowner patron, wearing a blue dress, but the work had been endlessly delayed and, in fact, was never completed. A year or so later he was told that Walter was preparing to start work on a portrait of his eldest sister Eliza – now married to a George Ranger – also wearing a blue dress. Whistler at once wrote to Walter saying that he had just heard of his plan and, kindly but firmly, warned him, "Now, my dear boy, just reflect for a minute and don't let my pet pupil unconsciously do what he would be indignant if another were to attempt, for you know my picture of little Miss Leyland in blue cashmere and velvet – in short, the arrangement in blue – you know how jolly it is, and of course I shall paint it directly I have time."

He continued, coming more to the point, "Don't you see, Walter, you know how I continually invent – and invention you know is the cream of the whole affair and so easy to destroy the freshness of it. And you know that all the whole system of arrangement and harmonies which I most certainly invented, I brought you up in, so that it is only natural that I should expect my pupil to perceive all harmony in the same way – he must do it – for I have shown you that everything outside of that is wrong . . . Suppose you were to see any other fellow doing my moonlights – how vexed you would be. Well, nothing more natural than that you should do them and quite right that the tradition of the studio should go on through the pupils – but still for instance it would be absurd to paint another *White Girl*. Don't you know what I mean?"

But, in a rare moment of rebelliousness, Walter painted Eliza in a long blue dress as a pair to the full-length portrait of Tinnie in black and white. At first, the verdigris blue he had bought in Battersea looked magnificent but then, as he said years later, "It never did us any good to go against Mr. Whistler, for that verdigris blue turned green after all." Indeed the finished picture was entitled *The Green Dress*.

Occasionally Whistler had a word with a friend who organised the annual South Kensington Exhibition and, as a result, Walter's *Harmony in Blue-Grey* had been shown there in 1873 and Henry's *Harmony in White and Grey* a year later. It was their own idea to hold an exhibition of their work in their father's boat-house, but to this Whistler could have had no objection. So long as the brothers kept to their place in his life, The Master seems to have been kind, if not generous. But once they began to attract too much attention his self-arranged solar system became unbalanced and he reacted at once. He was notably displeased when he heard that, without asking his opinion, the brothers were talking of painting "up to Academy pitch". Whistler, who had not submitted a picture to the Royal Academy since the grudging acceptance of the portrait of his mother, considered that his pupils should automatically be his allies in the war against convention.

During the late eighteen-sixties and early 'seventies, Frederick Leyland had been his most powerful and devoted patron. The son of a Liverpool street pie-seller, he had worked his way to the top of the shipping hierarchy, then expanding dramatically with British trade. He had become immensely rich and, although without formal education, was a man of natural taste, determined to prove this not only in Liverpool but in London. He admired Whistler's portraiture and commissioned him to paint his entire family, paying in advance. The only portraits completed were that of himself and of his wife. Both were full-length and Whistler had so much trouble in painting his patron's legs that he hired a model to pose nude for a figure to be clothed in Leyland's elegant trousers. When the portrait had been given a body but not clothes – and, as Mrs. Whistler was at Lindsey Row, turned to the wall for propriety's sake – Whistler was away, leaving Walter in charge. One day Mrs. Whistler came into the studio and asked to see the Leyland portrait. Walter demurred, found excuses, but had not the nerve to tell her the reason for his hesitance. She insisted on seeing it and, when Walter finally turned it round, gasped, "Oh, dear! Oh, dear!"

Whistler's relations with the Leyland family were close. He and his mother often stayed at Speke Hall, their mansion near Liverpool. He was attracted to Mrs. Leyland, a pretty woman with the quick sympathy he required, and to her younger sister. Whether he knew of, or sensed, Whistler's attachment to his wife, Leyland showed no sign of it and when his original style so startled convention in the late 'seventies that it had become the fashion to mock at Whistler's unconventional style and put him out of fashion as a portrait-painter, he remained loyal. To help Whistler through a difficult period he commissioned him to join, in 1876, the assortment of leading artists and architects whom he had chosen to convert the inside of his newly-acquired London house – 49 Prince's Gate in Kensington – into a palace fit for a Medici.

The centre-piece of Leyland's fantasy was the bronze balustrade from the grand staircase of Northumberland House at Charing Cross, then being demolished, this supporting a group of gilded figures from the prow of a Venetian galley. This staircase linked rooms beside which even his friend Rossetti's conglomeration of curios seemed commonplace. There was Beauvais tapestry, Renaissance bronzes, oriental china, inlaid French furniture, mosaic floors, Genoese velvet curtains and paintings both by Old Masters and by the contemporary Rossetti, Burne-Jones, Watts, Moore, Ford Madox Brown and Whistler, who had also been asked to decorate some panels in the Japanese taste.

Leyland sought advice about the decoration of his dining-room, in which he planned to show off the best of his blue-and-white oriental china. He also planned to hang above the mantelpiece Whistler's *La Princesse du Pays de la Porcelaine*, which he had bought some years before and wanted to display in a flattering position. Norman Shaw was in overall command of the decorations, but the dining-room was given to another architect, Thomas Jeckyll, who decided to line the walls with old Norwich leather painted with Tudor pomegranates and red flowers. Whistler, called up from his painting in the hall to give his opinion, complained that the colour of the leather clashed with *La Princesse*. With Leyland's permission he gilded the red flowers but this, while harmonising with his picture, did not do so with its muted Tudor background. Leyland, about to take his family away to Speke Hall, agreed that Whistler might experiment with alternative schemes in his absence and departed. It was a rash move.

Alone with *La Princesse* and her unharmonious surroundings, Whistler began to toy with various rearrangements of colour in the room but nothing he could visualise was satisfactory while the leather dominated the room. Then, in a moment of daring he began to paint on the leather again. It was beautifully satisfying to lay paint on so smooth and expensive a surface, for the leather, which had hung for three centuries in a Norfolk country house, had cost

Leyland a thousand pounds. Once a corner of the leather had been covered with his own fresh colour, there seemed no reason why the whole room should not be his canvas and in a moment of revelation he realised that an elaborate pattern of oriental gold and blue peacocks, which he had once planned but not painted for another client, would perfectly harmonise with *La Princesse*. It was a large room and the work too much for one man. Walter and Henry Greaves were summoned and the walls and ceiling were smothered in a frenzy of blue and gold.

Walter and Henry laid on the gold hour after hour, day after day. Whistler had chosen the same verdigris blue that Walter had used for his portrait of Eliza and disregarded his warning that "it would not stand". Leyland had not, of course, been consulted about so melodramatic a solution to what had seemed a minor problem of interior decoration and, perhaps because Whistler sensed what his reaction might be, the three men worked at a frantic pace during their patron's absence that summer. They would often be up by six and at work an hour later and soon their hair, hands and clothes would be flecked with blue and gold as the peacock tide edged across the room.

Whistler was delighted with the result and began to ask his friends to Prince's Gate for private views of his progress. For the Greaves brothers this, once again, was a new experience in Whistler's company: the jollities in their parlour had given way to his studio parties and these to his dinners and Sunday breakfasts and now they were in a Kensington mansion of unimaginable splendour receiving guests more sophisticated and richer than ever before. Gallery-owners and other artists came to praise – including the otherwise critical Edward Poynter, whom Whistler had known in Paris – followed by the *bon ton*, including Lord Redesdale, the Marquis of Westminster and Princess Louise. Whistler was in his element, sparkling with wit and praise of his own work. When a Lady Ritchie called ("We found ourselves – it was like a dream – in a beautiful Peacock Room, full of lovely light and tints, and romantic, dazzling effects"), he seized her in his arms and waltzed round the room among the pots of paint.

Lord Redesdale had struck an unharmonious note, asking, "What of the beautiful old leather? And Leyland? Have you consulted him?"

"Why should I?" snapped Whistler, "I am doing the most beautiful thing that ever has been done, you know, the most beautiful room."

Such shadows quickly passed and Whistler and the Greaves brothers went on with this combination of a major work of art and an elaborate prank. Not enough guests were coming for Whistler's liking and he sent out invitation cards and arranged to have a bowl of them on offer in Liberty's store. Instead of entertaining two or three friends, he began holding receptions for strangers. At one, an uninvited figure slipped into the dining-room, gazed at it in horror and fled. It was Jeckyll, the architect to whom Leyland had entrusted the dining-room.

Another unexpected guest at a soirée in the Peacock Room was Mrs. Leyland, in London unannounced, who had let herself into her house and been surprised to hear the noise of a party in the dining-room and the familiar "peacock laugh" of Jimmy Whistler. As she reached the door somebody suggested that Leyland might not be happy with the transformation on his return. Whistler shrugged and in his most carrying tone, crowed, "Well! What can you expect from a *parvenu*?"

Leyland, on his return, was as shattered as his wife had been at this treatment from their old friend and protégé. He could stand the loss of his magnificent leather, but the Peacock Room, though gorgeous, was, he felt, far too ostentatious for a prominent man trying to live down his backstreet origin and prove himself a gentleman. But the masterpiece had been painted and the damage done. Leyland behaved impeccably, but suggested that Whistler need not complete the redecoration. Whistler insisted that he should and Leyland reluctantly agreed. Asked what his fee would be, Whistler asked for more than two thousand guineas. Leyland, after consulting Rossetti, gave him one thousand pounds. It was not so much the amount by which Leyland had reduced his payment that infuriated Whistler, it was that he had been paid in tradesmen's pounds, not gentleman's guineas.

Whistler took revenge swiftly and spitefully, as was his custom. The last touches to the room were to be two splendid peacocks at the end of the room, which Leyland would face when he sat at table with his back to *La Princesse*. Under the grasping claw of one he painted a pile of gold coins.

When Leyland saw the completed room his eye caught the symbolic peacock but, to his credit, he left Whistler's work exactly as it was. Even so Whistler had lost, or, rather, thrown away, the friendship of a kindly and powerful patron and a family with whom he had been intimate. Like a spoilt child, who has finally got out of hand and been caught and punished, he returned to sulk in Chelsea with the innocent and bemused Walter and Henry.

In retrospect, Whistler used to say that his misfortunes began with the affair of the Peacock Room. "Ever since," he said, "I've had no luck."

Walter Greaves, also looking back, could have said the same.

5

"*Les Refusés*"

The Greaves family were still at the far end of Lindsey Row, as they always had been, to comfort the resentful Whistler. But the cosy bosom of the Greaves household seemed a pitiful substitute for the splendours of life with the Leylands, the lazy weeks at Speke Hall, the introductions to the *haute monde* in London and, as much as anything, the prospects of dazzling conversation at table in the Peacock Room.

At this time all Whistler's deep-buried feelings of personal inadequacy and insecurity came to the surface. The American who had abandoned America; the Londoner who felt himself a stranger among its inhabitants; the West Point man who had stayed away from his country's civil war; the amoral bohemian who loved his puritan mother; the artist whose ideas were misunderstood and mocked. His art was primarily that of a superb decorator, inducing no intellectual or emotional reaction and demanding only admiration. A view of Whistler, as astringent and uncompromisingly critical as any of his own judgements, was given half a century later by James Laver and it cruelly shows him as perhaps he saw himself at despondent moments such as this. "If Whistler's art reached down to no rich subsoil," Laver wrote, "if it tapped no profound source of human impulse, it was because he was essentially a plant in a pot. He proved extremely successful in drawing nutriment from the air around him; he developed an exquisite bloom of hitherto unknown variety, but his roots turned in upon themselves, and he left no seed to propagate his kind. His art was as exquisite as a prize in a flower show, as barren as a hybrid, as shallow as cosmopolitan culture must always be."

Yet Whistler exercised immense influence, directly upon taste and, less directly, upon art. His influence on the lives of those who

The last Chelsea regatta. In 1871 Walter Greaves etched and painted in oils the traditional festival that was about to be ended by the demolition of the old waterfront and the building of the Embankment. Racing at low water, the competitors were cheered by crowds on the balconies of the Adam and Eve tavern, the steamboat pier below Battersea Bridge and the foreshore.

Intimacy with the river at Chelsea. Turner's cottage with its wrought-iron, roof-top balustrade faces the Thames across a narrow lane and upstream stand the trees of Cremorne. A drawing by Walter Greaves.

Intimacy lost. Walter Greaves painted himself and his sister "Tinnie" on the newly-built Embankment to the west of Old Church Street in the eighteen-seventies.

came into prolonged contact with him was permanent and he left the stamp of his personality upon the place where he lived longest, Chelsea. Of his acquaintances, those few who were his match, in resilience at least, bore the scars of the relationship with pride or anger for the rest of their lives; those who, caught in his web were too weak or bemused to escape, were emotionally maimed. Among these were the loving Greaves family and, in particular, the devoted Walter.

In 1877, Whistler was in a highly sensitive and combative mood. He would admit to no scrap of blame for the quarrel over the Peacock Room, blaming Leyland for Philistinism and meanness. Having lost this bridgehead into the world of art patrons, he badly needed another and timely help came in the person of Sir Coutts Lindsay, who that year was preparing the first exhibition in the Grosvenor Gallery, which he had opened in New Bond Street as a rival attraction to the Royal Academy. Sir Coutts himself was to be the arbiter of merit and the artists he invited to submit paintings that year included both the grand, marble pillars of High Art – Leighton, Millais, Alma-Tadema, Richmond and Poynter – and a selection of rebels and the *avant-garde*, such as Rossetti, Burne-Jones, Holman Hunt and Whistler. Delighted as he was by this honour, Whistler was dismayed by the decoration of the gallery, the gilded furniture, the crimson silk damask and the green velvet, which were splendid for the traditionalists but fatal for his own delicate work. This, he knew, demanded simplicity, plain, subtle colours and the most sensitive balance in the arrangement of the pictures on the walls.

The exhibition opened in May and the gallery was crowded with smart Londoners, delightedly gathering round their old favourites, each painting telling a story which could be a talking-point at dinner for the next week.

Whistler was prepared for the scorn of the critics, indeed this was becoming so familiar an experience and his counter-attacks so telling that his repertoire would have been incomplete without them. But most of these critics were, in his view, ill-informed, uncultivated journalists. When harsh criticism came from an artist or intellectual, whose praise he would have welcomed, it still hurt. One of his paintings at the Grosvenor Gallery brought a rebuff so savage from so eminent a source that it could not be ignored or lampooned.

The painting was his *Nocturne in Black and Gold: The Falling Rocket*, a shower of golden sparks falling out of the night sky over Cremorne. To Walter Greaves, who attempted and sometimes achieved the same effects in several media, the subject would have been instantly recognisable. To Whistler, of course, the subject was of no consequence, and to him and his sympathisers it was enough that he had produced a beautiful and original harmony of colour.

But the most distinguished critic of the time had almost certainly never been to Cremorne and, in any case, had several years before spoken of the "absolute rubbish . . . scrawl or daub" of a painting which could only have been by Whistler. But John Ruskin – or "Ruskin" as he was always known, for he seemed too grand to have ever been called "John" – was Slade Professor of Fine Art at Oxford and had for years been preaching to the British public, dictating their taste. His theories were muddled and his causes many – he praised Turner's sunsets but despised Whistler's twilights, he supported Pre-Raphaelite escapism while seeing a practical Socialist purpose in art – but he proclaimed his creed with a passionate eloquence which demanded his audience to stop and listen. Ruskin was now an irascible sixty-eight, a miserable personal life behind him and mental illness close ahead; both were contributory to the unbalanced ferocity with which he now spoke and wrote.

Shortly after the opening of the Grosvenor Gallery exhibition, Whistler, alone with a friend, the painter George Boughton, in the smoking-room of the Arts Club, came upon Ruskin's review. One passage in it seemed to strike him in the face: "For Mr. Whistler's sake, no less than for the protection of the purchaser, Sir Coutts Lindsay ought not to have admitted works into the gallery in which the ill-educated conceit of the artist so nearly approached the aspect of wilful imposture. I have seen and heard much of cockney impudence before now, but never expected to hear a coxcomb ask two hundred guineas for flinging a pot of paint in the public's face."

"Sounds rather like libel," suggested Boughton.

"Well – that I shall try to find out!" replied Whistler, and the celebrated legal contest began. When Whistler sued Ruskin for libel, the excitement was intense and the prospect was said to be like that of a fight to the death between an elephant and a tiger. The opponents prepared their cases with relish, seeking support from those whose position in public esteem would weigh heavily in court. To defy Whistler was only to feel the cut of his sarcasm or risk a bloody nose; but to challenge Ruskin was to defy the custodian of the canons of High Art. The former was therefore hurt and worried when so many of those artists, whom he had thought to be sympathetic, made embarrassed excuses for their unwillingness to stand beside him. In the fever of the moment it seemed to Whistler that anybody who was not for him was against him. In his anxiety, even the support of his pupils was important.

After the exhibition closed, Whistler asked the Greaves brothers whether they had seen it. They replied that they had not and, seeing sudden anger in his eyes, added, as Whistler himself later recounted, that they had not "meant anything" by not going. They were embarrassed but could not have realised the implications of this stumbled apology. Before Whistler's anger had cooled he heard from a mutual friend that the brothers were, in his words, "painting pictures on the method of Whistler up to Academy pitch".

This was the turning point in the long relationship of the artist and the watermen. In retrospect they realised that, from this time, Jimmy employed them only for "fetching and carrying". At the time, buoyed up by memories of past happiness and present wishful thinking, they found plausible reasons for this apparent neglect. Whistler was leaving Lindsey Row.

A year before, Mrs. Whistler's health had begun to fail and she had gone to live by the sea at Hastings, while Maud took her place as chatelaine. Whistler himself had been out of fashion as a portrait-painter since the surprise attack by Ruskin and, to make money, he was planning to open the same sort of teaching studio that he had sometimes attended in Paris. There was not room for this in Lindsey Row, where he painted in a small room with a north light, so he was commissioning a sympathetic architect friend, E. W. Godwin, to build him a studio-house in his own taste in Tite Street at the far eastern end of the Chelsea waterfront.

Godwin and Whistler shared much the same views on art and

decoration and the former was not only agreeably unconventional but had a pretty wife, Beatrix, for whom he was to feel neither his familiar lust or acquisitive affection, but, possibly for the first time, deep love. The White House, as it was called, embodied all Whistler's theories of elegance. It's exterior – white walls and green roof – was to be severely simple, its windows spaced as asymmetrically as the few pictures on its walls. It was, in fact, far too plain for contemporary taste and, before granting a licence to build, the Metropolitan Board of Works insisted on the inclusion of ornamental mouldings in the façade.

Whistler left Lindsey Row in October 1878, having first supervised its redecoration for the new tenants. Although The White House was only five minutes' walk from the Greaves's house, Jimmy Whistler might have ascended into another world. Walter, passing old Battersea Bridge, still standing incongruously at the western end of the new Embankment, would walk over the site of The Adam and Eve and Arch House, past the Old Church and Albert Bridge, which for five years had crossed the river to Battersea Park, where Cadogan Pier had been suspended from its two handsome arches, and at the end of Cheyne Walk come upon a new and alien sophistication. From here to the Royal Hospital, on either side of the Physic Garden, which survived despite the loss of river water to its exotic plants, were being built palatial residences that seemed to belong to another time and place. The most sumptuous of these, Swan House, had just been completed in a mixture of *art nouveau* and Queen Anne styles by the *avant-garde* architect Norman Shaw on the site of The Old Swan tavern and its garden, from which Walter had often watched the finish of Doggett's Coat and Badge watermen's race from London Bridge. Facing the austere Embankment and, across the river, the young trees of Battersea Park, the new houses – like those replacing the Georgian terraces of Hans Town to the west of Sloane Street – seemed to have no connection with the busy, intimate life of Chelsea itself. Up Swan Walk, beside the Physic Garden, a reassuring row of eighteenth-century houses still stood, but, up the next turning, Tite Street, was a canyon of new houses in bright red brick, throwing into relief the startling simplicity of The White House.

Whistler's insistence on perfection had forced the builder's charges far above the estimate at a time when his money troubles were worse than usual. The time when he could frighten creditors away, or barter pictures, was past and his debts mounted so ominously that he had to pawn the portraits of his mother and Carlyle and several Nocturnes. Howell, ever ready with ingenious money-making ideas, suggested that Whistler print and sell some of his early etchings and this he did with success. The reprieve was temporary and it was no time to embark on litigation.

During these worrying months The White House was a great solace to Whistler and he delighted in showing round visitors, prompting their praise with exclamations of, "Pretty, eh?" "Perfect, what?" "A gem, ha?" Sometimes, Walter Greaves slipped in among the laughing guests like a shadow. He was not unwelcome but there was no place for him. The women were clustering round Whistler more possessively than ever: particularly Maud, now anxious for her future as mistress, and the young, attractive wife of Godwin, the architect, who was the cause of her anxiety.

There was no need for Walter Greaves at The White House as the day of the hearing of the libel suit drew near and the life of Lindsey Row was quiet and unexciting without the continuous display of wit and temperament in the Whistler household. Walter now saw himself and his brother as carrying on the artistic tradition of the district and both continued to wear Whistlerian dress: wide-brimmed black hats at a rakish angle and narrow, coloured ties fluttering from loose collars. But their shy manner could not match their dashing dress and, in Chelsea, they were regarded as being no more than local boys who had taken up painting and had been working in a famous artist's studio, instead of working sensibly in their father's boatyard.

In Battersea, however, they could cut a dash. Chelsea artists might paint the opposite bank of the river from their windows or the bridges, but they seldom went there and never thought of establishing a colony there – although a small close of studios was built off Albert Bridge Road. For Battersea was still, at heart, an independent village, grouped tightly round its riverside church. But the factories were increasing in number and size from the flour mill, the plumbago graphite crucible works and the candle factory, whose chimneys Whistler had painted. The market gardens were filling up with rows of little houses for the poorer classes, their façades often decorated in pathetic attempts to follow Ruskin's eulogy of the Gothic architecture of Venice.

Walter had regularly visited Battersea to collect Whistler's materials for sketching, painting and etching and, like his father, enjoyed walking in what had been the water meadows opposite Cheyne Walk. These were now Battersea Park, famous for its flower gardens, the bicycling on its perimeter road and its boating pond. The Greaves boatyard built skiffs for hire on the lake and Walter haunted the landing-stage where they were moored. He watched the growth of the park from its beginnings. From the landing-stage he sketched the lake in winter when there was ice on the water, snow on the artificial rocks of The Alpine Garden on the far shore and the newly-planted saplings stood black against the sky. In summer, the view from the boat-keeper's wooden hut inspired him to paint another highly original composition in oils, one that owed nothing to the influence of Whistler. *The Boating Pond, Battersea Park* was dominated by the concave curve of the wooden pontoons to which the skiffs were moored by the bow, and the white of the girls' summer dresses was balanced by the white of swans.

Rossetti and Whistler might be kings in Chelsea, but in Battersea they were unknown and Walter Greaves, with his chalks and sketching pad, was pointed out as a Chelsea artist. This could be his kingdom and, in some measure, the sight of crowds round the bandstand and the aviary and the young cockneys pulling their skiffs among the wooded islands in the lake compensated for the loss of the past excitements of the vanished Chelsea waterfront.

North of the river, the gladiatorial contest between Whistler and Ruskin was the talk of studios and *salons*. But when the court sat in November the action was robbed of its sensationalism by the absence, through mental illness, of Ruskin. Instead of a duel it was simply to be the baiting of Whistler by the Philistines; but that, in itself, was no unworthy spectacle. Principal witnesses for Ruskin were Edward Burne-Jones and William Frith, painters then at the peak of their fame, but the only supporters Whistler could get to court were the faithful Albert Moore and a reluctant William Rossetti, brother of Dante Gabriel.

Under examination, Whistler was at his best. The Attorney-General, who was counsel for Ruskin, questioned him about *The Falling Rocket*:

"This is Cremorne?" (*Laughter.*)

"It is a Nocturne in black and gold."

"You have made the study of art your study of a lifetime. What is the peculiar beauty of that picture?"

"It is as impossible for me to explain to you the beauty of that picture as it would be for a musician to explain to you the beauty of harmony in a particular piece of music if you had no ear for music."

When the *Nocturne in Blue and Gold: Old Battersea Bridge* was shown in court, the judge gazed at it in bewilderment and asked, "Are those figures on the top of the bridge intended for people?"

"They are just what you like."

"That is a barge underneath?"

"Yes. I am very much flattered at your seeing that. The thing is intended simply as a representation of moonlight. My whole scheme was only to bring about a certain harmony of colour."

Whistler won his case but was awarded damages of one farthing. The contestants each had to pay their own costs. Ruskin's was covered by his friends' subscriptions, but Whistler's attempt to raise money failed and he faced fees of about five hundred pounds. Fearing, quite rightly, that he might be declared bankrupt, his creditors crowded round him demanding immediate settlement. Charm and promises, or the offer of pictures, were not enough and writs began to arrive at The White House, Whistler receiving them with a magnificent display of nerve and showmanship, even persuading the bailiffs to wear hired livery and wait on his guests at table. Unaware of this, one lady remarked, "Your servants seem to be extremely attentive and anxious to please you." "Oh, yes," replied Whistler, "I assure you they wouldn't leave me."

Inevitably, Whistler was, in May, 1879, declared bankrupt. This meant that The White House and all its lovingly collected and arranged treasures would have to be sold. Meeting Walter Greaves,

Whistler told him to help himself to his Japanese etching paper before the sale. As a last gesture, he and his servant John one evening painted over the front door of The White House, "Except the Lord build the house, they labour in vain that build it. E. W. Godwin, F.S.A., built this one." It was a gallant, final joke, worthy of the Southern cavalier he imagined he was.

When The White House was sold for two thousand seven hundred pounds that September, Whistler was far away, losing himself in the back alleys and forgotten canals of Venice. He had left Maud in London, probably because her presence would have been too distracting without the balance of male companions. He had asked Walter Greaves to go with him, but neither had money and Walter refused, foreseeing the inevitable trail of unpaid bills, saying later, "I refused because I knew we should have trouble." In Venice, his place was taken by a gondolier, Cavaldora.

Whistler spent a year in Venice, Maud arriving soon afterward to share his poverty. He worked hard and his stay there is memorable not so much for the Nocturnes, for which he sketched and stared at the misty lagoon and the twinkling lights from Cavaldora's gondola as he once had from the Greaves's boat, but for the etchings and pastels of canals overhung with crumbling *palazzi*, alleys festooned with washing lines, and unkempt Venetians, all made beautiful by light and reflection, but a jolting surprise for those who thought of Venice in terms of Carpaccio, Canaletto or even Turner.

Returning to London a year later, Whistler prepared for another drastic change in his way of living. Still smarting at the loss of The White House, he took a studio nearby at 13 Tite Street, saying of its new owner, the art critic of *The Times*, "He obstinately stays there in the way, while I am living in this absurd fashion, next door to myself."

In compensation, new interests were crowding in upon Whistler. He was developing his interest in lithography under the guidance of Thomas Way who reproduced his sketches in pastel: portraits, Venetian scenes and figures in the manner of Albert Moore. The studio in Tite Street was now frequented by respectable painters on the brink of success and whereas the atmosphere in Lindsey Row had always been bohemian, here it began to show symptoms of the upper-middle-class artistic life that was shortly to become dominant.

Whistler had always wanted a male companion about the studio and for so many years Walter had been one of them, basking in The Master's favour as others came and went. But now a new companion was to be seen in his company, a man in every way the antithesis of Walter Greaves. The charming, precocious, soft and witty interloper was Oscar Wilde.

Whistler had not connected the pleasant, courteous young man, whose mother had recently settled in Oakley Street, with the tiresome undergraduate who, in reviewing the Grosvenor Gallery exhibition for a university magazine had written of *The Falling Rocket* and another firework Nocturne: "These pictures are certainly worth looking at for about as long as one looks at a real rocket, that is, for something less than a quarter of a minute." He saw Wilde as the ideal companion, although twenty years his junior. Here was a wit worthy of his own, entertaining but never dominant, because the young man would gracefully allow him the final thrust, or feed him a cue for a climactic witticism. Their duel of wit, playful fencing that inevitably came to sabre-fighting, was soon one of the most discussed social sideshows in the upper social and artistic sets. Before Whistler's jealousy destroyed their friendship there was much playful cuffing in their exchanges. Once, when *Punch* had published an imaginary conversation between them about art, Wilde had telegraphed to Whistler, "*Punch* too ridiculous. When you and I are together we never talk about anything but ourselves." He received the reply, "No, no, Oscar, you forget. When you and I are together we never talk about anything except me." As their relations began to turn sour, Wilde is said to have remarked that he wished he had made a certain pointed comment of Whistler's, at which Jimmy said, "You will, Oscar, you will!"

The older man's jealousy was not only of superior powers of sustained wit and conversation – for he himself was only master of the devastating retort or the uninterrupted monologue – but of the attention Wilde was attracting. Behind the dilettante pose there was a quick brain and a selective memory which sorted and stored the best of Whistler's talk about art for his own use. And Whistler, long accustomed to being the most stared-at dandy in Chelsea, the art galleries and the smart dining-rooms, found Wilde's more flamboyant fashions irritating. Once, seeing Wilde in a long, green, frogged coat he snapped, "Oscar – how dare you! What means this disguise? Restore those things to Nathan's, and never again let me find you masquerading the streets of my Chelsea in the combined costumes of Kossuth and Mr. Mantalini!"

The pupils, as the Greaves brothers had been, were now replaced by "Followers", young middle-class artists so devoted to The Master that they were willing to work as studio assistants in order to be at the ultimate source of wit and taste. In almost every case their relationships ended, sometimes after years, with Whistler savaging the younger man, usually for no valid reason. Some had the strength of personality and the original talent to shrug their shoulders and, once rejected, make their own way. Others either became sycophants, smiling under the lash, or crept away to rub salt into their wounds. At this time the two principal Followers were Walter Sickert and Mortimer Menpes, the former a clever, extrovert actor-turned-painter, the latter a well-to-do Australian. With these disciples to run his errands and, on expeditions, carry his copper etching plates, or even a heavy lithographic stone, there was no need for Walter Greaves.

For Whistler there was now an artistic court in Tite Street and uneasy domesticity in Pimlico, where Maud had been installed. She was pregnant and about to bear one of their two daughters, giving him an illegitimate family of at least three. They moved from Chelsea to a studio at 454 Fulham Road, which, with the help of Walter Greaves, Whistler decorated so startlingly that it became known as The Pink Palace. His relations with Maud were now uneasy and there are said to have been quarrels. Certainly, tension increased after the birth of their child as Whistler not only showed no inclination to marry her but was still unable to take her out to the houses of his respectable friends. Also, Mrs. Godwin was now separated from her husband and Whistler's desire for her was apparent, particularly to so sensitive a woman as Maud. There were quarrels at The Pink Palace and his long relationship with his mistress-model seemed near its end.

Before this came, they left Fulham to return to Chelsea, settling in The Vale, then a quiet, leafy cul-de-sac off the King's Road. They occupied a small, square, semi-detached house with a graceful Regency verandah and balcony and a wild garden. The few houses, set deep in their gardens in this rustic backwater were to become as significant a part of the artists' quarter of Chelsea as Cheyne Walk itself. But Whistler was not happy there. Maud became increasingly querulous as Mrs. Godwin's visits increased and then desperately worried when Godwin died in 1886 and she found herself the only obstacle between her lover and a respectable marriage. Tinnie Greaves, whose sympathies were with Maud, remembered a violent quarrel between her and Beatrix Godwin, when the latter called at The Vale. Whistler, exasperated by the shouting, pushed them both out into the garden and slammed the front door. Maud had burst a blood vessel in her rage and Whistler went up to the King's Road to ask a chemist to treat her.

Whistler was far less ruthless with his women friends than with men; it had needed a visit to South America and a change of address in Chelsea to rid himself of Jo. But now Maud herself was to provide him with the excuse he needed.

To his delighted surprise, Whistler was that year elected President of the Society of British Artists by the efforts of a caucus of young artists in defiance of a majority of disunited conventional members. At once he set about the rejuvenation of the Society and quickly succeeded in making it the most lively and progressive artistic institution in London. But he had many enemies quick to seize upon the smallest indiscretion.

Although success was about to return at last, Whistler was poor and Maud had had to resort to working again as a model, posing to other artists. One of these was William Stott, who not only admired and imitated Whistler's style of painting but, like the Greaves brothers, dressed in his fashion. Both Whistler and Stott had paintings hung in the British Artists' exhibition of 1887 and Maud had been the model for both. But Whistler's picture showed her smartly attired in bonnet and fur and Stott's showed her wearing nothing but her beautiful red hair. As Maud was known to be the President's mistress, the Society buzzed with gossip and the older members could say that this demonstrated the unsuitability of electing an amoral bohemian. The laughter more than the scandal infuriated Whistler and he asked the Stotts if Maud could stay with them for a time on account of her health. While she was with them, he left The Vale and, although Maud trailed after him for years, taking lodgings near to his, their love affair was over.

Whistler was in love with Beatrix – to him Trixie or Chinkie – Godwin. The daughter of John Birnie Philip, a Chelsea sculptor who had worked on the Albert Memorial, she understood the ways of artists and herself enjoyed a little genteel bohemianism. Many years younger than Whistler, who was now in his mid-fifties, she was dark and pretty but plump. She was also strong-willed and the only woman, apart from his mother, who could give orders to Whistler. In August 1888, he and Trixie Godwin were married in Kensington and his life set off on a new tack.

After a reception at his new studio in the Tower House, Tite Street, the Whistlers set off on a long honeymoon in France. On their return they settled for a time at 14 Upper Cheyne Row before moving to a large Georgian house, 21 Cheyne Walk, overlooking the river and a few paces from Rossetti's old house. But Rossetti had died in 1882, a year after Carlyle, and the three courts of the 'seventies had dispersed. Trixie was not sorry; for all her mildly bohemian attitudes she was at heart solid, respectable middle class, and wanted her husband to put all his raffish ways – and with them his old bohemian friends and mistresses – behind him. The degree of domination she was able to exercise was demonstrated by her ability to actually retouch his paintings in the presence of himself and his model. Once, it is said, he was painting the portrait of a young girl and, for better harmony of colour, was giving her brown instead of blue eyes. "Blue, Jimmy, blue!" cried Mrs. Whistler, taking up a brush and touching the canvas with the correct colour. Whistler could only moan, "Don't, Trixie, don't!" and accept her correction.

In her reorganisation of her husband's life one detail she insisted upon was that he drop the Greaves family; they belonged to the bohemian past. The rejection was easy because, for years Whistler had employed the brothers – particularly Walter – for the occasional menial task with a kind word or a quip in payment. With such strong memories of a quarter of a century of friendship, Walter put this down to Whistler's changing moods, for he always said that "he wanted knowing". There was no final quarrel, as in the case of so many other broken friendships, and on this Walter was always insistent, although there is a possibility that Whistler wrote him a letter of rejection. Walter afterwards said only, "People ran him down, I know, but he was a very nice fellow and very hospitable, too . . . Then one day he got married and vanished."

Walter sank away from the sun of Whistler like a small, extinct satellite pushed out of orbit, but still sadly hoping for a change of heart. In Tinnie, bitterness that had been growing over the recent years became acute and endured. The antagonism for the first legal Mrs. Whistler she showed by speaking of her as "that fat thing".

There may have been no overt brutality in Whistler's initial rejection of Greaves – that was to come later – but Walter was now lost and alone. For so many years The Master had been his inspiration. He had tried to follow his fashion in painting and etching and in dress, although in place of Whistlerian flair and dynamism was diffidence. Now he was left with memories of friendship, one of The Master's yellow ties and an assortment of scraps from the studios they had shared. Sometimes he had taken discarded canvases to paint himself and occasionally Whistler had made him a present of some little sketch or water-colour. Poverty prevented him from making a collection, although he did buy a small Whistler etching for fourteen shillings at the sale of Rossetti's belongings and was ready to bid up to one sovereign for an etching of Billingsgate, which finally sold for five.

The Greaves household had changed and shrunk since what now seemed the idyllic 'sixties. Charles Greaves had died in 1870 and his heir fifteen years later. Now Walter and Henry lived with their two unmarried sisters, Tinnie and Emily, and the house at the end of Lindsey Row was no longer the headquarters of "Greaves, Boatbuilders", but "Greaves, Artists". The brothers took their work with great seriousness, resuming their own style from which they had been seduced by Whistler. There was little or no market for their oil paintings, for these were regarded as no more than pathetic

Whistlerian imitations. But then, as Walter said, "I felt a longing for my own style, and something more my own did come back." They were sometimes able to sell their elaborately detailed drawings, water-colours and etchings of street scenes.

Again the brothers were jointly signing their large drawings and, while one was trying to persuade local shopkeepers to display their work, the other would be working on the next drawing. The tradesmen, who befriended them, exhibited their pictures and sometimes accepted them in settlement of small bills. But virtually the only market for their work was among visitors to Chelsea, looking for the houses once occupied by Carlyle, Rossetti and Whistler. So, instead of decorating the foreground of their pictures with figures of young ladies in tight-buttoned dresses or gambolling children, they now drew figures of Carlyle, Whistler as a young man, or a Chelsea Pensioner. Walter would sketch snow scenes of a terrible bleakness through which wandered a solitary figure, but, whereas Jimmy Whistler cared nothing for the identity of such a figure, it was for his pupil a self-portrait.

Whistler had painted many self-portraits and, at one period, had sketched himself every night before going to bed. Walter had tried to do the same, concentrating so fiercely on the drawing of his head with Whistlerian *élan* that the body might be out of true. His self-portraits – notably a fine one in oils based on the composition of one of Whistler's best-known self-portraits – now no longer showed an eager and ambitious young artist. Now he was over forty and he showed himself to be haggard and without confidence, yet still trying to hold himself proudly.

Several years after their rejection by Whistler, they seemed to be about to achieve success on their own. Their visits to Battersea, where they had always been able to stand on their own feet, had resulted in several useful friendships and one of these had resulted in their names being put forward among artists thought suitable for decorating the new Streatham Town Hall with murals. The brothers were chosen, probably because they were eager to accept "a bare living wage" for a commission on a scale that had never been offered to The Master.

For years, winter and summer, from 1890, the brothers walked five miles from Chelsea, across Battersea Bridge, through Clapham to Streatham High Road wearing, as a friend recalled, "the well-known garb, viz. silk hat and frock-coat, with cuffs much in evidence, wearing pink and yellow ties". The latter, which had belonged to Whistler, was worn by Walter. The work was arduous and, indeed, beyond their capacity. The huge rooms and high-walled corridors were dark and damp and the brothers had not been trained in the technique of preparing plaster for such painting, let alone the draughtsmanship it demanded.

As the murals – more than a hundred – were being completed in the autumn of 1895, numbers of visitors wandered through these strangely-decorated rooms and among them was a curious Beatrix Whistler. Having successfully excommunicated the Greaveses from their god, she was worried and annoyed to hear not only that they had been given what sounded like an enviable commission but that they were still signing themselves "Pupils of Whistler" without her husband's permission. What she saw turned her annoyance to rage and she at once sat down to write a letter to Jimmy.

"You have no idea how dreadful it all is!!" she began. ". . . you enter at the side into a narrow stone passage, as dark and damp as possible. I think it was painted grey with a dado and pictures above in panels – in fact, it is all alike, horrors in panels above a dado and there is no attempt at anything original . . . They have remembered anything and everything you ever did, even to the Japanese panels in your drawing-room, your brown paper sketches, the balcony, Battersea Bridge . . . They have painted the frames on the walls with yellow paint, with shadows and with the blossom pattern, the shells . . . etc., etc.!!!

"In the hall they are a mixture of you and Albert Moore – ladies in white, on a white sofa with azaleas in pots – too terribly bad, all out of drawing, absolutely childish! This is a recollection of one – a girl leaning on a marble balustrade talking to a man in white in a boat, supposed to be you I think . . .

"Then we went into the theatre – this was distempered a dull grey-green, with square panels of classic figures, done in a sort of monochrome and very like the decorations in country theatres, dreadful, dreadful, dreadful – then there was Carlyle!! Too funny

. . . for he looks as if he were balanced on one toe, at first I could not understand it, but, at last, I discovered that they had painted him on the same grey ground, had only very faintly outlined the top of the pedestal . . .

"On the end wall opposite the stage, is an awful thing – perfectly crazy!, of the . . . statue scene in *The Winter's Tale* – it is under this horror they have put 'Pupils of Whistler' . . ."

She went on to describe her dismay at each succeeding set of murals: ". . . Two or three classic ladies with pots, flowers on the floor, a travesty of *The Balcony* – two or three recollections of your peacocks. Another room with an imitation of *The Fire Wheel*, *Chelsea in Ice*. There! I can't go on– it was like a sort of hideous Whistlerian chaos, I felt quite mad and sick – I laughed out loud at last. I couldn't help it and turned round to find the man who showed us round was laughing too. It's frantic. My God, I could kill them – conceited, ignorant, miserable, gutter-born wretches. Don't write – write to them if you like and insist that they wipe out the pupil business. Don't, don't, my own dear darling love, draw any attention to them – besides the place will be rotten in ten years, it is running with damp and beginning to peal off. They have been at it for four years!!!!

"There are two rooms done with flowers, they are better, but recollected from you and the Japanese panels. They have even recollected the staircase at Leyland's. This must go . . . don't send more people to see it . . . Funny, they had only just left when we got there. Jimmie, it is exactly like the people on the pavement – *no better!!!*

"My darling, don't write to the papers. You must go and see yourself. I cannot give you any idea."

Her husband's reply, written to soothe her rage, showed that he still felt some affection for the brothers and perhaps even a twinge of guilt. He readily agreed that angry letters to newspapers would be inappropriate.

"Now, this matter of the Greaves is, Chinkie, of a certain *importance*," he wrote. "Very important, I consider. The situation may be made vexatious if I appear at all backward or disturbed – You see the letter is a public challenge – the two Greaves are not

The loneliness of Walter Greaves. A solitary figure in the snow, walking towards Duke Street past the northern end of Battersea Bridge, reflects the artist's desolation after his rejection by Whistler.

The celebration feast. After the sensational success of Walter Greaves's exhibition in May 1911, William Marchant gave a luncheon party at Les Gourmets restaurant. The photograph shows (*left to right*) William Nicholson, Walter Greaves, Augustus John and Marchant himself.

Rise and fall. Walter Greaves photographed posing proudly beside the Carlyle monument in Cheyne Walk after his first day of glory (*left*). A few years later, a forgotten, impoverished Walter Greaves was painted, wearing the same clothes, by William Nicholson (*right*).

only held up to ridicule, but are accused of imposition and falsehood.

"I am in a manner called upon to say that they are swindling or not swindling the authorities of Streatham, and, mind you, if I do *not* answer, the Greaves themselves may write to ask me, in the paper, to defend them – And then what a grand time for the critics! What would *they not say* of my unhandsome conduct! – attempting to hide the young man who had been loyal to me. Jealousy, envy and what-not I should be accused of – and things will be as hot as they can make it – whereas, if you will for a moment suppose that I have some wit, if not good feeling, nothing can be easier or prettier than the way in which I shall come out of it all – by as usual taking the initiative and looking down the muzzle!

"I have written a charming letter, which I shall first send you, there is time, though none too much . . . The thing is making a stir —

"As to the work in the Hall itself – it may not be all that good. It may be absolutely wild and uncultivated as decoration – the work of peasants perhaps, but, take my word for it, there must be some stuff in all that. *To have done it* . . . what others have *done* anything. Besides they were very intelligent and nice boys – and it would be a graceful act on my part – I feel kindly about them after all – Chinkie dear!"

Whistler wrote a tactful but firm letter of complaint to Walter Greaves but its wording has been lost.

Beatrix's prophecy proved right and this was sadly recorded by a sympathetic friend of the brothers, who could not bring himself to praise their pathetic attempts at epic painting. After visiting the Town Hall about ten years after their work was completed, he wrote, "One strolls in silent wonder through room after room, marvelling at the patient naïveté of these two earnest souls. The Entrance Hall, the Red Room, the Pink Hall – each filled with faded, ghostlike replicas of their favourite subjects. Here also are haunting echoes of Albert Moore, and there a friendly tribute to Whistler, but the plaster is falling off and all looks ephemeral and forlorn. Absorbing though it be . . . the work at Streatham does not add greatly to the Greaves brothers' esthetic laurels. Still it was at least lovingly and conscientiously done, and even in their most discouraging moments they never shirked or faltered."

About twenty-five years later there was a move in Streatham to offer for sale in America a mural showing the Harvard crew taking part in a universities' race on the Thames. The price decided upon was two hundred pounds, but it proved impossible to remove the painting from the wall. Eventually the building was sold and used as an engineering company's warehouse. Shortly before the murals were covered with white distemper, they were seen by the art historian William Gaunt, who wrote, "It was both mournful and exciting . . . Painted actually on the wall (frames are also painted round the pictures) they are pitted with numerous holes and gashes in the plaster. They are of the Thames rather than Chelsea in particular: the Pool; Mortlake with a lively crowd watching an American crew rowing on the Boat Race course; the old riverside inn at Battersea, the Red House; but they do include a view of the faintly Oriental 'Dancing Platform' at Cremorne with a number of the artist's typical black-coated figures standing round: and if rather cruder in style than his canvases, it conveyed, as a music-hall backcloth might – though on a smaller scale – a sort of shabby glamour."

The kindliness Whistler felt towards his disciples varied in accordance with his own relations with the individuals, groups and trends upon which his vanity depended. Nearly all of them found that, sooner or later, their devotion was rewarded with rejection on grounds which, in retrospect, must have seemed trivial. All but Walter Greaves were in some way equipped to face this humiliation. Mortimer Menpes, finally rejected after he had visited Japan, which The Master had not, tried to laugh at his banishment as one of Whistler's elaborate jokes but, when even he could no longer believe this, said to himself, "Whistler did not mean to hurt me – he was really very fond of me," and relied on his considerable income to cushion the blow. Walter Sickert, who had once been sent out to post letters for The Master, was almost as witty and arrogant himself, and when he was rejected – for the ultimate crime of being seen in conversation with the object of Whistler's current feud, by The Master returning his visiting card inscribed "Judas Iscariot" –

could snap his fingers, albeit with reluctance. The young artist, William Rothenstein, was far too sophisticated to tolerate such pettishness and when, after years of close affection for Whistler, he saw himself becoming another outcast for the same reason as Sickert, decided, "There were limits to the price one should pay for Whistler's friendship," and, again sadly, went on to follow his own talent.

For these, and other young artists who, for a time, were dominated by Whistler, there were now alternatives, of which the most important was the New English Art Club. A natural development of Sir Coutts Lindsay's Grosvenor Gallery exhibitions as a counter-influence to the Royal Academy, the Club was founded in 1886 to become the stronghold of English Impressionism, which Whistler worked so hard to promote. But he was now aged fifty-four and far too much of an individualist to belong to any movement which he could not dominate. So, in his own life-time, Whistler exiled himself from the artists and groups of artists he had inspired, becoming a grotesque mythological figure, an enlarged and heightened version of the wilful art student Du Maurier had described in *Trilby*.

Only one disciple was immune from his venom. Joseph Pennell, an emotional and excitable American etcher, had come to know Whistler in the 'eighties and he and his wife, Elizabeth, were not only compatriots but showed such slavish devotion that they seemed to him well qualified to become The Master's authorised biographers. So, for years, anything that Whistler said to the Pennells was spoken to posterity and their own place in the sunshine of his favour was unassailable.

It was while walking on Chelsea Embankment with Joseph Pennell that Whistler and Walter Greaves met again. Possibly, had his biographer not been present, Whistler would have crossed the road to avoid his old pupil, but this was impossible because Pennell "had been amazed to see approaching a strange faraway echo of Whistler, the chief difference being that the echo was shabby and wore a red necktie". The Master had no alternative but to briefly introduce the two men before walking on, adding a few words of explanation. That these were not generous is indicated by his mention of the brothers to Walter Sickert, who wrote, "Whistler gave me to understand that the 'Greaves boys' were negligible, that what they accomplished they had from him, and that when his influence was withdrawn they relapsed into the nullity from which he had lifted them for a while."

No doubt the chance meeting raised Walter Greaves's hopes of a reconciliation and certainly he put himself in the way of another. Outside Whistler's home, which was, at the end of the century, often in Paris, the most likely place to meet him was at the Chelsea Arts Club. So many artists had settled in Chelsea that there had become a need for a regular meeting place. For many years this had been – and was to be – The Six Bells public house in the King's Road, an old inn with a bowling green. Then, in 1891, a group of artists rented the upper part of 181 King's Road, near the Vestry Hall, from one of their number, James Christie, who had met Whistler at Barthe's life class in the 'seventies. There the club so flourished that, ten years later, it moved to more roomy quarters in two converted cottages at the northern end of Old Church Street.

Whistler was a founder-member of the Chelsea Arts Club together with the painters Wilson Steer, Frank Brangwyn and George Clausen and the sculptor Thomas Stirling Lee, who became the first chairman. Whistler was content, much to the relief of those who hoped for a quiet and efficient beginning for the club, at running the rules committee and any pique he may have felt at not being given a more prominent position were mollified by a reception held in his honour. At this, he replied to a laudatory address with characteristic verve: "It is right at such a time of peace, after the struggle, to bury the hatchet – in the side of the enemy – and leave it there. These congratulations usher in the beginnings of my career, for an artist's career always begins tomorrow."

Walter Greaves was not a member of the Chelsea Arts Club and, even if he had been considered worthy of election, he would not have been able to afford the subscription. Probably he did not even understand that election and a subscription were required because at a dinner given by the club for Whistler he appeared for a confrontation with The Master.

An account of this was given to the Pennells by Oliver Brown, who remembered Walter Greaves from Barthe's life class and had heard the story from another artist, possibly his father. "A little while before the dinner hour," he said, "some of the Committee, who were attending to the last details and who had never met Whistler, saw an elderly man come in with long overcoat and straight-brimmed hat and white gloves, thought it must be Whistler, received him effusively, and fluttered about him, until some of the older members of the Committee arrived, said he wasn't Whistler, and asked who he was. He said his name was Greaves and he was a pupil and a friend of Whistler's. And so, though he had not been asked, they gave him a good place at the table and insisted on his staying. Then Whistler came, presently saw him, put up his monocle, stared at him, said nothing and Greaves faded away."

Even then Walter did not give up hope of an eventual reconciliation. He was always about the Chelsea waterfront and even hung about the Chelsea Arts Club. A new member, the young painter A. S. Hartrick, remembered that "the first person I saw in the club – though I don't think he became a member – was Walter Greaves. He was wearing a flat-brimmed top hat and a flowing French tie, waiting possibly for Whistler, for whom we at first mistook him. Our impression was that he was very shabby and dirty-looking for such a celebrity, whom we had never seen up to that time. A lonely figure, he sat in silence, while we in truth were too shy to speak to him, imagining ourselves in the presence of a famous man."

Whistler himself did not appear that day but Walter lived in hopes and these encouraged him to make one last bold gesture of friendship.

6

Study in solitude

The turn of the century was the time of twilight for Whistler. The years since his marriage had given him achievement and happiness but also grief and frustration. His talents as an artist of originality and versatility were at last given the recognition he had sought by those whose opinion he valued, promising young artists hung on his words and, although he was essentially the rogue of the herd, he was flattered to be elected President of the new International Society of Sculptors, Painters and Gravers. He enjoyed the notoriety surrounding the idiosyncratic character he had been at such pains to develop and took an abnormal delight in picking unnecessary quarrels, which inevitably led to friends being forced into enmity or servility. His marriage had, however, given him complete and uncomplicated happiness, particularly during a long stay in Paris, and, for once, his emotion was entirely genuine when his wife died of cancer in 1896. He was crippled with sorrow.

A year later, Whistler's heart, which had long been weak, began to trouble him and worry, colds, influenza and climbing studio stairs hastened the onset of disease. He travelled restlessly from both Paris and London, where he would stay with his mother-in-law and sister-in-law in Chelsea, or with his friend William Heinemann, the publisher, in Whitehall Court. Finally, in 1902, he returned to the Thames, taking 74 Cheyne Walk, a new *art nouveau* house designed by C. R. Ashbee. This, within a hundred yards of the Old Church, he described as "a successful example of the disastrous effect of art upon the British middle classes", for the glaring beaten copper that covered its front door caught the eye as deliberately as did its inhabitant. But, once again, Whistler could look out on the changing lights of the river he had helped discover.

Looking out into the twilight from the house to which slowly encroaching heart disease often confined him, Whistler was unaware that, from the windows of a small public house, The Rising Sun, almost next door, Walter Greaves was sharing the experience. For twelve years after the death of Charles Greaves, who had inherited the boat-building business from their father, Walter and Henry had managed to support their mother and two sisters in the house at the end of Lindsey Row. But the hours of work they put into a single drawing would earn only a few shillings, and that might be considered fortunate. Often they were reduced to bartering their work with shopkeepers. Certainly, at this time, they exchanged drawings for coal and at Wright's dairy in Old Church Street, which had its own little meadow and farmyard behind the shop, they would barter pictures for butter, eggs and milk. It was a losing struggle against poverty and now that the brothers no longer followed their original trade there was no necessity to live on the riverside. Following the fashion they themselves had helped to set, artists and writers were eager to take houses or studios overlooking Whistler's Reach, as it was now often known, and, in 1897, the Greaves family gave up their old house and moved a mile inland, to 525 Fulham Road.

Walter could not bear to be parted from the river and almost every day he would pack a large portfolio with sketching paper and drawings he hoped to sell, and walk back to Chelsea, crossing the King's Road by The World's End tavern and cutting down the narrow World's End Passage to the river. There he would continually sketch the familiar scene. Surprisingly, this had changed little, although Old Battersea Bridge had finally tottered to the end of its days and been replaced, in 1890, by a new, wide, iron bridge. There had then been a plan to extend the Embankment westward from this point to sweep round in front of Lindsey Row, covering what the *Westminster Gazette* called "a malodorous stretch of mud . . . its condition is said to cost the parish an average of one life per annum". Already, *The Builder* journal had said of this reach, "If something effectual be not soon done, the power of steam will not suffice to drag vessels through the slime."

But, thanks to Whistler, this same reach had acquired a romantic aura and, at the same time, the *Daily Mail* rhapsodised, "The wide silver bay, edged with its low river wall, propped up by decaying brick buttresses of all colours, where the water strikes them, from sage green to deep crimson, and tufted here and there with timid plant growth. The old barges, either moored up at the wharf discharging their cargoes of yellow bricks, with their brown sails hanging listless on their curiously painted masts, or seeking in mid-stream to woo the wind . . . Everywhere the river glows with little bits of colour; the red of a steamboat funnel, or the spumey white where a buoy offers its resistance to the tide . . ."

Artists naturally saw the latter view and a number of the most fashionable, from Kensington and Hampstead as well as Chelsea, and including Poynter, Alma-Tadema, Frith, Watts and the historian of London, Sir Walter Besant, passionately opposed the embanking. So influential were the names signed under the petition of protest that the plan was abandoned.

But Walter Greaves miserably missed the view from the windows of the first-floor sitting-room of their house, which took on a new air of sophistication in 1901 with the arrival of its new occupant, the forceful and erudite Hilaire Belloc. So Walter had chosen The Rising Sun as a substitute. It, too, had first-floor windows from which he could study and paint the evening river. It was also within a few yards of Jimmy Whistler, whose mood, it seemed to Walter, would one day change as his moods always did.

But it was too late. Whistler was dying and, at The Rising Sun, the arrivals of doctors and friends were noted and understood. Occasionally, in the summer of 1903, the sick man would be seen being taken out for a drive. Those who were allowed by the maid and his sister-in-law through the copper door and upstairs into his grey-painted studio at the back of the house found a shrunken old man of sixty-eight with dulled eyes, capable occasionally of a desperate attempt to charm or amuse. In July, it was obvious that the end was near and, knowing this, Walter Greaves gathered up his courage for one last approach. He ventured for the first time to the copper door, rang the bell and gave his name to the maid. All he would say of his reception afterwards was that, "They wouldn't let me in." Whether it was *they* or *him* he was never to confide.

Some days later, on 17th July, a week after entering his seventieth year, Whistler died. The coffin was carried along the few yards of pavement to the Old Church for the funeral service. The congregation was meagre – too many old friendships had been left in fragments – but there was a pew of Academicians, including Alma-Tadema, and Mortimer Menpes was there. While the Pennells recorded with pique the lack of official representatives they failed to ask the name of an elderly woman in a corner of the church. It was said to have been Jo, once *The Little White Girl*. Unnoticed, across the road by the river wall stood Walter and Henry Greaves, sketching. Later, they drew the scene with all the reverence they felt for their past friend and all the painstaking detail that he had tried to take out of their work.

Whistler was buried beside his wife in the churchyard by the river at Chiswick, near to Hogarth. There were as few mourners at the graveside as in the church and the assembled police were not needed to hold back crowds. The grave was beneath an old wall hung with clematis and, for years before a magnificent monument supported by caryatids was set up, it was marked only by a low trellis on which grew roses. Walter Greaves and a companion, making a pilgrimage to the grave, had difficulty in finding it. When they did, the companion, a sentimentalist, said, "A nameless grave!" "It is his way," replied Walter. "He would say, 'Let all who want me find me.' "

Walter Greaves now walked alone in a Chelsea where every street had some memory of Whistler. West of Battersea Bridge, where little streets ran up from the river and hollyhocks and sunflowers stood above the cottages' green-painted palings, the memories were happy. East of Albert Bridge they were all of the bewildering, unhappy years when Jimmy was slipping away. But there were twenty years of friendship to remember and revere. On Walter's part it had been an intense and romantic friendship – "I went mad over Whistler," he would say, but now he was dead and the terrible rejection was irreversible. To dwell on it was too painful and it became clear to all who saw him that Walter Greaves was living in the distant past.

The Chelsea he now haunted was very different from the rough, jolly little river-port to which he had introduced Whistler forty years before.

The most essential change had been brought about by Whistler himself. Now Chelsea was established as the artists' quarter of London and, although Rossetti had been the king who attracted intellectuals to his court, Whistler had, virtually single-handed, given "his Chelsea" a dashing eccentricity of style. Long after the intellectuals had departed for Bloomsbury and Hampstead, and even after most of the artists had gone, this panache, although widely-spread and diluted, was to remain.

"Of course you will settle in Chelsea," Whistler had commanded the young Will Rothenstein in Paris, and he did. At the end of the nineteenth century there was much in the consistency of Chelsea to catch the imagination of any young artist, whether he were involved in Impressionism, Realism, or Romanticism. "The name itself," wrote Rothenstein, "soft and creamy, suggested the eighteenth century, Whistler's early etchings, Cremorne, old courts and rag-shops."

The influx of artists, which had begun in the 'seventies, had become a recognised migration and, by the 'nineties, some eighty Chelsea artists were exhibiting at the Royal Academy each year. Their studios were, at first, generally sheds in back gardens, converted greenhouses or stables and back rooms with a north light. But, from the 'eighties onwards, *avant-garde* architects were designing residential studios with a bedroom or two, usually opening on to a gallery, and with tiny kitchens and bathrooms. Some of the new blocks of mansion flats, put up in the 'nineties, had studio-apartments on their top floors. Studios spread throughout Chelsea, in rows lining the walls of old gardens long-planted with fig and mulberry trees, in stable yards and even in large blocks like Trafalgar Studios in Manresa Road and the stately studios of Tite Street.

But now Lindsey Row and Cheyne Walk were no longer the twin poles of artistic inspiration. Painters influenced by Whistler tended to settle in or near Tite Street, where the studios, such as those in the six-storey Tower House, were fit for gentlemen-artists hoping for the patronage of the rich. These included both Impressionists and followers of Whistler's style of portraiture. These included the American John Singer Sargent, who added a touch of swagger to a Whistlerian style in portrait-painting; William Orpen who inherited Whistler's early admiration for Manet; Charles Furze whose genteel Impressionism produced his *Diana of the Uplands*, beloved of county patrons; Augustus John, whom Whistler's ideas sent roaming into bohemia, and the forgiving Mortimer Menpes.

Only one of the prophets of the New English Art Club, Philip Wilson Steer, remained faithful to the west end of Cheyne Walk, where he settled his baggy-suited frame for forty-four years. A bachelor with a love of undisturbed routine, Steer lived in solid comfort at 109 Cheyne Walk with a housekeeper, a dog and a tabby cat, Chelsea porcelain figures, a collection of oriental *objets d'art*, bronzes and paintings that would have done credit to Rossetti, and a Nocturne by Walter Greaves. Here this quiet, lumbering man painted Impressionistic works of extreme delicacy in "the best bad taste" of anyone Will Rothenstein knew.

These men, and their like, had no intellectual pretensions. The intellectuals, the idealists and the romantics were attracted to The Vale, just to the north of the King's Road. Although Whistler had lived there the aromatic scent of Rossetti's *salon* was stronger than the whiff of turpentine. Rothenstein, when he followed Whistler's command to settle in Chelsea, found that his enquiring intelligence sent him towards The Vale. Oscar Wilde had taken him there to meet two heirs of both the Pre-Raphaelites and Whistler, Charles Ricketts and Charles Shannon, who shared a charming old house with "primrose walls, apple-green skirting and shelves, the rooms hung with Shannon's lithographs, a fan-shaped water-colour by Whistler and drawings by Hokusai." The most genteel of decadents, Ricketts and Shannon illustrated Oscar Wilde's books and designed the format, cover-plates, end-papers and illustrations for the publications of The Vale Press.

De Morgan was also a denizen of this grove of lilies and wistaria, his devotion to the ideas of William Morris and his Pre-Raphaelite escapism giving his pottery design much in common with the graphics of Ricketts and Shannon. It is curious, therefore, that he should have rented his house for a time to an artist so totally out of sympathy with the whimsicality of The Vale, Walter Sickert. Rothenstein had noted "Sickert's genius for discovering the dreariest house and the most forbidding rooms in which to work", but this pretty house was an exception. His love for the most realistic expression of human behaviour, deprived of the gloss of money and taste, was never fulfilled in Chelsea as it was to be in Camden Town, yet a friend recalled how he "loved the red-faced sporting men with big buttoned, box-cloth coats, who thronged the King's Road, and the racy retorts of the dingy little London *gamine* as she strolled the streets of Chelsea". It was strange that, professionally and personally, Sickert and Steer were so close when their taste was so strongly in opposition. Once, when walking together in Chelsea, the two friends passed a rag-and-bone shop and Sickert said, "That's how I should like my pictures to look," and Steer, unconscious that he was delivering a quip worthy of Whistler, replied, "They do."

That there was to be a *rapport* between Sickert and Walter Greaves is not surprising, for the two Walters, the one handsome, witty and sought-after, the other undernourished, diffident and lonely, were both involved in the harshest realities, one from choice, the other from circumstance. They shared, too, their memories of Whistler; they had both loved the man and been rejected by him, but both retained a sorrowful reverence for that friendship and a gratitude for much that they had learned at his easel. Musing on this strange combination of spurned friends, Rothenstein wrote, "How far Whistler was aware of Sickert's or Greaves's genius is problematical; I am inclined to believe he did not wish to recognise it . . ."

Still the river attracted the new settlers, as a young journalist, Arthur Ransome, recognised: "There is a time in the evening when the irregulars of these days cross the King's Road to usurp the Bohemia of the past. When it grows too dark for painters to judge the colours of their pictures, they flock out from the studios, some go up to Soho for dinner, some stroll with wife or friendly model in the dusk. The favourite promenade is along Cheyne Walk, where the lamps shining among the leaves of the trees cast wavering shadows on the pavements. Only the black-and-white men, working against time for the weekly papers, plug on through the dark. Now and again, walking through the streets, you may look up at a window and see a man busily drawing, with a shaded lamp throwing a bright light on the Bristol-board before him.

"For myself, I soon discovered that the dusk was meant for indolence, and always, a little before sunset, threaded my way to the King's Road, and so to the river. I would leave the spider strength of the Albert Bridge behind me and stroll on past Battersea Bridge to a promontory of embankment just beyond, the best of all places for seeing the sunsets up the river, and the blue mists . . . that mist so miraculously blue . . . A poet and a girl pass by arm-in-arm, with eyes wide open to that spangled loveliness that smiles undaunted by the stars . . ."

The social life of the studios at the beginning of the twentieth century was far from abandoned and a young artist, who came to live in Chelsea at this time, A. Egerton Cooper, remembered half a century later a "gentlemanly bohemianism". Certainly there was some heavy drinking and some unseemliness, as when a young woman singer took an upper studio in the three-storey Trafalgar Studios and so distracted the painters below that one of them beat a tom-tom and caterwauled below her window to such effect that she angrily commanded, "Stop, you elderly bounder!" There was also, of course, Augustus John to bring sexuality to Chelsea. A young sculptor, Charles Wheeler, remembered him at this time "walking with a not unbecoming hauteur beneath the plane trees . . . He is tall, erect and broad-shouldered, wearing a loose tweed suit with a brightly-coloured bandana round a neck which holds erect, compelling features – not unlike, indeed very like, the traditional countenance of Jesus Christ . . . He is red-bearded and has eyes like those of a bull, doubtless is conscious of being the cynosure of the gaze of all Chelsea and, looking neither to the left nor the right, strides on with big steps and at a great pace towards Sloane Square, focusing on the distance and following, one imagines, some beautiful creature he is intent on catching up with."

John defied the accepted rules of chivalrous gallantry that pervaded Edwardian England, and Dora Coates, wife of the Australian painter George Coates, to whom John had rented a studio in Manresa Road, wrote that he had "a compelling stare when he looked at a woman that I much resented".

This studio and the Coates's beginnings in Chelsea were typical of the period. As left by John, the studio was "as dirty as a rag-and-bone shop. Although a pink muslin curtain hung across the bedroom window, soiled socks and old clothes were lying about the floor amidst the dust of ages. The whole place had to be scrubbed with carbolic coap, but it was a studio with a splendid light and a fine tradition . . . here Holman Hunt had painted his *Innocents* and George began to 'feel' his work there the moment he started."

Entertainment in the studios was usually modest, with evening "coffee smokes", or long talks over cheap sherry or red wine about art rather than ideals, except in The Vale. There, discussion was often earnest until William de Morgan could be persuaded to tell ghost stories, for which his high-pitched voice, his tall, thin body and his wispy beard fitted him. Early in the evening, one group of friends would meet at The Six Bells. Egerton Cooper remembered being introduced to that circle by the writer Oliver Onions. A screen protected three tables each seating three or four near the fire and here would be found the élite of Chelsea. Hilaire Belloc, who had persuaded the others to drink red Burgundy, would have with him G. K. Chesterton, whom Egerton Cooper remembered dribbling as he talked brilliantly; the dapper little painter William Nicholson, who had a studio at The Pheasantry in the King's Road; Augustus John, who preferred whisky to wine; William Orpen; Ambrose McEvoy, the most flattering of fashionable portrait-painters, and George Lambert, a swashbuckling Australian artist. The conversation, which might be extended over a supper of sausage and mashed potatoes upstairs, was, Egerton Cooper considered, as fascinating as anything Boswell could have heard in the company of Dr. Johnson in Fleet Street.

As at The Six Bells, the company at the Chelsea Arts Club was exclusively masculine. Augustus John, with his red mane and single ear-ring provided enough bohemianism for all the members – and was to be long commemorated in the club by a sign over one of its baths reading, "Augustus John Slept Here". The general atmosphere was middle class and relaxed, tweeds were worn and briar pipes smoked and there was as much talk of sketching tours in Sussex as in Provence.

Eccentricities were few in comparison with those in Montmartre and Montparnasse. Egerton Cooper was to remember Joseph Pennell as being "excitable, conceited, a braggart but a brilliant etcher"; William Nicholson, the painter whose woodcut posters caused a stir, as "a dandy little man and very charming"; Sickert as "a hell of a swank but a very, very good artist"; Steer as "a huge farmer"; and Mortimer Menpes as "a comic turn". The young sculptor Roland Bevan was to remember Orpen as being "like a natty little City gent"; Steer, "like a reliable family solicitor"; John being "very intelligent and good company"; and Captain Adrian Jones, the sculptor, who was working on the giant Quadriga for the top of the Decimus Burton arch on Constitution Hill in a studio at the bottom of his garden next to the Chelsea Arts Club, wearing to the end of his life the long cavalry cloak which he had worn as an Army veterinary surgeon. Augustus John was not the only artist whose unconventional dress turned heads in the King's Road. Walter Greaves, the antithesis of the easy talent and the fertility-god reputation of John, still wore the fashions of the eighteen-seventies. Although, by rights, the doyen of Chelsea painters, he no longer belonged to the world of artists. Those who had known Whistler in his last years had often only heard of the Greaves brothers from others as shades from an earlier generation.

Walter's loneliness became suddenly more acute with the death, in December, 1904, of his brother. Henry had always been the junior partner. He had never fully understood or mastered Whistler's theories, but had stuck doggedly to his own style even when The Master was making him paint harmonies and arrangements. In photographs, the stance of his small, slight figure and the look in his eyes is defensive and only Walter's brush could give him a touch of the cavalier, black hat at a rakish angle and eyes boldly glaring over a shoulder. Henry died a bachelor and, for Walter, it was now too late to contemplate marriage. Materially, they had never had the money or status expected by a woman of their social position on the border between the working and lower middle class; family pressure and their own inhibitions might have prevented attachments with models or Cremorne girls. Emotionally, it is probable that they had been drained by Whistler. Walter had been a youth of seventeen at the most when they met and entering middle age when rejection destroyed his self-confidence. The devotion given to Whistler by him – as, later, by other heterosexual but more substantial disciples – and, to a lesser extent, by his brother dominated their lives and monopolised their affections. But the brothers had shared a love of their work and of Chelsea and had comforted each other in exile from the court of their king. Their mother had died soon after the move from Lindsey Row and Tinnie had increasingly resented their poverty, blaming Jimmy Whistler for luring the brothers away from their trade, exploiting their friendship and leaving them penniless. Now, when Walter trudged from Chelsea to Fulham for a meagre supper there were only the two sisters for company; Tinnie, in a yellow wig, low-cut dress and much imitation jewellery, to ask whether he had sold any drawings.

In his portfolio, Walter always carried a selection of drawings he hoped to sell. He never accosted strangers in the street, although artists would occasionally ask him if he had any Whistler drawings or etchings for sale and once Egerton Cooper bought one of The Master's watercolours of the King's Road for ten pounds. Sometimes he would sit on a bench by the river and open his portfolio then beckon to anyone who showed curiosity, inviting them to inspect the contents. Walter's own drawings he sold for whatever he could get, on at least one occasion only fourpence and in the bar of The Rising Sun he would sketch a portrait for a shilling or two. At first he had been shy of trying to sell on doorsteps but hunger drove him to it. The new red-brick blocks of flats, which had been built near the river – beginning with Carlyle Mansions in 1886 – had seemed promising and the landings, on to which their front doors opened, kept private his humiliation when rebuffed. Even this possibility was ended by prominent signs warning, "No Hawkers", and hall porters of military bearing were quick to see and turn away a visitor as furtive and shabby as he.

So he ventured round to the back of the flats where the tradesmen's entrances and service lifts were screened by high walls. There, swallowing his pride, he offered his drawings to the cheeky errand boys, who so often mocked him in the street. Perhaps one might act as his picture dealer and resell a drawing to a cook

The paintings that brought disaster. Whistler's *Nocturne in Blue and Gold: Old Battersea Bridge* (*left*) and Walter Greaves's *Passing Under Old Battersea Bridge* (*right*). That Greaves wrongly dated his work by about ten years is indicated by the distant view of Albert Bridge under construction, which can also be seen in Whistler's sketch of the two bridges (*below*).

Whistler's funeral, in 1903, elaborately drawn by the Greaves brothers from a rough sketch made at the time (*above*). The coffin is being carried from 74 Cheyne Walk, past The Rising Sun tavern to Chelsea Old Church.

Almost a Whistlerian dandy, Walter Greaves photographed at the wedding reception of William Marchant's daughter Josephine on 19th June, 1929. He died the following year.

upstairs, and then, perhaps, a potential patron might see it and want more.

One of the errand boys who regularly visited the service lifts of Cheyne Court, near the Embankment, with sleeked hair and spotless apron with his morning loads of groceries, was Freddie Ferebee. Sixty years later, he spoke of Walter Greaves: "He was quite a sad affair. There was nothing cheerful about him. He seemed to lead a very lonely life. You'd see him every day, but you never saw him with anybody. Wherever he went he had these pictures with him. He took his work very, very seriously. He used to show us these pictures and say, 'They're jolly good drawings. A lot of people admire them.' He'd try to sell them for a few shillings and I've known him sell them for half-a-crown. When there was no sale he'd toddle off.

"You could always find him down the end of Cheyne Walk, painting the boating. Sometimes he'd sit there all day, painting where they used to dry the kippers and bloaters in the sun – when I was a kid I used to think they'd come out of the Thames! But he was one of the figures you never took any notice of. He used to wear a top hat and a short coat and this funny collar with a couple of points. But he was a bit on the rough side – a bit haggard and sometimes unshaven – because he was going through bad times. He never said anything about Whistler to us. He never enlarged."

Most of the pictures Walter Greaves carried in his portfolio were wash drawings of the most popular river views, which he could sketch from memory. Now that Henry was dead it was no longer so satisfying to produce the large, elaborate drawings of street scenes, there was no market for his oils and the cost of colours made water-colours too expensive to paint regularly. But for a few generous friends he would have been near to starvation. There was a builder named Jameson to whom Greaves had tried to sell a drawing without success. At his refusal, Walter had asked him for the loan of two pounds to buy paints. Jameson, seeing his impoverished state, lent him the money, never expecting to see it again. Some time later, however, Walter appeared on his doorstep to repay and Jameson was so touched that he bought a picture. His purchase pleased him and he afterwards bought more.

His most consistent patron was a Member of Parliament living in Cheyne Walk, Lord Courtney of Penwith, a generous and emotional man, who could be moved to tears by reading a newspaper report of the ordeals of suffragettes. Regularly, according to Frederick Ferebee, he "used to help him on" with small amounts of money.

Now Walter Greaves was passing sixty, but he could not allow grey hair to remind him that his happy youth was so far past. One young Chelsea man, Harry Delaney, remembered, many years later, how boys had called out, "Just look at old Greaves!" He continued, "He used to put black lead on his hair and when he perspired it ran down in streaks over his collar. He was always dressed in a shabby, genteel sort of way in a very antiquated top hat and overcoat. He looked as though he'd been knocked round the ring a lot. He had a spirit of mild dejection and was always gazing at the ground. He looked despised and rejected and people didn't speak of him respectfully. The last time I saw him, he was dozing on a tram in Battersea."

The Chelsea in which Walter Greaves now wandered alone was again undergoing a period of change almost as drastic as that following the building of the Embankment. Among the changes that had followed that transformation was the closing of Cremorne. It had acquired an increasing reputation for depravity, prostitutes loitered in its arbours and wakeful citizens in the King's Road and along Cheyne Walk complained of drunken singing and brawling after the gates shut each night. Cremorne may have invited extinction, but it was never the Babylonian gardens its critics imagined. One of Whistler's younger artist friends, Anthony Ludovici, who had been used to the students' dance halls of Paris, wrote, "Cremorne seemed to me very formal, ceremonious, and very well conducted, but, oh, so dull when compared with what I had been used to!

"I remember well being reprimanded by the M.C. for holding up my leg whilst dancing a quadrille, and it surprised me very much to be obliged to comport myself as in a drawing-room, whereas we were dancing in a garden surrounded by ladies of loose morals and men taking their pleasures seriously. The holding up of a leg would suggest the *can-can*, and anything approaching loose French manners was not considered 'proper'. That word was always on people's lips . . ."

So, a year after the Embankment was opened, Cremorne was shut, its oriental dancing platform, its plaster goddesses holding flambeaux that had lit the shady path to "The Stooping Venus" above her fountain, its urns and vases and thousands of shrubs and flowers in tubs were sold by auction. The magnificent trees were felled and the gently undulating lawns and flower-beds sold in building lots. Within a decade, Cremorne had vanished under rows of mean little terrace-houses, one corner surviving temporarily as a nursery garden. Finally all that remained were the elaborate wrought-iron gates, opening on to a brewer's yard, and ornamental garden vases sprouting geraniums in Chelsea backyards.

Yet the final act of transformation, at what had been a wooded bank of the Thames, gave the place an entirely unexpected touch of dramatic spectacle. In 1904 a power station was opened at Lots Road, beside the site of Cremorne, to provide electricity for the new underground railways. Its four chimneys, two hundred and seventy-five feet high, stood stark and grand against the sunset seen from Battersea Bridge. In twilight they became something more mysteriously abstract than the campanili and palaces that Whistler had imagined on the distant bank and, as Battersea Church became part-hidden by growing factories, the four chimneys of Lots Road took their place as the centre-piece of Whistler's Reach.

Change in the west of Chelsea provoked mixed reaction but now, in the east, came another that was to be almost universally mourned. Since the Chelsea Bun House had disappeared and the Five Fields submerged by Belgravia, the scenery there had changed beyond recognition. To the east of the road linking Sloane Square with Albert Bridge, Chelsea Barracks had been built with a front so grandiose with towers and arches that it was rumoured that the War Office had mistakenly given the contractors plans for a projected barracks in India.

From there to the river ran the Queen's Road – now to be called Royal Hospital Road – and this had changed little. Between the Royal Hospital itself and the Embankment were little old shops, thirteen public houses and Paradise Row. These seventeenth-century houses, set behind gardens, had their place in Chelsea history as the setting of Jacobean and Georgian intrigues and flirtations, entertainments and literary and artistic discussion. They were the gentle heart of a Chelsea stretching back far beyond the artists' bohemia and in their walled gardens was tranquillity. Paradise Row had been admired for so many generations that its destruction seemed unthinkable, both to the recent settlers nearby and to the indigenous Chelseans. It came as a shock, therefore, to hear, in 1904, that the landlord, Earl Cadogan, who had inherited much of Chelsea from his ancestor, Sir Hans Sloane, planned to demolish the north side of this street, including Paradise Row, and build blocks of flats.

Chelsea was appalled and the middle-class intelligentsia organised a petition to Earl Cadogan, pointing out that the old houses could be renovated and let to such as themselves.

There was already hostile criticism of the new blocks of flats – notably of Carlyle Mansions, which dominated the skyline of Cheyne Walk beside the Old Church – and the petitioners continued, "There is a feeling among many residents and owners of property in Chelsea that the present extensive building of flats and tall houses will not, in the long run, conduce to the welfare of, or the value of property in the neighbourhood and we should deplore any further addition to the high buildings already in existence." But they were not dealing with a public body vulnerable to public opinion, as were those who had petitioned against the extension of the Embankment, but against an omnipotent landlord, bound by no strict planning regulations or preservation orders. Earl Cadogan ignored the protests and Paradise Row was destroyed.

The same landlord had already transformed the north-east of Chelsea, demolishing most of the neat eighteenth-century houses of Hans Town and replacing them with tall, narrow-fronted houses built of glaring red brick in a pseudo-Dutch style. Here, on the west side of Sloane Street, Belgravia and Mayfair pushed a salient deep into Chelsea, pressing up against the maze of little streets of Georgian dwellings, in which lived the bulk of the population. Some forty thousand people had lived in Chelsea when Walter Greaves was born, but the influx of country families to London and unbridled speculative building had, by the beginning of the new century, increased the population to ninety-five thousand.

Now it was the turn of The Vale to be laid waste and built over with expensive houses, hunched together to command the maximum rents where wild gardens had sprawled. Shortly before the demolition began in 1909, de Morgan gave what he described as "a house-cooling party" in several adjoining gardens, with more than a touch of Cremorne and Ranelagh: "The guests wandered into an unexpected Fairyland. Old Chelsea Pensioners in their scarlet coats guarded the lane, which was festooned with glowing lanterns . . . a band played softly while nymphs drifted over the turf in picturesque dances . . . choral singing was interspersed by the song of a living dryad among the bushes, hard by where the head of Pan looked out wickedly from a grove of grass-green lamps . . . in the flower-scented dimness . . . Then, by-and-by, there was supper and song . . . beneath the doomed trees wreathed with fairy lamps."

Changes in the Chelsea scene were not all for the worse. Although the old houses, which had once stood along the north side of Duke Street and then faced across the wide Embankment to the river, were finally demolished, they were replaced not only by the expensive Ashbee houses and flats but also by a medieval dining hall. Crosby Hall in Bishopsgate had been occupied by Sir Thomas More before he brought his family to Chelsea. Now its fifteenth-century hall was being used as a City restaurant, and was threatened with destruction. With a flash of imaginative magnanimity, the London County Council decided that the Gothic hall should not only be saved but moved piecemeal to Chelsea, where it could be re-erected on the site of More's garden as part of a new hostel for overseas women graduates. This was done in 1910, giving back to Cheyne Walk something of the old elegance it had lost, but, in making room for this medieval magnificence, the little house where Swift had lodged was demolished.

The rediscovery of Chelsea that Whistler and Rossetti had begun was hastened by the building of comfortable mansion flats, but now the modest houses which had been put up in the first half of the nineteenth century were falling into decay. Too small for the prosperous middle classes, who would be likely to need two or three resident servants, in addition to a usually large family, and too big and expensive for the poor, large numbers of houses, like those grouped round Paulton's Square, became lodging houses and sometimes workshops.

For the newly-arrived middle-class families, comfortably settled in the roomy houses of Oakley Street, Walpole Street or Tedworth Square, Chelsea was a place where some of the more rigid conventions could be overlooked. Captain Robert Falcon Scott, the Antarctic explorer, had chosen to live in Oakley Street with his sculptor wife; Mark Twain stayed in Tedworth Square and the actresses Ellen Terry, Lily Langtry and Mrs. Patrick Campbell all chose Chelsea. These were to be followed by the novelists Henry James and Arnold Bennett, the former choosing Carlyle Mansions in Cheyne Walk, the latter, Cadogan Square. The place was near enough to the West End, yet it was full of trees and quiet. It would have been unlikely, in 1905, that anyone who attended the fête in the garden of The Rectory off Old Church Street would have guessed at the sad prophecy in the choice of the bandmaster of the 1st Middlesex Royal Engineers (Volunteers) when he picked the march *Automobile* for his overture and *Motor Car* as the finale.

If one single social activity evokes the changed atmosphere of middle-class Chelsea in the first decade of the century it is the pageant, the masque and the fancy-dress party. These occasions, which survived many years in the Chelsea Arts Ball, owed their inspiration to Ranelagh and, perhaps, Cremorne. But it was a self-conscious inspiration lacking all the lusty undertones of the originals. Large private gardens were usually the setting and the real and imagined history of Chelsea the theme. Only to the sophisticates, who were unlikely to be taking part, did a Sir Thomas More with a waxed moustache seem ludicrous, and gentlemen wearing powdered wigs and smoking pipes posed solemnly for photographers as they arrived for rehearsals.

The performances were sometimes of an allegorical nature and Amy Lambert, wife of the Australian painter George Lambert and mother of Constant Lambert, the future orchestral conductor, recorded, "Pastoral plays make frequent demand on our time and interest. A very memorable and successful one was *The Awakening of Pan*, in which Lambert was persuaded to take the part of a sculptured god who is brought to life by a kiss from Flora.

"The make-up was perfect, he himself modelled the clay head from which the mask was made to his own exaggerated likeness, adding the luxuriant curls and the embryo horns . . . Skin-tight fleshings, goat-skin, pipes and grape cluster were added, and the whole coloured to the semblance of a garden-figure in moss-stained stone. For twenty minutes, Lambert stood immobile on his pedestal, and his sudden response to the embrace, and swift descent and capture and carrying off of Flora, left the audience breathless with surprise and admiration."

But the climate was not always conducive to such romps and Dora Coates sadly noted the failure of "a most beautiful garden pastoral, *Herrick in Love*, in which about fifty people, for the most part of Chelsea, were the performers", which was to include twelve poems and dances – "jigs, morris, country and sword dances". But, alas, on the day of the performance, and although "Mrs. Henry Poole was a very lovely little Electra", all was "spoilt by bad weather, and it was on a damp bier, strewn with wet, rain-drenched roses that Electra was borne away by the shepherds and nymphs, through grass saturated with moisture".

At the mock-baronial Whitelands College for training teachers at the corner of Cheltenham Terrace and the King's Road – later to become the headquarters of the British Union of Fascists – it was the same on May Day when "these young ladies, lightly-clad and flower-crowned, perform shivering evolutions in their garden and end by electing the Queen of the May for the year. They can be heard singing quite six yards off."

The other extreme of Edwardian life in Chelsea was to be seen in the poverty of the slums to the north of the King's Road, west of the new Hans Town and beyond World's End. Even in the centre of Old Chelsea, Lawrence Street, the site of the porcelain factory, had with its three taverns, its ancient doss-houses and its overcrowded little Georgian houses, acquired a rough reputation. Any local tough was likely to be known, in the slang of the day, as "a Lawrence Street 'erb".

Just as Walter Greaves could once have been seen to symbolise the artistic awakening of the Chelsea community and its enforced sophistication, so now his thin, unkempt figure illustrated its new urban poverty.

Both Joseph and Elizabeth Pennell came across the remnants of the Greaves family at this time but, while anxious to make use of their reminiscences for the forthcoming biography of Whistler, made no attempt to offer any help in return. First, Joseph Pennell, while helping to arrange the Memorial Exhibition of the late James McNeill Whistler at the New Gallery early in 1905, noted in his journal, "While I was there one of the Greaves brothers, who figure in Whistler's early Chelsea days, turned up. He also lent things."

A year later, while Pennell was making an etching of Chelsea Old Church, Walter came up to him and talked. Later, Elizabeth Pennell wrote of him, "Probably no one living knows more of Whistler in the old Chelsea days, and he told J. he would be delighted to recall all he could, if J. would go to see him. His memory is still fresh of the 'times' there had been in the evenings, of the people who came to the house and went out with Whistler on his father's boats. There had been noise. Whistler was always ready for it, he was always gay. But what affair was that of his? Why should he talk about that?"

But he did talk about it when the Pennells made three visits to him in Fulham, although he forgot their first appointment and Joseph Pennell was greeted only by Tinnie, now "an elderly woman in yellow wig and much jewelry, low dress and many necklaces". On his next visit Walter was waiting and then, and at subsequent meetings, was so eager to be of assistance that he later called at their house with more details he had remembered, although Elizabeth recorded, he was "repeating many things he had already told J., telling others in a disjointed fashion it is hard to follow". The last of these meetings was in the autumn of 1907 and the next – under extraordinarily different circumstances – was to be more than three years later.

There was no reward for this work and Walter had to search desperately for means of raising money. He had achieved a small success in 1907 when three of his Cremorne etchings were reproduced among the illustrations of a short book, *Cremorne and the Later London Gardens*, by an antiquary at the British Museum. But this did not amount to recognition. His most treasured possessions were bundles of letters from Jimmy Whistler to himself and other members of his family. Now, with two sisters to support, he had to make himself read through them and, keeping aside the most intimate and valued, sell the rest for the value of the autograph. In winter, when he could not afford fuel and the coal-merchant would no longer accept pictures in payment, he would tear his old canvases from their stretchers and break up the wood for his fire. The paintings themselves – Nocturnes and river scenes lovingly painted beside Whistler, with the same "sauce" as he had prepared for The Master – he rolled into bundles and stowed away in a lumber-room. He had now concentrated on drawings for so long and on selling old proofs of his etchings that he had had to abandon thoughts of finding a market for his paintings in oils. It was therefore as surprising as it was merciful that, at a time when he had been reduced to selling all but the few essential pieces of furniture, he should, in his eternal quest for a kindly dealer in the second-hand shops of Chelsea, find a shopkeeper who showed an interest in seeing his oils and, having seen them, offered to buy them for a few pounds. It was enough to keep the Greaves household in food and fuel for weeks.

The selling of dozens of cracked, filthy canvases, stuck together in rolls, must have seemed miraculous to Walter Greaves. He could never, even in the ambitious dreams he once had had, have guessed at the consequences of this act prompted by hunger. Nor could he have imagined any fantasy in which a future President of the Royal Academy, Sir Charles Wheeler, whom he knew as a young art student in Old Church Street, would one day have written of him, "We should have been incredulous if someone had ever said, 'There goes a considerable artist!' Yet so he was."

7

"*The New Master*"

In the late summer of 1910 the surface of the world of artists and art patrons was as unrippled as that of the lily-ponds that were shown in profusion on the walls of Burlington House. At the Royal Academy that year it was clear that the English Impressionists, the young rebels of the New English Art Club, who had followed the tossing plume of Whistler's white forelock, had been gently absorbed and dominated by conventional taste. Clausen had exhibited a wood nymph, Orpen an aristocrat wearing the cut of beard adopted by the new King George V. For every impressionistic canvas there seemed to be three on which medieval knights surprised bathing maidens; for each seascape there was a bobbing mermaid; for every exploratory portrait there was the flattering likeness of a potentate or his wife. The *bon ton* still liked their pictures to tell a story and those of 1910 included *Tumble, Froth and Fun; Sorrow and Sympathy; The Enchanted Shore; Love or Fame?* and *Pearls for Kisses*. The Academy galleries glowed with genteel, sunlit sensuality.

The heirs of Whistler – all but the stubbornly individual Sickert – had been seduced by colour. The rest – Steer, Orpen, Sargent, Nicholson, McEvoy, Lavery and even Rothenstein – were lured away from the low tones and delicate balances of Whistler by the delayed impact of Impressionism which had followed him across the Channel in a brilliant flood. In this opulent world the artist could share more fully than ever before. Any competent painter could make a comfortable living and the demand seemed insatiable for paintings to decorate the drawing-rooms of the *nouveau riche* and illustrations for popular magazines. This was the time of the professional illustrator, when American magazines might pay two hundred and fifty pounds for a single drawing.

The clear, shallow waters were undisturbed, for there was now no Whistler to spin a whirlpool. Yet one unexpected undercurrent was eddying in that September, touching only those who might be sensitive to it. Among picture dealers there was a rumour – a mysterious rumour, and any mystery was welcomed and cultivated at this uncomplicated time – that there had been something like a second coming of Whistler. Large numbers of paintings, thought to be by Whistler, had materialised from whence no-one knew. Among the first to hear of this were Joseph and Elizabeth Pennell, his biographers and the self-appointed guardians of his memory and reputation.

Walter Dowdeswell, a dealer of repute, wrote to them with the guarded but enticing news that he had "something of extraordinary interest" to show them. Elizabeth Pennell visited his gallery and, in an upstairs room, was shown more than a dozen paintings in oils and, although none was signed, Dowdeswell claimed them to be by Whistler. They were certainly Whistlerian and included Nocturnes and paintings of models in Japanese dress and the haughty poses The Master had required for portraiture, but their quality seemed varied, both between pictures and within a particular painting. Some work seemed too vivid and hard for Whistler but some, she admitted, was "fine", or "beautifully drawn". Dowdeswell suggested that any lapses in quality had been caused in the cleaning, restoration and re-touching which had been essential because of the appalling condition of the canvases when they had come into his hands.

All the canvases had had to be mounted on stretchers and some re-lined because he had bought them in rolls, filthy, cracked, blackened and sometimes stuck together. A collector, a Madame Frida Strindberg, the former wife of the Swedish dramatist, had sold him about fifty such canvases. She herself had found them at a second-hand bookshop in New Oxford Street.

Joseph Pennell was as intrigued as his wife had been when he saw Dowdeswell's canvases and quite as mystified. During the weeks that followed, they inspected all the pictures and sought the opinions of others who had known Whistler and his work intimately: his brother's widow; Alan Cole, at whose gallery Whistler had exhibited; William Heinemann, the publisher and a close friend of his last years; and the Ways, father and son, who had worked with Whistler on his lithographs. These and others, wrote the Pennells, "were bewildered, certain that some were Whistler's, uncertain about others, struck as we were by the difference in quality, many of the paintings being as commonplace as many were masterly."

It was certain, at least, that there was some very strong link with Whistler, but the clues only added to the mystery. At the time of Whistler's bankruptcy it was known that a considerable number of his canvases had disappeared from The White House, with and without his knowledge. Thomas Way had taken some and this had led to the inevitable rift, for he maintained he had bought the canvases and Whistler, insisting that they had only been on loan, demanded them back, saying, when Way refused, that he should never have associated with tradesmen. Now Way was confident that many of Dowdeswell's canvases were Whistler's, so could they be some of those he had acquired in 1879?

But then, said Dowdeswell, he himself had visited this same second-hand bookshop and bought, for twenty guineas, a packet of letters, all testimonials for Charles Augustus Howell, one signed by Whistler, others by Rossetti and Millais. Howell had been prowling round The White House like a jackal throughout the bankruptcy proceedings and it seemed more than likely that he had had his pickings. He had been dead for twenty years, but it seemed probable that the pictures might have come from his lair.

There was one further clue. Also in the bookshop were letters from Whistler to Walter Greaves and several canvases, which Dowdeswell had been offered but had refused to buy, signed by Greaves. Were these discarded canvases from Whistler's studio, completed or touched-up or over-painted by his old pupil?

To the Pennells this explanation seemed at least as likely as the other alternatives. They had never liked Walter Greaves, although he had told them all he could about his early days with Whistler when they had been preparing the biography. Perhaps it was Tinnie Greaves's bitter references to Whistler's meanness with money that had angered them. More probably, they resented the thought of having to share Whistler's past friendship, even though he himself had discarded that friendship and the friend appeared to be little more than a tramp, unworthy of even a temporary place among his courtiers. Glorying in their own privilege as the appointed biographers, the Pennells regarded Whistler and even the memory of him as being exclusive to them.

Whatever the suspicions, the mystery seemed as impenetrable as the old bookshop wherein the solution seemed to lie. Walter Spencer, who kept the shop at 27 New Oxford Street, invited only the privileged few into his gas-lit sanctum, past the windows packed to the top with early paper-backed editions of Dickens and Thackeray, rare first editions and prints, through a narrow ravine between tight-wedged shelves, piles of books and portfolios. Among those who had been invited had been Robert Louis Stevenson, Algernon Swinburne and William Ewart Gladstone. But inquisitive enquirers such as the Pennells were not welcomed and certainly not allowed up the narrow staircase into the upper rooms from which it was believed the canvases had come.

Dealers known to Spencer were, however, welcomed, and one of them had brought from his shop in Fulham a remarkable collection of Whistleriana: letters, some brushes and rolls of old canvases. Whether he had known the Ways and Howell was never revealed, but he had certainly known Walter Greaves, who, as poverty pressed him and his sisters, was forced to give up more and more of the hoarded reminders of happy years at Lindsey Row. For Walter himself the transactions ended there in Fulham. He had no idea of the interest the rolls of canvas had aroused, or of the involvement of the Pennells, whom he had not seen for three years, and certainly never knew that the strangely Whistlerian canvases were being sold, sometimes to American dealers, as unsigned works of The Master.

Another dealer, who had heard of the rumours and followed the trail to New Oxford Street, was William Marchant, successful proprietor of the Goupil Gallery in Regent Street, where Whistler and many painters of the New English Art Club had exhibited. The son of a Bristol iron-founder, he had been sent to school in France on the death of his parents and had, as a young man, worked at the Goupil Gallery in Paris. Now, a vigorous and perceptive man in his forties, Marchant presided over the London branch, always ready to encourage with financial support as with enthusiasm an artist of promise. Spencer showed Marchant not only more than fifty canvases, in the same poor condition as those Dowdeswell had bought, but about half that number of etchings. To Marchant they had a distinctive quality and were clearly not by Whistler, whose influence so many of them showed. He had heard of Walter Greaves and may have seen some of his work for he assumed that the unsigned works were by the same hand as the few that were signed. The collection that excited and captured his imagination were, he felt certain, the work of the half-forgotten pupil of Whistler.

Marchant bought the oils and etchings he had been shown for two hundred pounds and at once set about having them cleaned, restored and sometimes relined by the best craftsmen available. He then sought out Walter Greaves. This was not difficult. He still walked from Fulham to Chelsea almost every day to sketch, or try to sell his drawings. If it was fine, he might spread his work across a bench on the Embankment, as in a little gallery. Otherwise he might be found sitting in The Rising Sun hoping to sketch a portrait for the price of a drink or, along Cheyne Walk, in the King's Head and Eight Bells, where some eager young painter, like Egerton Cooper, might ask him about Whistler and buy him a glass of gin. The portfolio of work was always with him and his asking price for a drawing was five shillings, although he was ready to sell half a dozen for a pound. Egerton Cooper remembered him, at this time, always wearing a shabby frock coat, green with age, and always "down in the dumps".

Although Marchant had been prepared to meet a needy old artist, he was surprised by what he found. Walter Greaves was shockingly thin, his butterfly collar now many sizes too large for his scraggy neck. His sparse hair – and even a bald patch – were blackened and the blacking had flaked on to his shoulders. His moustache had been darkened, too, but above his lip tea or beer had washed it, showing the hair to be white. The features were still fine but he was puffy about the eyes, which seemed inexpressibly sad. Yet there was a dignity about him and a courtliness.

Marchant explained the circumstances of his buying the pictures from Spencer, that several had been signed with Greaves's name and asked Walter to inspect them and give his view on their origins. Soon after, Walter Greaves visited the Goupil Gallery and at once stated that all the works were his own. Delighted to see the canvases he had sold in tattered rolls restored to their first freshness, Walter chattered away, fascinating Marchant with his stories of Whistler, Carlyle and Chelsea. He was particularly excited to see his *Hammersmith Bridge on Boat Race Day* bright with its original poster colours because that, he said, had been his first painting in oils; he had painted it when aged only sixteen, and that must have been before he met Whistler. Another picture that Marchant praised, *Passing Under Old Battersea Bridge*, had been exhibited during the Great Exhibition of 1862 by Mr. Alan Cole, who had shown some of Whistler's work in the same South Kensington gallery. It would have been after that that Whistler had painted his own Nocturne of Old Battersea Bridge. Of course, Whistler had been a very great influence on him and his brother, although at first his ideas appeared strange and difficult to carry out. He had taught them to leave out most of the detail in their drawings – because they had been drawing and painting long before they met him . . . the Thames, Cremorne, both day and night effects. He had taught them to etch, too, and that was something they had never tried before.

Walter rambled on, spilling out his stories in no chronological order and Marchant's sense of discovery heightened with excitement. In his enthusiasm, it never occurred to him that hard times had made Walter an old man at sixty-five and that malnutrition had weakened a memory which had long been accustomed to follow Whistler's deliberate disdain for, and superstition of dates. The pictures were real enough and so was the artist. Marchant was a generous and sentimental man and the story of Whistler's forgotten pupil enthralled him, as he felt certain it would enthrall a public hankering for some new diversion.

Adrenalin was flowing in England in the spring of 1911. The Edwardian sense of comfortable self-importance remained and had been revitalised by the prospect of a vague but stimulating new era which the coronation of King George V would inaugurate in June. Dear, naughty old Edward the Peacemaker was being replaced by The Sailor King and there was an undefined hunger for fresh experience.

An astute judge of popular taste, William Marchant saw in the gaunt figure of Walter Greaves a unique blend of sentiment, subject for argument, and nostalgia sharpened by a genuine sense of discovery.

The first need was to rescue Walter Greaves from destitution and Marchant, who had been appalled by the poverty of the Fulham household, at once made him a gift of some furniture. Then, after a conference with his associates, who were then involved with the presentation of an exhibition of paintings by William Nicholson, whose lively elegance and immaculate taste well suited the public mood, told Walter that an exhibition of his works was to be held at the Goupil Gallery, at the fashionable gallery where The Master had been proud to exhibit. He added that, although Walter had no claim on any share of the proceeds, this he would be given.

With subtle showmanship, Marchant planned that the Greaves exhibition should open a few days after the apex of the artistic year, the private view of the Royal Academy. He knew that Burlington House would leave the crowds unsatisfied. It was likely to be little more than an extension of the previous year's exhibition; cosiness and daintiness would prevail and the tamed lions of the English Impressionists would purr reassuringly. He was right, for *The Art Journal* found it "a little bewildering. We do not regret particularly that there is not a so-called picture of the year; although we regret the absence of a group of pictures of sufficient novelty and interest to give as it were a fillip to the excellent work of the Academicians and Associates which is so well known to all of us . . . Not that it as a whole is dull; indeed, the general effect of most of the galleries is animated and lively. But, when we come to close quarters, the walls rarely yield the satisfaction which is evoked by art of real distinction. There are many large canvases, for instance, more than usual, with groups of people, gay in colour and lively in effect after their fashion; but so far as pictorial design, decorative quality, or more definite human interest is concerned, they are mostly meaningless and empty. They make one wonder why so much space has been occupied to say so little."

Now William Marchant was convinced that he was about to reveal pictures notable for their pictorial design, decorative quality and, above all, definite human interest.

When the Royal Academy revealed its mediocrity on 1st May, Marchant and his staff were arranging and hanging the Greaves pictures in the large and small rooms on the first floor of the Goupil Gallery. But first he asked Walter to add his signature to some of the unsigned canvases. The fifty oils hung in the large room, which was dominated by the full-length portraits of the Greaves sisters, dressed in green and in black-and-white.

A full-length portrait of a seated Carlyle – not painted from life – was also well hung and there was a self-portrait of Walter and a small portrait of Henry. Most of the paintings were of Chelsea and the river: Whistlerian Nocturnes, busy dock scenes and haunted back streets and, above all, the omnipresent river, sliding under Old Battersea Bridge at night, or sparkling as a blustering breeze whipped the sails of barges, the smoke of steamers and the skirts of ladies promenading to Cremorne. A few showed that the artist had ventured beyond his frontiers: to the Haymarket; to the shopping streets of Fulham, which he had painted at dusk illuminated by the new electric lighting in 1901; to the Pool of London; to Battersea Park boating pond and, most remarkably, to Hammersmith Bridge on boat race day.

In the smaller room hung twenty-four etchings and a water-colour. Greaves's needle lacked the sophisticated elegance of Whistler's, but his scenes of the river and Chelsea lived with grimy humanity, and his boats and barges sat on the water, or lay on the shingle, because they belonged there, and not because they formed part of an artistic composition.

Marchant prepared the catalogue in the same format and typeface as Whistler had used for the pamphlets with which he latterly liked to conduct his campaigns. As a preface, he summarised Walter's talk of his work and, with the artist's agreement, signed it with his name. In Press advertising, prominence would, of course, be given to Nicholson, whose work was hung in the ground-floor galleries, but Greaves's name was to be followed by the words "Pupil of Whistler" in brackets. Meanwhile, Marchant, whose reputation among art critics stood high, was in touch with Fleet Street, quietly advising his friends to expect surprises at the private view on Thursday, 4th May.

Wednesday was a wild day, with wind-driven rain emptying the streets. But Thursday was dry and warmer, though overcast, and there was a scent of spring in the air. To Marchant's relief there was little of excitement for the newspapers to report that morning. At home, a speech in support of the Daylight Saving Bill by Mr. Winston Churchill, M.P., at the Guildhall, had been interrupted by suffragettes. Abroad, there was some interest in the Moroccan war and it seemed that a French column was about to relieve the besieged garrison of Fez. During the day, the *Evening Standard* devoted columns of its front page to reporting Mr. Lloyd George's introduction of the Government's national insurance scheme, and it was confirmed that Fez had been relieved.

Marchant had sent out invitations to critics and his clients to the private view, and suggested that Walter ask friends from Chelsea. Both men stood ready by the door of the upstairs gallery to receive their guests and expectations were high. Guests were slow to arrive but Marchant's confidence was resilient and he was relieved when two or three critics came in, including Arthur Clutton-Brock of *The Times*. Among those Marchant was relieved to see was Elizabeth Pennell, whom he had invited with her husband as biographers of Whistler and likely to provide him with publicity by making the exhibition a talking-point in artistic circles. Neither he nor Walter Greaves had the faintest idea that this enquiring and interested guest should be a stormy petrel of dreadful portent.

In her journal for that day, Mrs. Pennell wrote, "In the afternoon I went to the Goupil Gallery to see the Greaves show . . . It seemed to me easy to see at a glance which were the pictures Greaves painted for himself, and which under the influence of Whistler. One or two blue nocturnes and one or two grey Battersea Bridges were obviously slavish attempts at imitation. The things that were entirely his own struck me as common in vision and treatment . . .

"Then I saw Greaves, who was jumpy. He told me Whistler had worked on the *Carlyle*, had come in to see him and his brother while they were doing it and criticised their work. They had painted the mount of the print on the wall white and he said it would never do and then painted it grey in tone with the wall . . .

"It was a private view, but nobody else was there except two men and two women, and an old man and his wife with whom Greaves was talking. He introduced them as old Chelsea people . . ."

Marchant, too, was becoming jumpy. The fashionable crowd usually attracted to his private views had not arrived, and there were rarely more than half a dozen visitors strolling through the rooms. As he told a friend, he was "somewhat ashamed that anyone should witness such a disastrous scene as an empty private view at the well-known Goupil Gallery". Walter, too, began to look even more grotesque with the blacking from his hair scattering on clothes which had been in fashion thirty years before. That the exhibition was, as Marchant described it, "an apparent fiasco" was bad enough for his reputation but, as a kindly man, he was desolate that he had raised such false hopes in Greaves and only succeeded in arranging his public humiliation. At last, in desperation, he pressed five pounds into Greaves's hand and suggested with embarrassment that it might be best if he made his way home to Fulham. But Walter seemed in no way disappointed and gently confided that all would be well and that his pictures would sell. Whereupon he departed and Marchant eagerly awaited the time when he could lock the door on what now seemed his failure of judgement.

Next morning, William Marchant did not turn to the newspapers with his customary eagerness. But he did hope that Clutton-Brock, whose opinion and friendship he valued, might have given the exhibition a kind reference in *The Times*. At first sight, it seemed that this was not so because the positions in which such notices were customarily placed showed no mention of the Goupil or Greaves. Turning to the main news page, opposite the leading articles, Marchant ran his eye along the headlines at the top of the page: NATIONAL INSURANCE SCHEME; CIVIL WAR IN MEXICO; ARMY AIRSHIP WRECKED; AN UNKNOWN MASTER. Beneath the last were the words, "Exhibition at the Goupil Gallery." Astonished, Marchant read Clutton-Brock's words: "Mr. Walter Greaves, in the catalogue of his pictures now to be seen at the Goupil Gallery, 5, Regent Street, describes himself as a pupil of Whistler. He tells us, in the short and simple account of himself at the beginning of that catalogue, that Whistler always insisted upon his describing himself so, and would not allow him to exhibit anything without his permission. Yet the fact remains that Mr. Greaves, though some of his pictures have a remarkable likeness to Whistler's, and were evidently influenced by him, is a perfectly original artist. We understand that he is an old man, and has lived and painted in London for most of his life. That being so, his obscurity is inexplicable. For he is not an artist who has produced one or two fine works, as it were by chance. There are 50 paintings of his in the exhibition, and scarcely one of them is not remarkable.

"At first sight one is struck by their likeness to Whistler's work, and at the same time puzzled by their underlying originality. But soon this originality asserts itself, and the Whistler influence seems to be a mere accident. Mr. Greaves tells us that his *Boat Race Day, Hammersmith Bridge*, was painted when he was 16; and, surely, no artist at that age has ever painted a more original picture. If it were exhibited without any history attached to it, it would be called Post-Impressionist. The figures crowded on the Bridge are painted with a primitive *naïveté*, yet they are all subordinated to the main design, while at the same time they preserve their character and propriety of pose and gesture. The *naïveté* persists in nearly all his work, and distinguishes it sharply from Whistler's cosmopolitan cleverness. Mr. Greaves tells us that his father was a boat-builder in Chelsea. He has, therefore, been familiar with the riverside from childhood, and his pictures of it seem to be rich with childish associations. He paints it as if he loved it for its own sake, not as if it were a new and interesting material for picture-making. No one has ever surpassed him in the drawing of boats, and he draws them as if they were human to him. Every house in his riverside pictures has its own character; and yet in most of his works the detail is almost as skilfully subordinated as in the best works of de Hoogh; and, as de Hoogh is intensely Dutch, so Mr. Greaves is intensely English. Whistler, no doubt, helped to make him an artist, but he did not make him a cosmopolitan like so many of his followers, and he has kept almost entirely free from the Japanese element in Whistler's art.

"He is at his best, perhaps, in works like the wonderful little night-piece, *The Black Lion, Church Street, Chelsea*, where there is nothing of Whistler. Here the houses all keep their character and definition in the darkness. The execution and the composition alike are almost childish in their simplicity. The picture looks as if anyone could have painted it, and yet no one has painted anything at all like it. There are three pictures of Old Battersea Bridge; and the longer you look at them the less you remember Whistler. Indeed, they have the same relation to Whistler's works that the Giorgionesque Titian has to Giorgione. Whistler defines only for the sake of his design. Mr. Greaves defines because he loves every timber in the bridge; and yet his design is almost as fine as Whistler's and almost as predominant. He is not a painter of moods, like Whistler, but a painter of things in which he is profoundly interested, like de Hoogh. Whistler has taught him some part of the science of picture-making, and that is all. In his portrait of Carlyle the influence of Whistler is evident; but notice the subtlety of expression and the manner in which he has invested the trousers with character – perhaps the most difficult feat an artist can accomplish. Again, in the portrait of Miss Alice Greaves the head is a masterpiece, and there is extraordinary boldness in the whole design, though the quilted dress is a little tiresome in its repetitions. Mr. Greaves tells us that it was rejected at the Grosvenor Gallery in 1876 for want of space. There are very few contemporary exhibitions in which it would not surpass every other portrait. If the Academy have not yet made all their purchases this year for the Chantrey Bequest, they have an opportunity here for making some reparation for the long public neglect, or rather ignorance, of a master, on whose discovery Mr. Marchant is to be congratulated."

Walter Greaves could not afford a daily newspaper but, that morning, a friend in Chelsea hurried to Fulham with a copy of *The Times* to read him the review, afterwards saying that he would never forget the pleasure of the moment. Walter listened to the praise attentively but with some bewilderment and, when his friend finally put down the paper with a triumphant, expectant look in his eye, said, "They call me 'An Unknown Master' – but I've been known in Chelsea all my life!"

At about the same time, Anthony Ludovici, an artist friend of Whistler, happened to walk past the doors of the Goupil Gallery when the porter, whom he knew, hailed him and remarked, "We have something upstairs which is going to bring the crowds here." He had not read *The Times*, but entered to find the two upstairs galleries crowded with celebrities and art critics. One of the latter, whom he did not know and presumably recognised him as an artist by his dress, assumed the exhibition was his and congratulated him, saying, "You are at last coming into your own!"

Then Walter Greaves himself arrived, pleased and puzzled, to find his pictures being worshipped by the sort of people he had not seen in such numbers since he had helped Whistler decorate the Peacock Room. Lord Curzon, Lord Rosebery, Lord Northcliffe and Lord Henry Bentinck, a rich patron of the arts, were among early visitors, as were Sir Arthur Pinero, the playwright, and the hostesses Princess Kropotkin and the Countess of Wemyss. Mr. Justice Darling and Mr. Justice Pickford were recognised by reporters without their wigs. Walter only recognised one celebrity, the old Socialist John Burns, now President of the Local Government Board, whom he had known in Battersea when they were both boys.

The reporters and photographers who jostled round Marchant that first heady morning all had the same request, to interview and photograph "The Unknown Master". Knowing Walter to be "of a timid nature, lacking the self-assurance and push of the modern artist", Marchant decided that he must first be instructed on the art of being interviewed and sent an urgent message to William Nicholson: "I wish you'd come down and look after Walter Greaves for me; I've got the place full of Pressmen, and poor Walter doesn't know what to do with them." Nicholson hurried to the gallery, bringing with him Augustus John, and they sat either side of him on a sofa explaining the habits of Fleet Street. In the midst of this Tinnie Greaves swept in, as Nicholson recalled, "looking like Queen Elizabeth in a red window-curtain". Catching sight of her brother among the famous and the rich, she exclaimed, "Well, Walter, we're going it, aren't we? One day we'll be able to have a motor-car with a footman sitting up behind and everything!"

Walter faced the reporters politely and without embarrassment, one of them remarking on his "quaint dress, hesitant speech and air of bygone courtliness and gentility". The first reports appeared in that day's evening newspapers.

Under the headlines THE MANTLE OF WHISTLER. LONDON'S RIP VAN WINKLE, *The Pall Mall Gazette* declared: "A new art planet has swum into our ken. But as often happens in a world that is tired of young prodigies, the discovery is a double paradox. For the 'new master' is old indeed. Mr. Walter Greaves is a septuagenarian who has been in London all his life and London knew him not. The fact is that he came into the world half a century too early and has paid the usual penalty . . . The mystery is how such a man has lived so long in our midst, unappreciated and unacknowledged – 'The world forgetting, by the world forgot.'"

The pictures had begun to sell fast – on this day fifteen oils sold, mostly for between one and two hundred guineas – and rows of red stickers on the frames of the etchings showed the number of proofs ordered. In celebration, Marchant took Walter Greaves, Nicholson and John to lunch at a smart restaurant, Les Gourmets, where they were again photographed at their table, a look of bewilderment on the face of The New Master. Marchant had already told Walter that he would be given an allowance from the profits but now he suggested that he take a studio for him nearby, so that the supply of his pictures could keep up with the demand.

Next morning the national newspapers were, in their different ways, as flattering as *The Times* had been. The *Daily Express*, reporting that Greaves's paintings which had sold for ten shillings were now commanding two hundred pounds, rhapsodised, "Those interesting dramas in which the hero after two or three acts of concentrated misfortune, victimisation and martyrdom, comes out an easy winner, are not often found in real life. But one of them – as complete an example as could be wished – is now exciting the attention of artistic London. Its first act was laid in Chelsea; its latest, though by no means last scene, is in the Goupil Galleries. The 'hero', who has just 'come out on top' is Mr. Walter Greaves . . . Recognition has only just come – suddenly and in a turmoil of acclamation."

Among the successful painters Walter was now to meet was William Rothenstein, one of the first visitors to his exhibition, who at once gave his opinion to the *Daily News*, which reported: "A remarkable feature of the discovery is the whole-hearted admiration expressed by the younger men of the art world, who, feeling that the veteran artist will not produce many more pictures, are working to secure a record attendance at the Goupil Gallery, and have hopes that at least one of the canvases may be secured for a public collection.

"One eminent pupil of Whistler, Mr. William Rothenstein, speaking to a *Daily News* representative last night, said it seemed incredible that a man of Mr. Greaves's talents should have remained unappreciated so long.

" 'An entirely new note runs through all his pictures. He was known to some of us as a kind of legend, the subject of many Whistler stories, but we had perhaps rather regarded him merely as a follower of The Master.

" 'Everything he has painted is the result of a rare passion and reverence, and there underlies everything he does a spirit of rare intensity, which is curiously suggestive of the early works of the Pre-Raphaelites. I think nothing quite like the portrait of his sister has been painted in England, and I hope that one or more of his fine pictures will find a home in the Tate Gallery.' "

Such praise was heady and stimulating enough, but, on this Saturday morning, a new note was introduced, transforming a sensational success into a sensational mystery. Lord Northcliffe, who was now proprietor of both *The Times* and the *Daily Mail*, was delighted that Clutton-Brock had, single-handed, generated the talking-point of the week, and now expected it to be followed by an equally startling revelation from Paul Konody, art critic of his popular newspaper. In this he was not disappointed.

Konody introduced his article with the now-familiar fanfare of praise: "To the list of the great English painters of the Nineteenth Century has to be added a name which will sound unfamiliar . . ." Then he came to the unexpected point of his theory: "How much of the astounding talent shown in these paintings was due to Whistler's teaching, and – one trembles to utter the blasphemy! – how much did Whistler learn from his pupil? From Mr. Greaves himself, whose worship of The Master, according to all accounts, amounted almost to self-effacement, it would be vain to expect enlightenment. But there is the evidence of his work. *Passing Under Old Battersea Bridge*, the most 'Whistlerian' of all his works, so like The Master's Nocturne at the Tate Gallery in arrangement and in the manner of applying the paint and especially of indicating the figures, bears the date 1862, and thus antedates Whistler's picture by over ten years . . . Thus . . . one is forced to the conclusion that Whistler himself may have benefited to no small extent by the example of his pupil."

On Sunday, *The Observer* supported this theory with the opinion that Whistler had been inspired by Greaves's *Battersea Bridge* and, on Monday, the *Daily Chronicle* reported that Greaves "has been hailed as a new and, in some respects, a greater Whistler".

The *Manchester Guardian* tried unsuccessfully to damp down the explosive potential of the sensation with the soothing words, "When a marvel does swim into the ken of the London Press the tendency is naturally to make it a cycle of miracles, and in the electric atmosphere that arises it becomes difficult for the plain man to keep his head. At the moment the difficulty is to refrain from saying that Mr. Walter Greaves . . . is to Whistler what Giorgione was to Titian." But the writer went on to deplore the effect of Whistler's sophistication on the simplicity of an artist who could paint the *Hammersmith Bridge*.

But by now the electric atmosphere was such that the cycle of miracles was global, inter-continental telegraphy making it as much of a sensation in New York as in London. Among headlines above reports from the London correspondents of American newspapers were WHISTLER DETHRONED; ART TRAGEDY SHOWS VANITY OF WHISTLER; NOW CRITICS ARE ASKING WHICH WAS THE MASTER?; WAS THIS ARTIST WHISTLER'S GHOST?; THE CRUSHED GENIUS; THE OTHER WHISTLER; CASTING WHISTLER IN THE SHADE.

However sensational, the publicity seemed heaven-sent and all the following week the exhibition was crowded. Most of the oils and all the etchings – usually several proofs of each – were sold, the purchasers including Nicholson, John, Orpen and Lord Northcliffe, who decided to present a painting to Chelsea Town Hall, writing to the Council, "I took the liberty of telling one of my Art critics to spend two hundred pounds in buying a picture, or some pictures of Walter Greaves, which I should be glad if you would hang on the walls of your collection."

Walter himself was still in great demand for interviews, being asked – with the reverence due to a reincarnated spirit – for his memories of Whistler and Chelsea in the days before the Embankment. He was constantly photographed. In Chelsea, he was posed beside the statue of Carlyle in Cheyne Walk, wearing a silk hat, frock coat and spats and leaning on a cane. He was photographed in a studio, brushes and palette in hand, beside an easel holding a canvas showing Lawrence Street or the river. In one photograph, William Marchant sits beside the easel, admiring the artist at work.

Marchant was generous, giving Walter arbitrary sums of money and making arrangements for a regular payment to him of thirty shillings a week. At last able to afford full meals, he put on weight so that he filled out the coat that had hung in folds from his thin shoulders. He had moved from the shabby house in Fulham Road to a small flat – 41 Churchfield Mansions – in New King's Road, nearer to the river. Marchant meanwhile had taken a studio for him in Crown Chambers, 9 Regent Street, a few doors from the Goupil Gallery. The studio, on the top floor at the back, had been last used by a popular landscape painter, Tom Robertson, who had left a few of his pictures behind. These Walter criticised with a new-found confidence, saying, "I like smoother surfaces. He could get just as good results with less pigment."

Almost every day, Walter climbed the long, twisting staircase to his studio. There he was visited by a sympathetic friend, who described him being "engaged chiefly on river scenes, both day and night effects; and though the hand had lost not a little of its surety, and the eye its precision, he seemed greatly to relish his work." He seemed to have little idea of the value of his pictures, although he gratefully received his cash allowances from Marchant because at this time he sold another portrait in oils of Carlyle for thirty shillings, the price he would have asked a few weeks before. When told that he should be asking at least a hundred guineas, he replied, "No, no, I can't. It really isn't worth any more."

London had settled back with a sentimental sigh of relief at the apparent happy ending of what the art critic Christian Brinton described as "one of the most pathetic and appealing narratives in the entire annals of esthetic endeavour". A sentimental public liked to see the recognition of Walter Greaves just as this same writer described it: "The last time I saw him was when he sat in the quiet gallery, with the pearl-grey twilight creeping softly about him, and the work of a lifetime on the darkening walls. There seemed a poignant tinge of contrast to it all. The pictures were still fresh and young. They were things of the spirit, and had been wrought in love and in hope. He himself was broken and enfeebled, for he was merely flesh. And yet the sunny optimism of the man has shown no sign of abatement. As we said good-bye I turned and asked him what he thought of doing now that he was comfortably off and well cared for, now that the battle of life had been won, so to speak, in the very last round. Without a moment's pause, and with a smile I can never forget – the smile of one to whom his work is more than anything else in the world – he cheerily replied, 'Oh, I shall go on painting a bit!' "

On Saturday, 13th May, disquieting rumours that had been muttering below the horizon like a summer storm took shape in a visitor to the Goupil Gallery, demanding to see William Marchant. This was Joseph Pennell, whose wife had made the swift visit to the private view. The American appeared not only excited, which was his frequent state, but "angry . . . ominous, not to say antagonistic" and announced that he wished to speak of "a most serious affair".

Marchant had expected Pennell to be annoyed by some of the critics' sneers at Whistler but he cannot have foreseen that any specific accusation was to be made. But now he claimed that Greaves had not exhibited his *Battersea Bridge* in 1862, as was stated in the preface to the catalogue. He had searched the catalogue of the International Exhibition for that year and there was no mention of any work by Greaves. The assertion that it had been shown in that year – many years before Whistler's own Nocturne on a similar theme – would therefore have to be substantiated.

Pennell's bearing was so threatening and heavy with the prospect of further accusations, that Marchant could give no immediate answer, only promising to look thoroughly into the allegations. He was going abroad the following day and so asked Pennell if the matter could await his return in about a week's time. Pennell agreed to take no further action until then, and, meanwhile, Marchant began his own enquiries into the viability of the date which had given Konody the clue to his remarkable theory.

Pennell had had more evidence than he revealed. Another painter, examining the questioned picture closely, had told him that the date had been painted on a separate piece of canvas fixed to the painting and the join concealed with varnish. And, at the Athenaeum Club, Pennell had met Alan Cole, whom Greaves had named as being responsible for the 1862 exhibition. Not only did Cole, who had succeeded his father as art director of the exhibition, confirm that there was no reference to Greaves in the catalogue but, disclaimed all personal involvement, with, "my father thought me a genius, but even he would not have chosen me as art director at the age of sixteen".

Unable to contain himself in the face of what he described as the "most scandalous attacks" on Whistler's reputation, Pennell broke his promise and, on 16th May and before Marchant's return, wrote a letter to *The Times* repeating the charges he had made to Marchant, adding, "I think, therefore, that it is only right that Mr. Greaves should be asked by you, sir, to produce some more positive proof, and reliable data, as to the date at which this work was shown. The first reference to Mr. Greaves's exhibiting, I believe, is 1873."

This first letter was not published but talk of it spread and the art critic of the *Daily Chronicle* strengthened the rumours by writing, "The Greaves exhibition is certainly the most interesting and debatable exhibition in London. Already the art world is divided into two camps – those who accept Greaves as an artist of remarkable gifts, who late in life has come into his kingdom, and those who deny his originality."

A week later Marchant, back in London, was able to confirm the truth of Pennell's accusation. Walter Greaves readily agreed that his memory must have been at fault – and there was plenty of evidence in other pictures to illustrate his wild inaccuracy in dating his early works – and next day the preface was cut from all copies of the catalogue.

That no deliberate deception was intended could have been proved conclusively by more exact study of the painting. Between the piers of Battersea Bridge could be seen a distant bridge, curiously unlike any spanning the Thames. Presumably, at the time, it was taken to be an imitation of some Whistlerian fantasy of the same bridge in Japanese distortion. Yet a drawing of this view by Whistler himself clearly shows that it was a real bridge: the single span of Albert Bridge under construction. While the painting showed only the curved span supported by piers, the drawing, executed later, but many months before the suspension bridge was opened in September 1873, also showed scaffolding around the huge uprights which were to carry it. Had Greaves given careful thought to the date of the picture, his recognition of the structure in the background would certainly have led him to bring it forward by ten years.

But it was too late. Pennell had called upon the services of William Heinemann, whose name he rightly thought would carry greater weight at Printing House Square, and two days after Marchant admitted to the mistake, a long letter was published in *The Times* stating the facts that were already accepted at the Goupil Gallery. "The sensation created by the exhibition of Mr. Walter Greaves's pictures is due to the impression given . . . that he actually influenced and, in some directions, led Whistler," wrote Heinemann. He went on to list other apparent discrepancies: Greaves's claim to have painted "night effects" before he met Whistler, and etchings dated 1859, before it was thought that the two had met. He concluded, "I feel certain that Mr. Greaves has no desire to mislead, or to claim for himself greater distinction than the fact that he was a pupil of Whistler's." And he called upon Greaves to modify all "the misleading statements" in the preface, despite the fact that this had already been withdrawn.

Clutton-Brock now stepped in with a letter in his newspaper, which could have been expected to end the controversy. "Mr. Greaves was praised in *The Times*, not because of the likeness of his works to Whistler's, but because of their unlikeness. They seemed to me most interesting when they were most original; and I said so," he reasoned. "A masterpiece is the work of the man who made it, no matter what he may have learnt from others. But while the dates of Mr. Greaves's pictures have nothing to do with the merits of Whistler, they have also nothing to do with the merits of Mr. Greaves . . ."

This letter was supported by another from Marchant, admitting to the mistaken date and quoting Greaves as saying that he had never intended to suggest that he had invented the Whistlerian Nocturne. Heinemann seemed satisfied, for he replied, "My object is achieved since 'history is put right'." Finally, *The Pall Mall Gazette* wound up with a leading article remarking that on the principal that "no incense could be more grateful or appropriate to the Elysian shade" of Whistler than "the dust of controversy", "Mr. Greaves approves himself a loyal pupil, for he is stirring the vortex of art criticism to its depths . . . There is an assured place for Mr. Greaves in the art of Victorian England, but we feel that his reputation will be all the stronger directly it is stripped of the pathetic fallacy which attaches, very naturally, to a long-neglected master coming tardily and suddenly into his own."

Yet the piquance of discovery had already turned sour and several critics began to react against the first enthusiasm with the sharpness of *The Outlook*, which made the comment, "To some of us the sweet pea will never be quite the same again. Journalism has blown upon its freshness, has touched it with a tawdry popularity . . . Under the eye-catching, empty title of 'The New Master'; a subject of descriptive writing in the evening ha'pennies, with his hat's shape and the colour of his gloves made public, Mr. Greaves too has been most unfairly thrust on to an unenviable position. His false fame, which he surely must despise, will just last out the exhibition of his work. Then inevitably the long drop to reasonable estimation will wound."

But this was not to be the end of the affair. Heinemann's gentlemanly bowing out of the quarrel, once he felt that honour and history had been satisfied, was not enough for Pennell. He and his wife were in a state of feverish excitement, perhaps imagining that they were inspired by The Master's own love of combat, and they had enlisted, among other allies, their fellow-American, John Singer Sargent.

An appreciative article about Greaves appeared in *The New York Times* on 21st May and this, too, seemed to call for a rebuttal from Joseph Pennell, who was well aware that in New York he was not as hampered by the law of libel as in London. Like others, Pennell had been intrigued by the startling variations in quality of Greaves's work. Now he had formulated a theory. Not only were some unauthenticated paintings, sold as Whistler's in the United States, really by Greaves, but the best of Greaves's work on exhibition in London could only have been by Whistler.

On 24th May, *The New York Times* printed, under the headlines WORKS BY GREAVES SOLD AS WHISTLER'S. ART SCANDAL THREATENED. BIOGRAPHER OF WHISTLER ALSO ASSERTS THE MASTER PAINTED SOME OF THE WORK EXHIBITED AS GREAVES, another attack inspired by Pennell. Repeating at length the story of the mistaken date, this continued: "Mr. Pennell declares that there is intrinsic evidence that it was Whistler's hand that painted the background of barges that is the chief feature of the Greaves picture of Battersea Bridge. He adds that several other paintings in the Greaves exhibition owe their chief merits to Whistler's brush, instancing the background of one painting entitled *The Balcony*, and the head of Greaves in the portrait of himself, supposedly the work of the latter artist. 'Whistler began his portrait and Greaves finished it – finished it in more ways than one,' said Mr. Pennell succinctly to *The New York Times* correspondent today. Mr. Pennell believes that unless steps are at once taken exactly to determine Greaves's place in the world of art there will result confusion between his work and Whistler's which will become an outrageous scandal."

On the following day *The Nation* published in New York an article signed "N.N.", which was generally accepted as Pennell's *nom de plume*. In picking over the controversy, point by point, the strident note became hysterical. Taking up Greaves's ready admission that Whistler had sometimes helped him in his work, Pennell wrote of an etching, "There is one plate that is at least half done by Whistler and must be added to his work." Two oils, he maintained, "look like canvases which Whistler, dissatisfied, had thrown away, only that their fate should be to have Greaves take them up and ruin them." In sneering at the murals the Greaves brothers had painted in Streatham Town Hall, Pennell described them as being "the uttermost rubbish and banality, though several are copied from Whistler, the designs of whose frames even are stolen."

Meanwhile, in London, Pennell was determined that the controversy must not die down and wrote detailed letters, which were published in *The Sunday Times*, *The Star* and *The Art Chronicle*, taking up yet again Greaves's lapse of memory. Marchant had to reply to each not only to defend Greaves's reputation but to correct Pennell's reference to his company as "Goupil's", a triviality which had already been the subject of a lawsuit in a different context.

By this time, Pennell's sustained animosity had created what Marchant described as "an atmosphere of suspicion and even prejudice . . . around Mr. Greaves." Among the rumours circulating in London that he had heard and now listed, were that Lord Northcliffe had engineered the sensation as "a newspaper stunt"; that Marchant had bribed the critics; that Greaves was impersonating another artist; and that the reason for Marchant's decision to limit the exhibition to ten days was that he had discovered all the works in it were by Whistler.

Marchant was quick and forceful in his defence. For a start, he asked Greaves to start work on a Nocturne under his own supervision. This painting, *Battersea Bridge, Moonlight*, although painted from memory, was in the same high Whistlerian manner that he had been trained to adopt by The Master in the 'seventies, and helped refute Pennell's accusation that Greaves had painted the foreground of the bridge over Whistler's background of the river in his *Passing Under Old Battersea Bridge*. As additional evidence he had the questioned painting closely examined and was able to produce greatly enlarged photographs showing that the paint on the background slightly overlaid the paint on the foreground. As to the etching, *Barges, Lime Wharf, Chelsea*, which Pennell had claimed was partly by Whistler, Greaves was able to affirm that he himself had strengthened the somewhat weak original with dry-point retouching, and that Whistler had never even seen the plate.

But now it was a scandal within a sensation and had gone too far to stop. In *The World* of 30th May, the critic, A. J. Finberg, wrote that the revelations had "pricked the Greaves bubble". Marchant reacted quickly with a threat of litigation and Finberg instantly retreated, writing that he had only meant to say that "a great deal too much fuss had been made about Greaves's work" and that he had not had the slightest intention of imputing dishonesty.

A more violent attack now appeared in *The Saturday Review* by Rowland Strong under the title THE GREAVES HUMBUG. In this Whistler was assaulted as furiously as his pupil. "The trouble with Mr. Greaves," wrote Strong ,"is that he is artistically speaking, deaf, dumb and blind . . . The cold lamb and mint sauce effects in which Mr. Greaves drivels so industriously . . . in obedience perhaps to the misleading counsel of his 'master' whose own work was technically quite as bad . . . The portraits of Carlyle and Miss Alice Greaves are among the cruellest pictures that I have ever seen. They constitute the documentary 'give-away' of the whole bag of Whistlerian tricks."

The accusations of plagiarism, false representation and even theft had become so serious and were having so disastrous an effect upon the demand for the paintings, which Greaves was producing in his new studio, that a counter-attack was essential. Marchant was fortunate in having most of the heirs of Whistler – Sickert, Steer, Nicholson, Rothenstein, John and Clausen – ready to do battle. The obvious champion was Walter Sickert, who commanded wit and style to match Whistler's own and, above all, had a far more intimate and more discerning understanding of The Master than had Pennell. He therefore wrote *L'Affaire Greaves*, which was published in *The New Age* on 15th June.

"It appears that Mr. Pennell, who has appointed himself official scold to the memory of Whistler, is dissatisfied with some of Mr. Walter Greaves's painting," he wrote. "Mr. Pennell is an able black-and-white man, an effective etcher and transfer-lithographer, but not so far as I know, a painter. As a critic he cannot be noted for balance or temperance. I do not therefore find myself disturbed by Mr. Pennell's Constantinopolitan perturbations . . .

"My acquaintance, oddly enough, with Walter Greaves's work dates from the third day of this glorious June. I had heard of the boom, did not believe in it, was bored by it, and I told everyone I knew that I was sure it was a *coup monté*, and that there was nothing in it . . . However, so far as I am concerned, all's well that ends well. I came, I saw, and was bowled over, and herewith make publicly an act of penitence. Walter Greaves is a great master. Henry doesn't count. Walter announces himself with an immense painting of

Hammersmith Bridge on Boat Race day, a work of extreme youth. Simon Bussy once told me an enchanting story: A painter, entering the studio of a colleague, is so struck with the work on the easel that he seizes it and rushes to the door with it. '*Malheureux, ou allez vous avec mon tableau?*' '*Au Louvre!*' To the National Gallery with Hammersmith Bridge! . . .

"The Hammersmith picture is a masterpiece. The only thing that it reminds me of in painting is Carpaccio. It is a staggerer. Its perfect *naïveté* results in purest art . . .

"Let anyone look at *The Thames, Bright Morning; Unloading the Barge; Mountebanks, Chelsea; The Old Haymarket; Lawrence Street, Chelsea; Cremorne Gardens at Night, Showing the Entrance to the Theatre and the Stooping Venus Fountain; The Boating-Pond, Battersea Park; Battersea Church*, and *Old Chelsea and the Adam and Eve*, and say that here is not a little master in the front rank. In the portrait of Miss Alice Greaves, Walter Greaves has accomplished what Whistler spent his life trying to do. It is odd, tragic, humorous, *cocasse*, anything you like, that it should be so, but there it is. The ways of providence are inscrutable. The boatman's son is the great gentleman. The humble and meek have scored in this dramatic manner, as they have scored before, and as they will probably score again to the end of time. '*Au Louvre*' with Tinny Greaves!

"Now the reader will ask, What about the Whistler influence? What especially about the Greaves Nocturnes? Of the bulk it may be said that here was a fine artistic personality deflected from time to time from its orbit. Greaves did many Whistlerian Nocturnes, not one of which could be mistaken by a connoisseur for a Whistler Nocturne. Whistler, trained in Paris, taught and influenced Greaves; Greaves, the professional armorial painter and boatman, inspired Whistler and suggested subjects to him. To be dragged out of your orbit round the town, like a tin kettle at the tail of a dog, by a stronger personality may appear to the unphilosophical experience merely painful. The truly philosophical kettle returns, dented, it is true, but enriched by, and grateful for, ecstatic experience . . . Any nagging about mutual indebtedness is sordid and trivial in such a case. It is as if two lovers should quibble under the bough of a lime-tree about which of them it was that made the other happy."

And he concluded, "As to Whistlers and Whistleriana, I am perhaps the person living who is most qualified to speak, and that is why I have been at the pains to write this article."

But even this was not enough. The vendetta that the Pennells had launched was so vindictive that its poison had already spread far beyond remedy. Marchant himself published a full and factual account of the affair in a booklet entitled *A Reply to an Attack* and this, together with a laudatory and somewhat over-sentimental monograph by Christian Brinton, accompanied an exhibition of Greaves's work to New York the following year. However, Elizabeth Pennell recorded gleefully, "Unfortunately for him and the owners of the galleries, Joseph happened to arrive in New York while the exhibition was being held and he exposed Dr. Brinton's mistakes. The pictures were disposed of at auction, fetching small prices, and Greaves has not often been heard of since."

The fame of Walter Greaves had lasted, untarnished, for exactly three weeks.

8

The gentle art of making friends

The scandal bewildered Walter Greaves as desperately as had his rejection by Whistler. Himself a man without malice, he could never understand why Joseph and Elizabeth Pennell should pursue their vendetta against one who had, after all, also been a friend of Jimmy's. But the couple maintained their antagonism both in London and New York, openly expressing satisfaction when, as a result of their campaign, the fashion for Greaves's work faded as quickly as it had begun. Pictures that had been sent to America did not sell well and, when the residue were sold by auction at Christie's saleroom in London six years later, they recorded that the prices averaged between one and seven guineas. Their persecution of Walter Greaves reached a climax when *The Whistler Journal* was published ten years after the scandal of 1911 and a whole chapter of the book was devoted to an attempt to discredit Greaves, written in so vicious a style that it probably did more harm to the Pennells than to the old artist, who had again sunk back into obscurity.

"I never could make out Pennell's reasons for going on as he did," Walter told a friend years later. "I had never done him any harm, and he came along to me when he was writing Whistler's *Life* to ask me for what I knew. But don't let's talk about Pennell."

In Chelsea, at least, he was free from the *canards*, for there he was known, as a character if not as a notable artist. He now had the memory of being accepted by the most distinguished painters of the time as an equal. Those who lived and worked in Chelsea would still recognise him with a kindly word as he again hawked his drawings for a few shillings. But his brief fame had given him a grain of self-confidence and pride, because, it was now noticed, his dress was worn with a pathetic attempt at Whistlerian dash. Charles Wheeler, the young sculptor, had lodgings in Old Church Street at this time and often saw Walter visiting the little antique shop below in the hope of being allowed to display a drawing in the window. More than fifty years later, when Sir Charles Wheeler had been President of the Royal Academy, he wrote of Greaves in his memoirs: "He was one of the Chelsea characters and the butt of rude little boys. He wore a tall and battered silk hat with square-cut frock coat and concertina-ed, pin-striped trousers. His boots were always immaculately polished – turning up a little at the toe-cap – and his hair oily and ebony black hanging in serrated locks over his coat collar . . . Greaves had a down-at-heel appearance as, detached and flat-footed, he plodded along Church Street, Cheyne Walk, Paulton's Square, Glebe Place, King's Road and all that part of Chelsea we considered to be the hub of our universe. His coat was greenish black . . . and was surely made for someone else. The tattered portfolio he invariably carried also may have belonged to another artist, J. McNeill W. perhaps, but was always full of drawings of the riverside of earlier days; for when I remember him he was very old with a wizened face and thin, drooping moustache, like those of mandarins painted on Chinese vases. He would hawk around his sketches for a few shillings each . . . None of us knew his canvases and he was a figure of some amusement, but he kept the 'even tenor' of his way."

One of his most comforting friends was William Nicholson, who had a studio in The Pheasantry. He attempted to give Walter confidence by introducing him to his circle as a distinguished painter. On one occasion he took him to an exhibition of French Impressionists in the West End. To give the expedition an extra sense of occasion Nicholson stopped the cab at two grocers' shops to buy a basket of plovers' eggs and some red pepper but later reported that Walter, eating the delicacy for the first time in his life, munched them with an expression that showed he regarded it as an overrated luxury. Nor was he impressed with Cézanne, Picasso and Van Gogh, remarking, "Expensive, those bright colours. You don't want to use a lot of bright colours like that."

Many other artists and critics had been touched by the rise and fall of Walter Greaves and one Chelsea friend wrote in a booklet, published in the King's Road after the Goupil Gallery exhibition, that his story "calls forth every feeling of brotherhood in man". Yet most were too immersed in their own affairs, for now Chelsea had an art industry and there was work and a good living for any artist ready to conform to public taste in portraiture, illustration and graceful paintings to decorate middle-class drawing-rooms.

The hub of this world was the Chelsea Arts Club, which, unassuming as it was, had become one of the most envied male strongholds in London, advertising itself flamboyantly each New Year's Eve since 1908 with the Chelsea Arts Ball evolved from a studio dance initiated in the 'eighties. Girl artists' models could make a good living between Sloane Square and World's End and for them the Models' Club was opened in 1913, in which was combined an employment agency and a hostel and where "every room is a smoking-room, for there are two things which are essential to the comfort of the girl-model, and they are cigarettes and chocolates".

While at the northern end of Old Church Street, the artists drank beer and wine while they argued the merits of newly-marketed colours, or the latest portable sketching equipment, their models entertained young men down by the river. One such visitor described his initiation: "From an open door trickled the tones of a cheap piano and the mellow, philosophic chant of the 'cello. They were playing Elgar's *Salut d'Amour*. The room was dark save for one candle at the piano and the dancing firelight. People were sprawled here and there, but to distinguish them was impossible. I fell over someone's foot, and a light treble gurgled at me, 'Sorry, old boy!' I caught a whisk of curls as the thin gleam of the candle fell that way. I fell over some more feet and collapsed on a low settee. I found myself by the side of a lady in solemn crimson. Her raven hair was hanging down her back. Her arms were bare. She smoked a Virginia cigarette vindictively . . .

"Out of the smoky glooms of the room came light laughter and merry voices. One saw dimly, as in a dream, graceful forms reclining gracefully, attended by carelessly dressed but distinguished young men. Some of them raised their voices, and one heard the self-proud accent of Oxford. The music stopped, and the girls sprawled themselves more and more negligently, nestling to the rough coats of the boys. The haze of smoke thickened. One of the

Oxford boys said he knew an awfully good story, but it was rather risky, you know. I pricked up my ears. Did we know the story – story about a fellah – fellah who had an aunt, you know? And fellah's aunt was most frightfully keen on dogs and all that, you know . . .

"I never heard the finish of it. I became rather interested in a scene near the window, where a boy of about my own age was furiously kissing a girl somewhat younger. Then the lady at my side stretched a long arm towards me, and languished, and making the best of a bad job, I languished, too . . .

"I decided to slip away, and fell down the ragged stairs into Chelsea, and looked upon the shadow-fretted streets, where the arc-lamps, falling through the trees, dappled the pavements with light. The skies were dashed with stars and a sick moon. It was trying to snow."

In this last winter of peace, many such innocent adventurers were discovering an escape in Chelsea, as if unconsciously flinching from the years to come. It was now possible to dine by candlelight at creaking oak tables at The Blue Cockatoo, overlooking the river. The food was cheap, the candles in their wobbling brass candlesticks and the coals in the welcoming Georgian grate cast shadows on panelled walls. Beyond the steamed windows, the river swirled under Albert Bridge and tugs hooted in the night.

Where artists had found beauty, stimulation and companionship, the new arrivals found whimsy unlimited, which journalists were quick to enhance finding "something curiously feminine and intoxicating in its charm, something that evokes the silver-pensive mood. One visions it as a graceful spinster – watered silks, ruffles, corkscrew curls, you know, with lily fingers caressing the keys of her harpsichord. Pass down Cheyne Walk at whatever time you will, and you are never alone; the little companies of delicate fancies join you at every step."

To these visitors, Walter Greaves and his portfolio were as much part of the romanticised bohemia as the proud stallion parading of Augustus John. His may have been a picturesque poverty, but it was very real. The Pennells had succeeded in destroying the demand for his oils and the shock of August, 1914, generated a universal sense of urgency, no mood to help the sale of gently nostalgic drawings of Victorian Chelsea. There seemed no purpose in sketching the riverside, when the portfolio was always full, and Walter was seen less in the streets, the alert grocer's assistant, Frederick Ferebee, later remarking, "I reckon he disappeared when the war broke out."

The First World War appalled the cosy world of artistic Chelsea that for so long had seemed an impregnable haven of comfortable culture. Dora Coates, living in Glebe Place, wrote, "Never shall I forget how suddenly Chelsea seemed to become an armed camp. Soldiers were bivouacked in Ranelagh Gardens and the Royal Hospital grounds, Army motor lorries were rattling noisily along the usually quiet Embankment, and those hot nights we lay awake listening to the heavy, ominous rumble of laden troop-trains, all night long, slowly steaming out of Victoria Station. It was a heart-breaking sight to see the young men of all ranks going up the steps of Chelsea Town Hall to enlist . . ."

Yet it was in the four years of suffocating horror that followed that the discovery of Chelsea was completed. Middle-class girls were coming to London to take up "war work" as nurses, secretaries and drivers and many of them took lodgings in boarding-houses off the King's Road. At a time of drabness there was some excitement in the idea, if not the reality, of a rented room – the "bed-sitting-room" – in the *Quartier Latin* of London. Tea was brewed on gas-rings and toast made at the red-hot asbestos grills of gas-stoves. Here in her "bed-sitter", the nicely-brought-up English girl felt liberated from convention. The tradition of Chelsea as an avenue of escape for young people was thus founded.

The younger members of the Chelsea Arts Club joined the Artists' Rifles, which had been founded by Lord Leighton, and the older men, such as George Coates, became medical orderlies in nearby military hospitals. Painters were engaged as official war artists but, while Orpen, John and Rothenstein were finally commissioned to record the battlefields, the occasion demanded fresher eyes more ready with immediate emotional reaction and younger painters interpreted the carnage with more impact, notably Paul Nash and Christopher Nevinson. But there was even a little "war work" for Greaves. Early in 1917 a charity matinée in aid of Miss Lena Ashwell's Concerts at the Front was arranged at the Chelsea Palace of Varieties, which had been built by the Edwardians on the site of Wilkinson's sword factory opposite the Town Hall. The revue was called *Chelsea on Tiptoe* and its cast included Fay Compton, Lena Ashwell herself, Gerald du Maurier and Owen Nares. Augustus John designed the cover of the programme, which announced that Scene Four, *In Whistler's Studio*, had scenery made "from a design by Mr. Walter Greaves".

William Marchant was still giving him thirty shillings a week, but this had to be shared with Tinnie and Emily, and Walter's poverty was such that he was made small grants of money and gifts of clothing for himself and his sisters by The Artists' General Benevolent Institution. One opportunity to make a substantial amount of money did, however, occur. Since his discovery, Walter had remained friends with the bookseller Walter Spencer, who would say of him that he had never known a man "more destitute of heat or resentment". Sometimes Walter would make his way to the shop in New Oxford Street, where Marchant and Dowdeswell had found the rolls of old paintings. In summer, Spencer said, "he carried a cane, wore a yellow ribbon tie and carried lavender gloves and a light overcoat over his arm". In winter, the two men sat and talked over the fire in the back office. Sometimes they talked of Whistler and, on one such occasion, Greaves showed Spencer about thirty "very personal" letters that Whistler had written to him. Spencer read them through and said that they were extremely valuable. At once, Walter took them back from him, and, said Spencer, "tore the letters up and put them on the fire. 'They were private letters,' he said. 'Now I can never be tempted to destroy that privacy.' "

Now Walter was able to help a friend in distress. William Nicholson had suffered a shattering tragedy. His wife had caught influenza from their favourite son, who was on leave from France, and died. Within three months, the son was killed in action. Walter had often visited Nicholson at The Pheasantry and now he helped console him at his new studio in Eaton Square. Walter, for all his quaintness, had seemed a normal part of the Chelsea scene to Nicholson, but, seeing him among the elegant stucco-fronted terraces of Belgravia, he was struck by the engaging incongruity. In this studio one day, Walter leant against a white grand piano, forming a composition so curious that Nicholson asked him to pose for his portrait in that position and so produced one of his most striking paintings.

On one of his visits to Eaton Square, Walter found Nicholson painting a portrait of General Smuts, the South African war leader, and was introduced as "a famous painter".

"Well, Mr. Greaves," said Smuts. "So you're another of these London painters. Why don't you people come out to South Africa? You'd see some light and colour there."

"I don't know so much about that," replied Walter. "Jimmy says —"

"Jimmy?"

"Jimmy Whistler. Everybody knows Jimmy. Jimmy always said, in London there's atmosphere. You don't want all those bright colours, do you? A bit of Antwerp blue and white and black's all you want. And *paint thin*." When Walter took his leave, he turned at the door and repeated, "Don't forget, General, you don't want a lot of colour. You *paint thin*."

The war ended, the restfulness and sense of apartness from the metropolis that Chelsea still offered, again attracted those in search of both escape and excitement. The new fashion for "bed-sitters" brought in young people, young men starting careers in the City, as well as art and drama students, and all were avid for reminders of the imagined Golden Age of bohemianism and this Walter Greaves unconsciously helped provide. "Students congregate hither," ran one account of the immediate post-war Chelsea. "Here also are adventure, zest, experiment and every heresy and the gay camaraderie of Bohemia . . . One veteran Bohemian, who erstwhile worked in Whistler's studio and who was 'discovered' and had an exhibition of his own some years ago, flits through the streets like a shade with a portfolio under his arm."

When in Chelsea, Walter still made The Rising Sun his base for sketching and hawking expeditions. Small boys might jeer at him but here he was at least recognised. Ralph Burchett, son of the owner of stables in Old Church Street, often saw him at the door of the public house, when his father would say, "Oh, there's Mr. Greaves. I must have a word with him." Young Burchett remembered him at this time "always wearing a long cloak and a black, Spanish-type hat. A very sad man, he looked dejected."

No part of Chelsea had changed less than the narrow streets and courts behind the Old Church. A few of the old buildings had been converted into studios – it was in Justice Walk that Charles Wheeler had mistaken Rudyard Kipling for an encyclopaedia salesman when he called to commission a memorial plaque to his son, killed in the war. But it was still an astonishingly village-like community, noisy with horses' hooves and jingling harness, cocks crowing and the hissing of geese. Old Church Street was noted for its stables, some of them on two storeys communicating by a ramp, and at times more than a thousand horses were quartered there.

One young writer, Patrick Brand, acquiring a coveted garret in Chelsea, described the yards and gardens behind Cheyne Walk to the west of the Old Church. Beneath his window "arose the cackling of a neighbour's hens, the barking of a dog in one of the backyards, the clink of a spade in a back garden. When I opened my door . . . it was frequently to be confronted by the goose that for twelve years had made free of the street, disdaining dogs and motor cars and hissing its own back at the cats, and waddling unconcernedly into the passage and up the stairs of any house that left its front door open. Looking out over . . . the higgledy-piggledy collection of studios, chicken-runs, back-gardens, it needed the dull rumble of the traffic along the Embankment to our left and the King's Road away to our right to remind us that this was really London."

In 1919, the remnants of the Greaves family moved deeper into Fulham. Some relations lived in Lillie Road and, as both Tinnie and her elder sister, who was now in her eighties, were in poor health, Walter found lodgings next door, at Number 33. From here his shortest route to Chelsea lay through Brompton Cemetery, among the mausolea, catacombs and neo-Classical necropolis. Shuffling through the autumn leaves, Walter would pass the splendid *art nouveau*, copper-green tomb of Frederick Leyland and his wife.

Although he was now aged seventy-three, and was again emaciated through malnutrition, Walter was physically resilient. Yet, with his sisters failing, the prospect was one of loneliness, relieved only by visits to Chelsea, and eventually the prospect of old age in a workhouse. At this moment his fortune changed again, and by chance.

William Rothenstein had returned from painting the battlefields to move his family to London and, while searching for a suitable house, called on William Nicholson. In his studio he again met Walter Greaves. After the old man had left, Nicholson told Rothenstein of his plight and the two agreed that action must be taken. Walter must not only be provided for, they agreed, but honoured. A subscription list was opened by the Chelsea Arts Club and George Clausen arranged that the Royal Academy would make Walter an annual allowance of fifty pounds from the Turner Bequest.

In 1920, Walter Greaves attended another formal dinner at the Chelsea Arts Club, where Jimmy Whistler had snubbed him so brutally. This time he himself was the guest of honour. Lord Henry Bentinck was chairman and Walter Sickert the principal speaker. Many distinguished painters were there including some younger men without Whistlerian connections, such as the sculptor Roland Bevan, who came to do him honour, although privately considering him "a bit past it – always talking about 'Jimmy' and living in the past". Max Beerbohm, who had admired the Greaves exhibition of 1911, wanted to come but wrote to Rothenstein from Rapallo, "My dearest Will, I wish I could be at the dinner to Greaves. Put my name down by all means, and let me contribute to the 'purse'. How much are people giving? Would £5 be a correct sort of sum? If so, put me down for that, and I will send you a cheque." After the speeches of praise, the presentation was made. Rothenstein described the scene: "When a cheque for £150 was handed to Greaves he was quite taken aback; he had never, he said, had so much money in all his life! He spoke simply and unaffectedly of his years as a painter; had Pennell been present even his hostility to Greaves would have been disarmed."

Although full and untarnished recognition was at last his, and modest financial security assured, his sisters' health was a constant worry. In December, 1921, Tinnie died and, weakened by shock, Emily followed a few weeks later. But now Walter had powerful and generous friends and they were quick to help. As an immediate gesture of sympathy, the Chelsea Arts Club elected him an honorary member; ironically the only other painter to have been so honoured having been Sargent, who had sided with Pennell in 1911. Marchant set about arranging another exhibition at the Goupil Gallery. The loyal old artist friends took up Sickert's original suggestion that *Hammersmith Bridge on Boat Race Day* be bought for the nation and, to a fanfare of congratulations from the younger artists, it was bought by the Chantrey Bequest and put on permanent exhibition at the Tate Gallery. Thanking Rothenstein for his part in this, Walter wrote from Lillie Road, "I do feel really honoured that one of my pictures should be bought for the nation, and as you have always been so kindly disposed towards me and my work, I reckon that you have been very instrumental in bringing me forward before the public."

More had to be done, and the Artists' General Benevolent Institution applied, early in 1922, for his admission to the Charterhouse hostel for impoverished gentlemen as a Poor Brother. Their appeal was supported by Marchant ("Not only is Mr. Greaves a great artist . . . but also a perfectly honourable, straightforward and self-respecting man, a true and loyal friend."); Lord Henry Bentinck (". . . his kindly disposition and gentlemanly-like manner . . ."); Rothenstein (". . . modest and uncomplaining, full of zest for work and of interest in life . . ."); Nicholson (". . . unfailing pluck and energy. If any first-class painter ever deserved a comfortable old age it is certainly Walter Greaves . . ."); and Clutton-Brock of *The Times* (". . . a remarkable and accomplished artist, the value of whose work is obscured for some by that simplicity which is one of its greatest virtues. For many years he has practised the art of painting patiently and most disinterestedly, without receiving the rewards or recognition which were long ago his due. Therefore his character no less than his talent deserves admiration. If he had practised the arts that win popularity, he might long ago have been rich."). Eulogies came also from Charles Aitken, the Director of the National Gallery of British Art ("The Tate"); Ronald Gray, the honorary secretary of the Chelsea Arts Club; and Archdeacon Bevan, Rector of Chelsea, who described him as "a man of outstanding genius . . . greatly respected throughout this Borough."

Meanwhile Marchant was preparing the exhibition, which opened in May. Of nearly a hundred pictures, half were watercolours, many of them the large Chelsea views which Walter and Henry had worked on together and jointly signed. It was the first time these watercolours had been exhibited outside the windows of Chelsea shops or, earlier, in the Greaves's boatyard, and Marchant included in his catalogue some of Walter's reminiscences of Victorian Chelsea. In his foreword, Marchant renewed his counter-attacks on the Pennells, whose final slurs had just been published in *The Whistler Journal*, describing them as "those people who in the past were audacious enough to accuse Mr. Walter Greaves of having appropriated as his own productions certain works which really were Whistler's" and who had "striven to keep alive the atmosphere of suspicion". But this time he was taking no chances and wrote that "as the publication of one single date in the catalogue of the 1911 exhibition resulted in certain people losing their heads, and – in consequence of their antics – others nearly losing their reputations, Mr. Greaves and I decided to erase all dates from the present exhibits, except those which were engraved on the copper plates."

The exhibition was no echo of the sensation of 1911, but it was a modest success, giving Walter Greaves an assured place among English topographical artists and offering a graceful tribute to the work of his brother. Although these pictures did not aim so high as his oils, the newspaper and magazine notices were appreciative and *The Times* concluded a long review on a note which stood as the basis of future recognition of his work: "Mr. Greaves is not a great artist as Rembrandt or Titian is great. He is limited, provincial, naïve; but his sincerity has a kind of greatness in it and makes even his inferior work interesting . . . when he is good, he is very, very good; and when he is bad, he is still Greaves."

At this time Manchester City Art Gallery acquired both his largest and one of his most striking canvases, *Chelsea Regatta*, and Nicholson's portrait of him beside the white piano.

Marchant and Rothenstein helped with the plans for retirement and soon the latter could write, "There was no difficulty in Greaves entering the Charterhouse. 'No expenses, a pound a week pocket money and everyone kind!' It was luxury for Greaves. But when I went to visit him, his hair, which had been unnaturally black, through the offices of the Matron and a cake of soap, had turned white in a single afternoon."

It was a wrench to leave the familiar streets of Chelsea and Fulham, for the Charterhouse was in the City, near Smithfield. But Walter took with him his sketching materials and continued to draw Chelsea from memory, decorating his little room with some of his smallest paintings. He kept, too, the old portfolio, stuffed with drawings he no longer needed to sell, including a pencil sketch of the young Jimmy Whistler on the back of a printed table of distances by water from London Bridge. Marchant stored quantities of canvases – Nocturnes, river scenes, portraits of Whistler, laughing or scowling, portraits of Tinnie and Henry striking the haughty poses that Jimmy had liked – together with stacks of drawings and etchings. Among the few he could keep to admire was a little framed sketch of Cremorne lit by fireworks, shadowy figures among the trees.

William Marchant remained a staunch friend, inviting Walter to spend his summer holidays at Hove, where he had a house. There, his young daughter Josephine would play Strauss waltzes on the piano and Walter himself would beat time, or himself try to strum the tunes he had heard on the dancing platform at Cremorne. Josephine was acutely embarrassed at having to take him for walks along the sea-front, where she might be seen by her friends because, particularly in Hove, Walter cut a remarkably eccentric figure. His final recognition had given him confidence, and he attempted to carry himself with the style of, say, Nicholson, or John, or even Jimmy. "He was not exactly a dandy," Josephine Marchant remembered. "But he was particular about his appearance although he was rather frayed."

Then, in 1925, William Marchant died suddenly at the age of fifty-seven. He was sadly mourned by the artists, Sickert writing in *The Times* that "he was so naturally honourable and generous that it never occurred to him that he was either the one or the other", and having "inherited from the period of Whistler the hobby of perpetual controversy" had "fought like a merry tiger to rehabilitate Walter Greaves and place him in the position of dignity and comfort that this country owed him". His widow, Cicely, took over the direction of the Goupil Gallery and moved to London. Walter would be invited to dine and play the piano at their house in St. John's Wood and he visited Mrs. Marchant at the gallery. On Quarter Day he would always call on her there to collect his allowance from the Royal Academy, and afterwards take her out to tea in a café with a quartet, which would play nothing more modern than Gilbert and Sullivan. In 1929, he attended Josephine's wedding, being given a chair beside the bride at the garden reception. He sat there, a black Homburg hat tilted forward on his thick white hair, smoking cigarettes, seeming to be conscious of recognition as a celebrity.

At the Charterhouse, he spent much time painting and drawing Chelsea from memory and set off on long walks through the City each day, dressed in a soft black hat, long coat, fawn gloves and yellow tie. As one of the sixty Brothers, he lived among elderly men from backgrounds socially superior to his own, yet was always considered not only "quaint" and "lovable", but "gentlemanly". Always, when setting out on his expeditions which were often to watch shipping from Blackfriars Bridge, he would exchange pleasantries with the porter, who remembered, "He said he loved music, but that when music was sent out into the air it was lost, while the thoughts one put on canvas were there for all time."

Chelsea, so much in his thoughts, was now half an hour's journey away by motor-bus. Much of it appeared exactly as he had known it. The little family businesses were still there and the old inns. Bowls were still played on the green behind The Six Bells, and Chelsea Pensioners were ready to tell stories in return for pints of beer, but now about Germans and Turks as well as Boers and Zulus. The place was still alive with artists and, even if some were now rich enough to have moved to houses in Sussex or the Cotswolds, they still visited the Chelsea Arts Club. Sargent and Conder were both dead, but Nicholson, Rothenstein, Clausen, Sickert, Steer, Orpen and, of course, John were still painting. Now his old friends were distinguished painters: Nicholson, Rothenstein, Beerbohm, Clausen and Orpen to be knighted, John to be awarded the Order of Merit.

Chelsea had become not only the artists' quarter but the artists' caravanserai and, at some time during the 'twenties and 'thirties, everyone of note was to be seen there visiting if not working. The sculptor Jacob Epstein became a notable Chelsea figure and Henry Moore and the painter Graham Sutherland both taught at the Chelsea School of Art. In their wake was arriving a new migration of the intelligent middle class, who might be working in the theatre, publishing, journalism or the new British Broadcasting Corporation. It became the fashion for "newly-weds" to set up house in small Chelsea houses and, in 1925, a stir was caused by the conversion of a Georgian slum-cottage into a smart little town house with green shutters.

To those brought up in the austere cliff-dwellings of Kensington and Bayswater, the discovery of Chelsea was a revelation. Behind the enchanted sweep of Chelsea Reach, lilac and laburnum overhung Tudor walls and gas-light illuminated Queen Anne façades. There were the cries of lavender-sellers; the muffin-man with his bell, balancing a tray of muffins covered with green baize upon his head; street-singers; and an old couple, who would appear after the lamp-lighter had made his rounds, wheeling in a small perambulator a harp to be played in the pools of light beneath gas-standards which had lit Chelsea since Walter Greaves was a boy.

On Saturdays, costermongers returning from Hampstead Heath to Battersea and Brixton, rattled through Chelsea in their painted pony-carts and stopped to drink and dance to barrel-organs outside the public houses. At the Chelsea Palace of Varieties a seat could be had for ninepence and then roller-skating rinks were converted into cinemas, and, finally, palatial cinemas with electric organs cast a red glare of neon-signs into the night above the King's Road. Despite the long habitation of the Sitwells – Edith, Osbert and Sacheverel – in Carlyle Square, Chelsea was never to be fully established as an intellectual quarter, such as Bloomsbury or Hampstead. In the late 'thirties, the boisterous studio party, or the display of television after dinner to guests in evening dress, was customary entertainment.

Chelsea, like Whistler, was always ready to mock pretentious intellectual fashion. In the 'thirties, a Chelsea novelist, Guy Pocock, wrote the story of a middle-aged schoolmaster, Stubbs, venturing into the farther fringes of the *avant-garde*:

" 'Are you an artist, sir?' asked Stubbs.

" 'Indeed I hope so,' said Gabriel.

" 'A painter?'

" 'Indeed no. I am a poet.'

" 'How interesting!' said Stubbs with his disarming smile. 'Have you written anything lately? Anything that I might hear, I mean?'

" 'I don't write my poems,' said Gabriel, smoothing his little silky moustache. 'And you can't hear them. They are not verbal or articulate; they are subjective and intercommunicative. You see, I compose object-poems only.'

" 'Oh, really?' said Stubbs. (I *must* get out of the way of saying 'Oh, really?' he added mentally. But people in Chelsea did say such incomprehensible things that as often as not it was impossible for him to say anything else.)

" 'I have an object-poem here, which I have been composing during the last three weeks,' said Gabriel; and proceeded to draw from his pocket a flat cardboard box which reminded Stubbs of the larger Valentine-cases of his extreme youth.

" 'I call this *The White Soul's Wish*,' said Gabriel, opening the Valentine-box and displaying certain objects fastened on to the bottom with white cotton – two white feathers, a white shoe-lace, a plaster-of-Paris egg, two bone buttons, and a cockle-shell and a Turkish cigarette. There was no writing, no explanatory sign of any sort.

" '*The White Soul's Wish*,' Gabriel repeated softly. 'You can see how the poise of the feathers and the rhythm of position give what one might call optative quality to the general falling cadence.'

" 'Oh, really?' said Stubbs."

However much the migrants from the professional classes might appreciate Chelsea, their arrival brought about some drastic changes where landowners recognised the possibilities of exploitation. The principal private landowners were the heirs of Sir Hans Sloane, the Sloane Stanley and Cadogan families. In 1927, Major Cyril Sloane Stanley announced his intention of demolishing Lombard Terrace and replacing it with luxurious houses of pseudo-Georgian design. At once a petition of protest was organised by the Chelsea Society, which had been founded in that year by Reginald Blunt, the son of a rector of Chelsea, to prevent a recurrence of a tragedy such as the demolition of Paradise Row by the Cadogans. Lombard Terrace was a row of four houses surviving in Cheyne Walk to the west of the Old Church, the last reminder there of the pre-Embankment scene. Describing Lombard Terrace as "the most beautiful spot of old Chelsea that is left to us", Sir William Orpen wrote that the proposed destruction made him weep. But it was to no avail for, as Blunt recorded, "the matter was, as the owner frankly admitted, a financial business" and Lombard Terrace was doomed, although its demolition was, in fact, preceded by that of some old houses on the far side of the Old Church, including the last fragment of Shrewsbury House.

At the same time, destruction on a far larger scale was being planned in Chelsea by the Cadogans. This aroused much less concern than Lombard Terrace because, as *The Times* remarked of the buildings concerned, "it cannot be said that they have any historic or sentimental value". They had however sentimental value, at least, to the hundreds of working-class families who lived in the little Georgian streets between the King's Road and Fulham Road, to the east of St. Luke's Church.

Evictions were not new in Chelsea. In 1909, the *Daily Chronicle* reported that over twenty thousand people were to be driven from the borough and "the members of one particular family enriched". But Edwardian tenants were more docile than Londoners who had experienced the First World War and the General Strike of 1926.

In 1929, Earl Cadogan sold fourteen acres of Chelsea to Sir John Ellerman in what *The Times* considered "the most important transaction in real estate that has been announced for a long time". Streets of cottages, most of them in bad structural condition, were to be levelled on either side of Sloane Avenue and blocks of flats erected in their place. The original inhabitants, some of them belonging to families that had lived there for more than a century, were to be evicted.

This time there was no petition signed by aesthetes, but the formation of a Defence Army by the tenants. A force of three hundred men – "Most of us are ex-Servicemen, so we know how to arrange it," said one – took over the streets and *The Star* reported, "A portion of Chelsea has been turned into an armed camp. Despatch riders, both cycle and motor-cycle, spies, look-outs, and men carrying thick sticks are in every portion of the area concerned. There are at the same time at least a score of police and C.I.D. men as well." The tenants prepared to defend their homes with force and, although militant Socialists and probably Communists were among the leaders, the *Evening News* reported that "bearded artists in black hats" were emerging in numbers from their studios to offer their support. A wave of shocked sensibility spread through middle-class Chelsea.

Despite the Defence Army, the tenants stood no chance. Police dispersed street meetings as the bailiffs took over the property, house by house. For a few days, rioting seemed possible, then *The Star* reporter wrote, "Several families already have been turned out and the doors of their houses padlocked by the agents. Four families, with nowhere to go, went into the workhouse, and one man of 70 had to be taken there in a taxi by the bailiffs who evicted him . . . The next man who has to go, we hear, is an ex-soldier named Kelly. He has six little children and lost a leg in the war."

The outcome was inevitable. The thousands of personal tragedies were remembered in smouldering resentment not only in Chelsea but wherever the exiles finally settled. The evictions of 1909 and 1929 were primarily responsible for the population of Chelsea declining in the first thirty years of the twentieth century by thirty-six thousand.

The street scenes that vanished from Chelsea remained in the memory of Walter Greaves. "I think I could draw all old Chelsea by heart," he told a visitor. "I don't suppose I'd get it extraordinarily exact, but I can *see* the place all right as I do it."

The visitor was young John Rothenstein, son of William, just down from Oxford and preparing his first book, *The Artists of the 1890's*. Writing to ask for an interview, he had received a warm reply, asking him to come after lunch one day, adding, "I suppose I can call myself 'a bit of old Chelsea', the Old Bridge Houses and Cremorne Gardens have all vanished, I often think of those happy days there, please remember me to your Parents . . ." Rothenstein found Walter "one of the most delightful old men I have ever met: enthusiastic, serene, utterly without guile or ill-will".

Greaves's place in this book, which was published in 1928, was beside Sickert, Steer, Conder, Beardsley, Ricketts and Shannon, Beerbohm, William Rothenstein and Whistler. Described as "one of the most important artists of the period", Walter, wrote John Rothenstein, was "a man for whom the world, with its controversies, its admirations, its hatreds, has no meaning . . . His own attitude towards his work is fully contained in a reply to a question once put to him. We were talking of his boyhood, and I asked him how early he started to paint. 'I never could help it,' he said, 'Chelsea was so beautiful that you couldn't but paint.' Such an attitude makes theory superfluous. Pride and jealousy had no place in his character, but all the while he had a consciousness of his own power, a sense of satisfaction which came from the ability to express his innermost feelings. But transcending all other differences between himself and Whistler was the fact that he was entirely unlike his cosmopolitan master in being intensely national, even local, in his outlook and his technique . . . Greaves about whom there was always something childlike and direct went straight for the qualities which he felt."

Like all who understood Greaves, Rothenstein was moved by his story and concluded his chapter, "And when we last parted, and I saw him – a small, grey, lonely figure in the sunlight, waving me goodbye from his door in the Charterhouse – I became poignantly aware of his situation. Nor was it possible for me to remain unmoved in the contemplation of this aged man, one of the great artists of his time, sitting alone and forgotten in his little room, sketching old Chelsea from memory because he 'couldn't pass the time without it'. And the man who first hid his light under a bushel was his jealous god, Whistler."

This meeting had a lasting effect upon Rothenstein and he wrote, "The consequence of my coming to know Greaves was to make me feel it both a privilege and a duty to preserve against oblivion some memorials, however slight, of artists I have known – especially those whom fashionable opinion passes by."

It was extraordinary and appropriate that this same young art historian, son of one of his most faithful friends, should, more than twenty years later, become the Director of the Tate Gallery, having in his care not only *Hammersmith Bridge on Boat Race Day* but seven other of Greaves's paintings. It was largely due to Rothenstein's enthusiasm that Greaves's recognition by those whose opinions mattered was kept alive, because he feared that *Hammersmith Bridge* had "assumed the character of an anonymous masterpiece, like a folk song or a medieval building, than of the work of a particular man". Nearly forty years after their meeting, Sir John Rothenstein, living in Chelsea, remembered, "Walter Greaves was a charming old man. He had a gentle, rather hoarse voice and spoke deliberately and utterly without guile. He seemed fatalistic but pleased that I had visited him.

"His *Hammersmith Bridge* far surpasses anything else of its sort in the nineteenth century. His paintings of Chelsea have a candour and sense of 'place' that has never been sufficiently appreciated. Like Utrillo's feeling for Paris, Greaves evokes Chelsea. If he had been an American or French painter he would have been held in immense regard."

Rothenstein was to regret that he could pay no further visits to Greaves, but many of his old friends, including Walter Spencer, were to feel the same. Twice before he had faded from memories and now, cared for in the Charterhouse, but still a relic from a vanished past, few remembered that he was still alive.

The beginning of the 'thirties were celebrated at the Chelsea Arts Ball in the Albert Hall with a fancy-dress extravaganza. The setting, designed by Augustus John, was on the theme of Noah's Ark, but for the grand parade the Slade School of Art designed a torpedo-shaped float representing that unimaginable possibility, a rocket-ship to be fired to the Moon. Five thousand dancers swirled through the great rotunda, reminiscent both of Ranelagh and Cremorne, ushered by such stewards as Orpen, Steer, Captain Adrian Jones, H. M. Bateman, the cartoonist, and, of course, Augustus John. For, in succession to Rossetti and Whistler, John was now king in Chelsea.

By 1930, Walter Greaves had had to give up painting, but was still able to sketch. He passed his eighty-fourth birthday that July, but now his closest surviving relations were the two sons of his elder brother, Charles, one of whom had emigrated to Australia and the other, Archibald, settled in Bristol to work as a French-polisher, although he, too, had ambitions as an artist. Yet Walter seemed to have achieved a serenity in his memories of the past and, at the Charterhouse, he was surrounded with affection. In November he collapsed in the dining-room and was taken to hospital. Pneumonia developed and on the twenty-third of that month he died. That evening, the bell of the Charterhouse tolled a curfew of fifty-nine notes as was the custom when one of the sixty Brothers was gone.

Fleet Street was generous with its obituaries and the sensation of 1911 was described beneath headlines that recalled those heady weeks. His fellow-artists were appreciative. Augustus John was quoted as saying, "I greatly admired Walter Greaves as an artist and loved him as a man. He went through life unembittered by adversity, retaining to the end his simplicity, sweetness and integrity of character." William Rothenstein, who was to be knighted the following year, said "I believe his work will live".

Walter Greaves was buried in the Charterhouse cemetery in the churchyard at Little Hallingbury, near Bishop's Stortford, in Essex, beside the lych-gate. Among those who followed his body was Marchant's loyal widow, who sadly said, "It was pitiable to see that only myself and one or two others who had known him were present at the funeral of a distinguished artist and, in his day, a really great man". Walter had died intestate but surprisingly having saved three hundred pounds. The lack of a will can only have been due to his impracticability, for the Marchants received just his own collection of his favourite work, his unsold pictures and a large, shabby portfolio, once so familiar in Chelsea.

The following year she arranged a memorial exhibition at the Goupil Gallery, and, while Whistler lay beneath a bronze cenotaph beside the Thames, and Greaves beneath a small institutional headstone in Essex, the old controversy flickered again. "Whistler himself was happiest in evasion while Greaves was by nature explicit, and, moreover, his art was positively inspired by the subject interest that Whistler thought unimportant," ran the notice in *The Times*. "The example of Greaves is, in fact, a standing proof of the inadequacy of Whistler's aesthetic gospel – except as a means of concealing his own limitations."

Their own passions spent, the thoughts of the two men were, as Walter Greaves had said to the porter, "on canvas for all time". Nor was their art their sole memorial. It remains at Chelsea, soon after the setting of the sun. As the light lessens, the shapes of ships and barges, warehouses and factories are thrown into strong relief, the tide flows and this is the river of Walter Greaves. Then the light blurs and the poor buildings lose themselves in the dim sky and the tall chimneys become campanili and the warehouses are palaces in the night and this is the river of Whistler. But, for a few moments in the fading of the light, it belongs to them both.

9
Epilogue

Chelsea had evolved into the artists' quarter of London over a century. This began with Turner and reached its climax with John, and, of the hundreds of artists who worked there, none lived there longer or painted it more lovingly than Walter Greaves. His life covered almost the span of this century, he flitting through its changing scenery like some mythological spirit. Long after he had gone, his friends would find themselves imagining that they had caught a glimpse of him, portfolio under arm, lit for a moment by gas-light or vanishing round the corner into Justice Walk.

The century can be defined as 1840 to 1940. It began with the creak and splash of oars as a boat from Greaves's yard, introduced Turner, and then Whistler, to the river and it ended to the howl of air-raid sirens along Cheyne Walk. With its naval and military academies, the Royal Hospital and its barracks, Chelsea had never been far from the thought of war, but – apart from the random dropping of a few small bombs from German Zeppelins during the First World War – it had not known the reality since the Romans fought for its ford.

That this innocence, too, was about to be lost was already apparent when the artists' colony still flourished. In 1937, the year before Hitler invaded Austria, the retired admiral in charge of Air Raid Precautions in the borough warned, "Chelsea is strategically probably one of the most vulnerable boroughs and the one which is likely to be singled out for the brunt of the air raids." To those living in the quiet backstreets, involved in bowls at The Six Bells, the Chelsea Gardens Guild or the Chelsea Arts Ball, this might, at first, have seemed alarmist. But news from Ethiopia and Spain and still-vivid memories of Flanders had been a warning. Chelsea was surrounded by potential targets. On the western boundary, Lots Road power-station; across the river to the east, Battersea power-station and gas-works. Crossing the river, three road bridges and two railway bridges, the westerly of the latter linking the southern and northern main-line systems. There was Chelsea Barracks, of course, but, more dangerous, were Westminster and Whitehall lying a few seconds' flying-time to the east.

Chelsea prepared seriously for war and, in 1938, at the time of the Munich crisis, the ARP services received fifty-three thousand gas-masks and one hundred and sixty-three thousand sand-bags. Trenches were dug in squares and gardens, basement rooms of middle-class houses were made "gas-proof" and, at the height of the crisis, the gas-masks were issued. But there was to be a reprieve for a year, so this was a dress-rehearsal.

When war came, Chelsea was as well-prepared as any civil community in Europe. While the Guards marched out of Chelsea Barracks and the Territorials mobilised at the Duke of York's Headquarters and the children of Chelsea were evacuated to the country, the remaining citizens prepared for aerial bombardment. This did not come for nearly a year, so, once the preparations were complete, there was time to become accustomed to a new environment of empty roads and dark nights. Again, perhaps for the first time since Whistler painted his Nocturnes, there was a consciousness of the beauty of night. But after the evening mist clothed the riverside with poetry as with a veil, as Whistler had seen it, there were now no golden pin-points of light to be reflected on the water, no moving patterns of colour at Cremorne. A ghost of Old Battersea Bridge was conjured up when a wooden bridge was built, to replace any that were bombed, between Cheyne Walk and Battersea Park in an unconscious and unnoticed arrangement for a Nocturne.

The first German bomb exploded in Burton's Court, outside the Royal Hospital, at the end of August, 1940, and the curious were charged sixpence towards a patriotic fund for a close look. During the next five years the six hundred and sixty acres of Chelsea were struck by more than three hundred and twenty high-explosive missiles and many thousands of incendiary bombs. Of its population, reduced by half to about thirty thousand, five hundred and thirty-four were killed and hundreds wounded. Hundreds of houses were destroyed, or damaged beyond repair, and few remained unscathed.

It was a long ordeal marked by what were officially described as "incidents" of exceptional ferocity. One evening in November, 1940, a bomb struck Sloane Square underground station as the staff canteen was crowded with a new shift of railway workers coming on duty. "Two great flaming jets guarded the pit which had once been the station," wrote one who was there. "The bomb had severed the gas main . . . and the newly-built station had just disappeared into the depth below . . . The bomb had fallen as a train was leaving the station, and the rear carriage was caught directly – the remainder of the train was shot by the blast almost to South Kensington station. This incident was most ghastly as regards the holocaust of human flesh . . ." Dustbins were filled with arms and legs and, three days later, thirty-eight bodies had been assembled from fragments and seventeen of those who had been in the station could only be reported as missing.

A crowded shelter in Beaufort Street was struck with heavy loss of life and houses were blown to rubble singly and in groups. The most memorable night was in April, 1941, when parachute-mines designed to produce maximum lateral blast, were dropped on Chelsea. One of these exploded at the base of the Old Church tower. The church itself – and the five ARP workers within – were destroyed, as were the mock-Georgian houses that had recently replaced Lombard Terrace and mingled together in heaps of Caroline and 'thirties bricks. The loss of the church and its familiar, reassuring tower, shocked Chelsea more than any other destruction in London. At dawn next morning, an ARP worker described his first sight of the ruin: "It twitched the heart to look at it; and a small group of people were standing by the barrier across the road like mourners at the grave of Chelsea's first monument."

The Blitz of 1940 and 1941 was followed by a comparative lull until, at the beginning of 1944, the *Luftwaffe* delivered a series of sharp night attacks on London. These raids, although shorter than the night-long throbbing of bombers' engines of that first autumn, winter and spring, were made in the face of powerful defences, so that the explosions of bombs and the glare of fires were often lost in the noise and light of the defending guns, rockets and searchlights which, over Chelsea, presented a display of pyrotechnics such as the most ambitious impresario at Cremorne can never have imagined in his most fevered moments.

On one such night, as German aircraft were caught in the beams of dozens of searchlights and streams of red tracer-shells converged upon them, one dived over Chelsea and watchers on rooftops saw a huge billow of red smoke erupt from the site of Cremorne. The bomb-load had missed the power-station but struck blocks of low-rent flats and, in the bloodiest moment of the war in Chelsea, seventy-five people were killed.

Andrew Butler, an architect employed to report on the condition of bomb-damaged houses, left telling reports of the interiors of Chelsea homes. After a bomb had opened a block of flats like the front of a dolls' house, he wrote: "Take a typical drawing-room in one of these flats, probably belonging to an old-fashioned and comfortably-off couple. The walls covered almost entirely with pictures, chiefly of sentimental value only. A thick carpet with mats on top of it. An elaborate brass fender requiring constant polish. Two sofas, several armchairs and a large number of odd chairs standing about all over the room, most with elaborate arms and legs inviting dust. One small bookcase, glass-fronted and holding the memoirs of colonial officials and books on shooting. On top of this, two large vases with flowers and five or six framed photographs, standing in echelon. A green lacquer cabinet on a stand with gilt legs, very fine and rich, with a large Chinese pot on it and more flowers in that. Then two occasional tables, both with spindly legs and glass tops and precious things inside – snuff-boxes, rings, little ivory plaques, with a fan or two. And a thing the French call a *vitrine* – a glass cabinet on legs with rare pieces of china on its shelves and a bit of carved jade or a jewelled and painted box. Finally, a small and elegant writing-table with drawers at each side shaped to its pretty curling front, with a silver-covered blotter on it and behind the blotter a receptacle for notepaper, delicately made in rosewood. A large ink-pot – well-filled – stood beside that and a big framed photograph of a girl in Court dress, looking happy and signed in a scrawled hand 'your loving Marcia'. Imagine all that, nice and tidy and dusted daily . . .

"Then visualize it wrecked as I found it. All the plaster off the ceiling, of course; the door just splinters and the windows voids. Plaster off the walls, too – bulged inwards by the blast and knocking everything towards the centre of the room . . . That writing-table had its back broken and its drawers were burst open on the floor, so that I saw – projecting from the usual plaster filth – bundles of old letters, receipts and documents which looked like securities and insurance certificates or even wills. The *vitrine*, in a French frenzy, had flung itself face downwards, bursting . . . so that there was an intermingled mass of Old Chelsea, Spode and Worcester vomited on the carpet. I walked on powdered Sèvres and caught my foot in something hard and cutting which was Marcia's crumpled silver frame and her photograph torn across. The whole muddle was so hateful that – for an instant – I almost hoped the owners of these things had perished too."

Sometimes they had, as when Butler saw the body of a dead woman wrapped in a blanket: "Only her feet and ankles showed at the end of the bundle – neat and pretty ankles with silk stockings and nice shoes. But the feet to me seemed the wrong way round . . ."

Most Chelsea houses were not so substantial. Instead, wrote Butler, "about eighty years old, neat and ladylike in front, plain and sometimes squalid at the back . . . Three storeys and a basement; the bulge at the back; a strip of garden; a slate roof with a leaking valley in the middle; often a pillared porch, steep steps and some crumbling stucco enrichments . . . They were not built for resisting blast."

Distinctions of class and riches had seldom been marked in Chelsea and now virtually disappeared. In what came to be called Civil Defence and in the Home Guard militia, efficiency was the criterion.

Patriotism, national and local, was intense and, despite the recurring horrors, morale remained high. Two elderly sisters, who ran a boarding-house in Oakley Street, refused to increase their modest rents throughout the war "because that's what Hitler wants us to do". A young librarian volunteered for the most grisly tasks in the mortuary because "somebody has to do it". Brave acceptance was normal behaviour. John Strachey, who was to become a Minister in the post-war Labour Government, recalled that one evening before the sirens sounded "a Chelsea Pensioner, his full-dress, cherry coat glowing in the last of the light, came slowly down the street . . . He said, with great simplicity, 'Have the angels of death begun to sing yet?' Probably you had to live in the Royal Hospital and to be eighty years old to get away with a remark like that."

The Royal Hospital and its grounds were struck by a parachute-mine, twenty-four high-explosive bombs – of which ten failed to detonate – and more than a hundred incendiary bombs, killing more than twenty old soldiers and members of the staff. The last missile to strike Chelsea, hit the hospital. A medical officer there had decided not to send his young family away from London because, he used to joke, his house had been struck by a Zeppelin bomb in The Great War and this could not possibly happen again. Early one morning in January, 1945, a V2 rocket dived out of the stratosphere on to his house killing all within.

The life of the artists' community survived fitfully, but Chelsea was the scene of a remarkable confrontation. General Sir Bernard Montgomery had returned to London from commanding the Eighth Army in North Africa and Italy, to lead the invasion of France, and, in the spring of 1944, commissioned Augustus John to paint his portrait. One day, while Montgomery was in the Tite Street studio, George Bernard Shaw was announced. This meeting of the practical soldier and the philosophical pacifist was as remarkable a confrontation as that of Whistler and Carlyle. There was a display of Shavian banter.

"General, I will tell you when the war is going to end," said Shaw. "When money goes to five per cent. All wars end then."

The two men liked each other and later that day Shaw wrote to John, "This afternoon I had to talk all over the shop to amuse your sitter and keep his mind off the worries of the present actual fighting. And as I could see him with one eye and you with the other – two great men at a glance – I noted the extreme likeness between you." And the difference. "You, large, tall, blond, were almost massive in contrast with that intensely compacted hank of steel wire, who looked as if you might have taken him out of your pocket."

The end of the Second World War, about four months after the rocket struck the Royal Hospital demonstrating the likely form of future wars, was followed by what seemed like years of penance. Food rationing was more rigorous than it had been in wartime, the roads remained empty and, with moral and material austerity, the new Labour Government began trying to piece the nation together again. At first it seemed that Chelsea would, in time, find its way back to the privileged niche it had made for itself in the capital. Living remained cheap, for most of the mid-Victorian houses on the big privately-owned estates were still let on long leases at rents which had seemed economic in the nineteenth century. The boarding-houses filled with young people returning from war service to resume or begin academic or professional education. The pleasures of Chelsea were its few little restaurants, its cheerful public houses, its cinemas and, as after the First World War, relaxed sexual morality for which the gentle bohemianism of the place provided a quietly romantic setting.

It was immediately clear that life for the artists would not be as it had been, at least for some years to come. Photography had almost entirely replaced graphic illustration, although there was still a demand for humorous drawing and cartoons. Few of the former patron class could now afford to commission portraits. Advertising remained the one expanding field for the artist. By 1950, it was estimated that as many as ninety per cent of the artists still working in Chelsea depended for their livelihood upon commercial art.

This, it was realised, need only be a temporary slump. Soon artists would be able to combine their chosen work with some teaching in new art schools. Television and increasing popular interest in design would offer opportunities. With increasing national prosperity there would again be a demand for portraiture and for drawing-room pictures and book illustrations, as two brilliant and very different Chelsea artists, Sir Alfred Munnings and Mervyn Peake, were to show. Later, without doubt, there would be a demand for further experimentation in painting and new markets for lithographs, etchings and reproductions as well as originals. This, indeed, was to come.

The principal long-term doubt was whether artists would be able to remain in Chelsea. At the beginning of the 'fifties it was reckoned that of some three hundred professional artists working in Chelsea, less than half had their own studios. Before the war, there had been three hundred and sixteen studios designed as such (as well as countless others converted from shops, garages and out-houses). Of these, about thirty were destroyed during the war and so many damaged that at least fifty more could no longer be used. During the war, when many artists had been away, others had been taken over and some converted for other purposes. It was now said that twenty-four had become offices or warehouses, twelve were the homes of writers or musicians and another eighty-seven occupied by new arrivals with no connection with the arts.

The artists struggled to retain a hold on their quarter. They exhibited through their societies, and a few local galleries and continued to raise funds for the Chelsea Arts Club at the New Year's Eve ball, although this was becoming less of a frolic and more of a beery roughhouse each year. Chelsea Borough Council promised to build studios as an integral part of new housing development and successfully did so. But it was still easy for landlords to raise the rents of the studios and replace the artists by prosperous settlers, to whom the idea of comfortable – and usually respectable – bohemianism appealed.

The social and economic forces brought to bear upon Chelsea would have quickly overwhelmed a more resilient community. Since the war, Mayfair, the smartest residential district of London since the eighteenth century, had been invaded by commerce. Great houses, which none but millionaires could afford to maintain privately, became offices, or were demolished to make way for blocks with maximum floor-space. The migration was again westward. Bayswater, once so grand, had become one of the shabbiest quarters of London during the war, and now its northern reaches were filling up with Irish labourers engaged on the rebuilding of London. Kensington remained, prim and expensive as before, and only Chelsea seemed to offer an agreeable escape, for those who could afford it, from the pressures of city life.

While the artistic life of Chelsea declined, other strains in its ancestry came to the surface. For the first time since the closing of Cremorne, it became a place of popular entertainment. The Festival of Britain in 1951 brought some pleasure gardens to Battersea Park, cluttering the beautiful river walk with kiosks and mechanical fairground machines. Across the river, the longing for a return to good eating and drinking was at last satisfied. On Sunday mornings, young people took to drinking beer as near to the river as possible, notably at and around the King's Head and Eight Bells, still a Victorian public house patronised by artists, Chelsea Pensioners and darts-players. Then the first of many small, expensive restaurants of quality – The Ox on the Roof – opened in the King's Road. A few years later, came the first of the coffee bars, where young men and girls could flirt over small cups of strong coffee extracted from gleaming, steaming Italian coffee-machines. Chelsea began to compete with Soho in the variety of its gastronomic attractions and, for the sentimentalist, there was a temptation to trace this trend as far back as the Bun House, Don Saltero's and Cremorne. All had been established because of Chelsea's reputation as a place for physical relaxation and mental stimulation.

Just as Ranelagh had attracted a type then known as "The Chelsea Macaroni", so, in the 'fifties, appeared another recognisable type, known collectively as "The Chelsea Set". Few of them seemed to live in the borough, but had been attracted by the whimsical descriptions of Bohemia-on-Thames, which still appeared in newspapers, and were themselves soon to become material for gossip-columnists as avid as "Bo-Peep". The sons and daughters of well-to-do parents, and their raffish camp-followers, affected unconventional dress, either a careful disarray, or an over-emphasised Edwardian dash. But they contributed little to contemporary life and were, in fact, as transient and of no more consequence than "The Bright Young Things" had been thirty years earlier, except that they emphasised the exhibitionist but unproductive aspects of Chelsea character.

This was offset by a sudden and unexpected revival of the theatre in Chelsea. Although actors and actresses had long lived in Chelsea – with the actor-producer Sir Lewis Casson and his wife Dame Sybil Thorndike as their loved and unchallenged king and queen for half a century – the amount of theatrical activity within the borough had been small. But the small Royal Court Theatre in Sloane Square had achieved a reputation for productions modest in scale but high in quality. Among these were the series of farces by Sir Arthur Pinero in the eighteen-eighties, and, in the years before 1914, plays by George Bernard Shaw and W. Somerset Maugham. Such success did not last and, during the 'thirties, the theatre was used as a cinema. Then, in 1956, the year of the Suez War and of suddenly heightened political awareness among young people, its fortunes changed when it was acquired by the new English Stage Company.

During the first two years of the new management, thirty-two plays, most of them new, were produced at Sloane Square. Of the young playwrights, whose work made so revolutionary an impact upon the British theatre, the archetype was John Osborne, who first attracted attention with his *Look Back in Anger*. There was more than a dash of Whistler in Osborne's public personality and attitudes. England and the English seemed to arouse in him – as in Whistler – both heat and warmth, affection and rage, venom and nostalgia. Like many young theatre people of his generation he suffered political passions, following a Leftward course, but enjoyed the profits earned by his plays and film interests and settled among the rich in the pseudo-Georgian comforts of Chelsea Square. Like Whistler, Osborne seemed to revel in controversy, both generating his own and joining in others in the correspondence columns of newspapers. Like Whistler, he counter-attacked his critics with particular ferocity. Like Whistler, he appeared to relish his capacity to disturb.

Another significant arrival in Chelsea at this period was a girl dress-designer aged twenty-one, Mary Quant. With striking originality and imperturbable self-confidence, she produced fresh fashions for young girls with the aim of giving them a feeling of assurance and releasing them from the tradition of dressing in imitation of their mothers. These clothes were first sold in a Georgian house at the corner of Markham Square and the King's Road. Not only did the designer's enterprise expand into a major fashion and cosmetics concern, but stamped Chelsea as a centre of an expanding luxury industry, much as had the milliners, hairdressers and fan-makers of the eighteenth century in Sloane Street.

By 1960, the pattern of change was set. The streets of artisans' cottages, surviving from the mid-Victorian years, had almost all been converted into smart, if cramped, town houses, commanding prices between fifteen and fifty thousand pounds. The pressures to create another Mayfair in Chelsea were enormous but were resisted by laws protecting tenants and controlling rents, by the preservationist efforts of the Chelsea Society and the loyalty of the established inhabitants to their surroundings. But it could no longer be described as the artists' quarter of London. The Chelsea Arts Club survived – and, when it opened its doors to those without the artistic qualifications it had formerly demanded, was again to flourish – but the Chelsea Arts Ball had degenerated so much that it had been abandoned. Probably, the proportion of artists was higher in Chelsea than in any other part of London, but now it was a quarter to be shared with businessmen, journalists in the various media, antique dealers, restaurateurs and the garment industry.

There was much talent – artistic in the widest sense – in Chelsea. Although the most important writers disappeared from the scene with the Sitwells and T. S. Eliot, so many biographers, historians, novelists, poets and journalists worked there that it would be difficult to list them, particularly because many were transient. Of the journalists, roving foreign correspondents found Chelsea both restful and conveniently on the route between Fleet Street and Heathrow airport. It was possible to meet a war correspondent walking in the King's Road with mud from Borneo still on his shoes, or coughing outside the Old Town Hall from the effect of vomit gas he had breathed in Saigon the same week.

The most modish figure in London at this time was the photographer. Usually a very young man, his interest would have been initially in fashion photography but often he would widen his lens and sharpen his focus to study contemporary life. More self-conscious than the photographers who had evolved a new form of journalism for magazines such as *Picture Post*, edited for years by Tom Hopkinson, who lived in Cheyne Row, their work showed startling visual impact as often as precocity.

The appearance of Chelsea had, inevitably, altered and was still changing. In one respect, this was for the better. After the bombing of the Old Church, it had been discovered, not only that the small, beautiful More Chapel had survived almost intact, but that most of the monuments were only slightly damaged. Now the church was rebuilt as an exact copy of the original, the cost being met, for the most part, by the people of Chelsea. In 1958, the flag of St. George again flew from the tower, the church wholly restored.

In the ruined foundations of the houses where Lombard Terrace and Whistler's last home had been, neighbours had, for years, cultivated little gardens. This site was now acquired by Chelsea Borough Council and converted into a formal sunken garden as if in expiation of Major Sloane Stanley's cupidity.

The other heirs of Sir Hans Sloane again became active. The rebuilding of Georgian Sloane Street began and, elsewhere in the hundred acres of Chelsea belonging to the Cadogan Estate, long leases began to fall in. The houses on the corner of Cheyne Walk and Oakley Street – including the handsome, stucco Pier Hotel, The Blue Cockatoo and one of a group of three *art nouveau* houses, in all probably the most characteristic, if not the most architecturally valuable, group of houses in Chelsea, were demolished after Earl Cadogan had sold them to a property-developer. A sentimental writer with memories of long and satisfying evenings at The Blue Cockatoo, bought its elegant Georgian grate from the demolition gang and this survived in an old house in Lawrence Street. The rest was rubble.

Perhaps remembering his forebear's eviction of tenants in 1909 and 1929, Earl Cadogan planned, in demolishing and rebuilding some ten acres around Tedworth Square, to rehouse all those who wished to remain at rents they could afford. This, however, involved the erection of gigantic tower-blocks of flats as well as luxury houses and, so many were the objections on aesthetic as well as social grounds, that the plan was abandoned. Constant vigilance by the Chelsea Society prevented the worst excesses of some landlords, but among the lost buildings was The White House, where Whistler might have found contentment, and in its place arose an opulent private house.

In the 'sixties, although many of the backstreets would still have been recognisable to Whistler and Greaves and certainly to Augustus John, the transformation of the King's Road began. Talk of "The Chelsea Set", John Osborne, Mary Quant and the rest, had given Chelsea a new, smart connotation far removed from the relaxed past. It became as much an objective of tourist pilgrimages as the *Quartier Latin*, although most of those who gave the place its flavour had gone. Sharply-rising rents forced out the small shopkeepers of the King's Road and in their place appeared expensive antique shops, restaurants and the flashy little shop-windows of the garment industry, which its boards of directors chose to call *boutiques*.

The restaurants attracted not only gourmets, but the more exhibitionist celebrities from the film industry, television and any activity that relied heavily on personal publicity. As smart little restaurants rose and fell in favour, their patrons, dressed to catch and dazzle the conventional eye, vied with one another for the most favoured tables and the widest smile from the proprietor. In their wake followed those who wished to be taken for celebrities and, while the resulting scene was almost as colourful as a masque at Ranelagh, those who chose a restaurant solely for its combination of food and price could find themselves going hungry amid all the emotional greetings, exchanges of kisses and hissed confidences.

This gaudy display attracted large crowds of young people and, on Saturdays, the street became at times almost impassable. Many of these visitors to Chelsea wore eccentric clothes and hair-styles not, like past eccentrics, because of any galloping individuality but as a uniform of revolt against discipline. Deprived of former disciplines and ambitions, whether in the context of family, religion, the British Empire or war, and finding only fleeting and sometimes synthetic crusades in the quickening pace and change of world affairs, they, too, sought escape. This was sometimes in narcotics but, more often, in the studied flouting of convention in the Whistlerian manner. This was usually harmless, sometimes entertaining and was more than counterbalanced by a growing humanity among young people. But it gave Chelsea a spurious reputation as an over-scented garden for lotus-eaters.

The commercial exploitation of the main street of Chelsea gave new prosperity to the hamlets of shops serving small but distinctive districts. Here the exploiters met with conservative opposition, as when a brewer gutted and vulgarised the old King's Head and Eight Bells and the bulk of its former patrons sadly left it to the tourists.

Lying on the western approaches to central London, Chelsea suffered more than most districts from traffic and noise. When London Airport had been sited at Heathrow, near Hounslow, in the late 'forties no authority seemed to have recognised that aircraft would grow in power and size so that, within twenty years, airliners landing there would fly over south-west London at little more than a thousand feet, the howl of their jet engines stopping conversation below and interrupting sleep.

Both the King's Road and the Embankment were often choked with traffic, most of which was composed of private cars carrying their owners to work or shop in London, or heavy industrial traffic on passage to the docks east of London. The problem of attaining, or regaining, the peace for which Chelsea had been renowned became an inescapable problem of the later years of the twentieth century.

Under such pressures, some retreat into nostalgia was inevitable. This, for Chelsea, was supplied by Walter Greaves. In the years since his death, *Hammersmith Bridge on Boat Race Day* retained its place among the notable paintings of his time. For the rest, his work quietly receded to the state of recognition granted to interesting, but minor painters, mostly of curiosity value. Then, at the beginning of 1967, he once again came to the fore. An exhibition of his work was held in Lord Leighton's mock-Moorish mansion in Kensington, organised by the recently-merged Royal Borough of Kensington and Chelsea. Again, *The Times* recalled the old controversy, the art critic William Gaunt praising the river paintings of "Whistler's gifted and long-suffering admirer" as having "a mastery of their own". At the same time, oils by Greaves were hung prominently in an exhibition, "The Influence of Whistler on English Painting", in the West End, and the following year, numbers of his pictures were included in an exhibition called "Whistler and Chelsea" at the Chelsea Arts Club and he was given an exhibition to himself at Chelsea Public Library, which was opened by the biographer of Whistler, James Laver. Most telling of all symptoms, his work appeared in the saleroom catalogues of Christie's and Sotheby's for their collections of "Important English Pictures". Sometimes, in these, Walter Greaves shared a page with Jimmy Whistler.

In his history of Chelsea, William Gaunt praised in these pictures "the combination of fact and aesthetic feeling . . . by Walter Greaves, who if we leave Whistler out of account, is to be considered as the artist of Chelsea *par excellence*". In Chelsea, it is impossible to leave Whistler out of account and Greaves would have been the last to wish this. Yet, in his work he has captured and defined something of the spirit of Chelsea that eluded Whistler. It is not simply nostalgia for sunlit barges and gaslit hansom cabs. It is neither the subtlety of his Nocturnes nor the quaint naïveté of his street scenes. There is, as William Rothenstein said, "a rare passion and reverence" in his way of recording a gentle and kindly way of life. He himself received less than his share of kindness but, as he said to the porter at the Charterhouse gate, "the thoughts one puts on canvas are there for all time". His were loving thoughts – for Jimmy Whistler, for his family, for Chelsea. These and pictures were all he had to leave behind.

Bibliography

Beaver, Alfred. *Memorials of Old Chelsea.* (1892)

Blunt, Reginald. *By Chelsea Reach.* (1921)

Blunt, Reginald. *Red Anchor Pieces.* (1928)

Brand, Patrick. *A Garret in Chelsea.* (1935)

Brinton, Christian. *Walter Greaves.* (1912)

Burke, Thomas. *Nights in Town.* (1915)

Butler, A. S. G. *Recording Ruin.* (1942)

Carr, J. Comyns. *Coasting Bohemia.* (1914)

Coates, Dora. *George Coates.* (1936)

Edmonds, Richard. *Chelsea: From the Five Fields to World's End.* (1956)

Faviell, Frances. *A Chelsea Concerto.* (1959)

Faulkner, Thomas. *An Historical and Topographical Description of Chelsea and its Environs.* (1829)

Gaunt, William. *The Aesthetic Adventure.* (1945)

Gaunt, William. *Chelsea.* (1955)

Gregory, Horace. *The World of James McNeill* Whistler. (1961)

Hare, Kenneth. *London's Latin Quarter.* (1926)

Jacomb-Hood, G. P. *With Brush and Pencil.* (1925)

Jones, Adrian. *Memoirs of a Soldier Artist.* (1933)

Lambert, G. W. *Thirty Years of an Artist's Life.* (1938)

Laver, James. *Whistler.* (1930)

Ludovici, A. *An Artist's Life in London and Paris.* (1926)

Marchant, William. *A Reply to an Attack.* (1911)

Moorehead, Alan. *Montgomery.* (1946)

Pearson, Hesketh. *The Man Whistler.* (1952)

Pennell, E. R., and J. *The Life of James McNeill Whistler.* (1908)

Pennell, E. R., and J. *The Whistler Journal.* (1921)

Pocock, Guy. *Stubbs at Fifty.* (1937)

Ransome, Arthur. *Bohemia in London.* (1907)

Rothenstein, John. *Artists of the 1890's.* (1928)

Rothenstein, John. *Summer's Lease.* (1965)
Rothenstein, William. *Men and Memories.* (1931)
Steen, Marguerite *William Nicholson.* (1943)
Strachey, John. *Post D.* (1941)
Sutton, Denys. *Nocturne: The Art of James McNeill Whistler.* (1963)
Way, Thomas, R. *Memories of James McNeill Whistler.* (1912)
Wheeler, Charles. *High Relief.* (1968)
Whistler, J. A. McN. *The Gentle Art of Making Enemies.* (1890)
Wroth, Warwick. *Cremorne and the Later London Gardens.* (1907)

The quotations from letters on pages 127–9 are published by permission of the University of Glasgow, which holds them in the Reserved Collection of the Birnie Phillip Gift.

Index

KENSINGTON
SQUARE
Albert Pla.
Blackmans Riding School
St. Albans Rd.
Clarendon Rd.
Eldon Road
Christ Ch.
Queens Gate Terrace
Queens Gate Gardens
Queens Gate
GLOUCESTER ROAD
PRINCE ALBERTS ROAD
HORTICULTURAL SOCIETY'S GARDENS
INTERNATIONAL EXHIBITION
INTERNATIONAL BAZAAR
SOUTH KENSINGTON MUSEUM
CROMWELL ROAD
Red Field Lane
BROMPTON
Alfred Place West
Harrington Road
Market Gardens
OLD BROMPTON
HEREFORD SQUARE
ONSLOW SQUARE
Selwood Lane
Cancer Hospital
Sydney Street
South Parade
TRAFALGAR SQUARE
Priory Farm
Nursery
BOLTONS
Drayton
LITTLE CHELSEA
Seymour Place
CHELSEA PARK
Park Lane
OAKLEY SQUARE
Chelsea Workhouse
Stanley Villas
CAMERA SQUARE
PAULTONS SQUARE
Limerstone Street
William Street
Lindsey Row
St. Marks College
Market Garden